# CENTURY OF REVOLUTION

# A WORLD HISTORY, 1770–1870

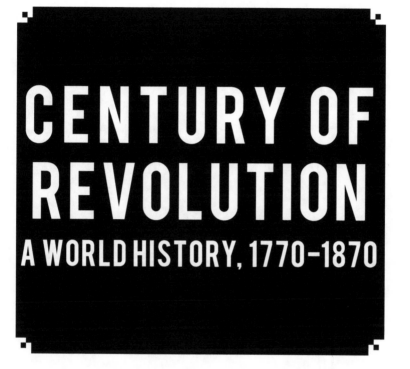

# CENTURY OF REVOLUTION
## A WORLD HISTORY, 1770–1870

Edmund Clingan

iUniverse, Inc.
Bloomington

# CENTURY OF REVOLUTION
## A WORLD HISTORY, 1770-1870

iUniverse books may be ordered through booksellers or by contacting:

iUniverse
1663 Liberty Drive
Bloomington, IN 47403
www.iuniverse.com
1-800-Authors (1-800-288-4677)

ISBN: 978-1-4759-9342-4 (sc)
ISBN: 978-1-4759-9343-1 (e)

Library of Congress Control Number: 2013909828

Printed in the United States of America

iUniverse rev. date: 6/5/2013

# CONTENTS

# PREFACE

Twenty years ago, I began teaching world history at Hunter College. I have subsequently continued and refined my courses at the University of North Dakota and Queensborough Community College. It was soon apparent that a survey of world history from 1500 was unsatisfactory in every way. It overwhelmed the students with material, jumped from place to place, and did not allow enough detail to reveal the subtle connections of modern world history. One needed shorter time spans in order to teach the history of the globe effectively. But how should one divide these periods? The era of the Second World War and the long period in the shadow of that conflict are obvious divisions. The year 1870 makes for a good dividing point as united Italy and Germany, modern Japan, and a transformed United States emerged and dominated much of the historical narrative. The demographic, political, and social changes mark the 1870–1930 period as distinct from the earlier nineteenth century. Coming from the other chronological side, Columbus in 1492 and Vasco da Gama in 1498 definitely mark the beginning of modern world history (indeed, I might say real world history). When did this "age of exploration" come to an end? Exploration of the polar regions and the detailed mapping of the continental interiors are way too late. Captain Cook's Pacific explorations and landing in Australia are an excellent ending point.

This leaves us with the hundred-year period between 1770 and 1870. There were so many political, social, economic, and intellectual movements recombining and competing with each other around the world that focusing on one or two would distort the rest. I have settled on revolution as the organizing principle. This borrows from R.R. Palmer's marvelous *The Age of the Democratic Revolution*, but I am moving beyond the Atlantic world and I do not see most of the revolutions as particularly leading to government by the people. I attempt to explain revolutionary theory in the first chapter and separate out the adjectival *revolutionary* from the noun *revolution*. The English Civil War and even the Glorious Revolution were revolutionary in certain ways, Shaka's military reorganization was revolutionary. But none was a revolution that was self-aware and pushing to a new order. The American Revolution is a clear and successful revolution. Palmer showed how the idea of revolution spread from there, even to the Comoros islands. The French Revolution and Napoleon caused many more inspirations. No one seems to have picked up on how Andrew Jackson reimagined himself on the model of Bonaparte. Revolutionary ideas and movements went back and forth across the Atlantic. These revolutions affected Africa and the Muslim world and caused revolutionary developments, but no definitive revolutions. The Taiping rebellion was a revolution that failed to dislodge the Qing monarchy in China. The book ends with a genuine revolution in Japan.

This is a coherent period in world history, and I am teaching a course on the subject. Alas, there is no textbook. Palmer's book is limited in chronology and scope. Lester Langley's *The Americas in the Age of Revolution* provides an excellent comparison of the North American experience with those of Haiti and Iberoamerica. But nothing integrates Africa, Asia, and Australia into this story. I offer this modest essay in the hope that readers will better appreciate the connections of the revolutions around the world.

As with my previous textbook *An Introduction to Modern Western Civilization*, I pledge that any profit made on this book will be donated to the Queensborough Community College Fund.

# WHAT DOES "REVOLUTION" MEAN?

## Revolutionary Theory

The world experienced a century of revolution from 1770 to 1870. What do we mean by revolution? The *American Heritage Dictionary* notes that the word comes from "revolve": to turn upon an axis. It defines revolution as "an assertedly momentous change in any situation."

A revolution is not simply toppling a ruler or staging a peasant revolt. These events have occurred from time immemorial. It is not shifting a political system. The ancient Greek philosopher Aristotle described political systems going in cycles from monarchy to despotism to aristocracy to oligarchy to democracy to mob rule and back to monarchy. Italian writers of the Renaissance called it a revolution each time power shifted from one elite party to another.

A revolution means remaking society in a progressive manner to bring it closer to God's kingdom. It requires the Christian idea of progress in a linear fashion. This does not mean that revolutions only occur in Christian countries. Revolutionaries are self-aware. While revolution involves religious and ideological underpinnings, it must also avoid the trap of the pure being "above politics." A key moment came with Thomas Aquinas' *Summa Theologiae* (1268) stating that politics is natural to man, not a result of the fall of Adam and Eve. Revolutionary movements are preceded by the spread of Christianity. Many things are retrospectively called "revolutions" in ancient and medieval times, but those leaders were not planning a full overhaul of society and politics. Movements were grabs for power or returns to the past (the Gracchi, Caesar) or slave and peasant revolts (such as that of Spartacus).

# Roots

Following the line of thought suggested by Martin Malia, the first proto-revolutionary movement probably occurred in Hussite Bohemia in the fifteenth century. Two strands combined here: firstly, the century-long crisis of the Catholic church and the challenges to its monopoly of religious interpretation; these ideas had migrated from England via the advisers to Anne of Bohemia, wife to the English king Richard II, who was murdered in 1400. Secondly, there was a growing resentment from the Bohemian Czechs against German rule in their land.

**John Huss** (1370–1415), a preacher in Prague, combined these ideas. Huss arrived at the Catholic Council of Constance in November 1414 and was tossed in jail. In July 1415 the Council degraded Huss from the priesthood and turned him over to the German Emperor Sigismund, who burned him. Bohemia erupted in war. By 1419, Hussite nobles and cities had united against the Emperor's power. The most radical Hussites seized Prague and massacred the town council. In 1434, the moderate Hussites defeated the radicals and signed a treaty with Sigismund guaranteeing Hussite practices and the equal right of Hussites and Catholics to hold public office. The Bohemian assembly, which the Hussite nobles controlled, eventually gained the right to elect kings.

# The Reformation and Revolution

Martin Luther's posting of the *95 Theses* in 1517 was not itself revolutionary because Luther backed the power of the princes and did not endorse an overthrow of the political or social system. However, his challenge to religious authority soon triggered a revolutionary radical reformation.

The Lutheran Reformation was not for everyone. A massive peasant revolt (condemned by Luther) was led by an Anabaptist. This was a radical group that sought to return to the early Christian communities described in the New Testament. A central tenet was that adults should choose their religion and be rebaptized if they chose, thus the name **Anabaptists**. They shared goods and refused to take oaths, pay taxes or fight in a king's army. Because Jesus had opposed all violence, they were usually pacifists. They began in Germany,

Switzerland, and Netherlands, but spread to Bohemia and elsewhere. They called for religious, social, and economic reform and stressed the individual conscience and private revelation made by God. They promoted free will and full religious liberty. They remained a tiny group, but their ideas upset kings and Catholics and Lutherans alike.

In 1532, a particularly radical sect of Anabaptists, the Melchiorites, took over the German city of Münster. They were led by a baker and a preacher and turned communist, polygamous, and violent, believing that the kingdom of God was at hand. Catholics and Lutherans joined together to obliterate this community in 1535.

None of these revolutionary movements was successful, but they were the first ones to bring ideological fervor to remaking society and politics in a progressive manner. While they could be inspired by the past and even claim to be restoring a true faith, they still saw their movement as progress along God's path for humanity.

# THE STATE OF THE WORLD IN 1770

There are four basic things to understand about the world of 1770:

## 1) It was united

The world of 1770 was partway through a transition. The world of 1500 had been divided into three separate areas at varied levels of development: a) the Old World, which includes all of Europe, Asia, and Africa; b) the New World, which includes North America, Central America, and South America; and c) Australia, which was still a Stone Age economy and society. These three areas had their own plants, animals, and diseases. By 1770, all the major areas had been united. There were still significant areas of the interiors of the Americas, Africa, Asia, and Australia that were outside of the world system because of disease and/or difficult transportation, but those areas were shrinking each year. By 1870, the "unknown" areas of the world were just a few pockets. By 1770, there had been a full exchange of plants, animals, and diseases with extraordinary results. Disease, especially smallpox and measles, had killed most of the native population of the Americas.

## 2) It was agricultural

For the previous 3,500 years, virtually every suitable area of the world supported agriculture. The non-agricultural areas of the world were too hot or too dry. Most of every economy rested on farming and most people farmed for a living. Before that time, hunting and gathering had been more rewarding because more animals were available, wild cereals were not yet abundant, and people had not yet developed inventions for collecting, processing, and storing cereals efficiently. Population pressure had remained low. In 1770, hunting and gathering were restricted to many of the marginal areas not yet tied to the rest of the world.

Agriculture had developed at different rates. This profoundly affected development. Southwest Asia had developed an agricultural complex around wheat around 8500 BC. China had developed a crop complex around rice and millet by 7500 BC. But Mesoamerica did not develop agriculture around rice until 3500 BC, and the Andes developed a complex around the potato about the same time. Adding to the later start was the relatively slow spread of domestication in the Americas along the north-south axis as Jared Diamond noted in *Guns, Germs, and Steel.* Since technology flowed from farming to animal domestication to pottery to metal technology, this lag time was fatal to American cultures. Agriculture also led to development of cities, greater population densities, and created favorable conditions for certain diseases and parasites. Cities appeared in the Middle East by 3500 BC, but not in southern Africa until AD 1100. Writing had been known from the Middle East and Egypt by 3000 BC, but not in western Africa until AD 700.

## 3) It was rural

Most people still lived outside of cities, even in the states of Western Europe. The rural setting produced most of the economy, even manufacturing. Wage-paying jobs were scarce in the cities. The unemployment rate in cities was very high in the best of times. Many who tried to move from the countryside hoping to find a job would end up dead of hunger, cold, or violence.

## 4)It was dominated by absolutist empires

Rural, low-density populations made effective communication and transportation, and therefore control of the population, very difficult. Most of the civilized world was under the control of monarchies. **Monarchy** comes from a Greek word meaning "one man rule." We may use the term **absolutist** to describe these monarchies: **a political system where a great degree of power is concentrated in a pre-industrial centralized monarchy or administration**. "Politics" refers to the exercise of power. "A great degree of power" is not total power. Kings had to share power, most commonly with **noble** families who inherited their wealth and power rather than earning it. They often were the richest people and usually owned land. They kept order in local areas for the king, and the king gave them privileges in return. Because most kings and nobles gained wealth and power through a lucky accident of birth, they were often stupid, lazy, and incompetent. The ordinary people had to pay for this (sometimes with their lives) in the wars started to satisfy a king's vanity. Sometimes a king was so incompetent (or just a boy) that advisers and officials of government would run his nation. You did not need a strong or skilled or smart king to have an absolutist government.

Absolutist governments also controlled their nation's official churches, which were Roman Catholic in France, Spain, and Austria, Orthodox in Russia, Protestant in Prussia, and the Church of England. The governments would accept or appoint the leaders of these churches, and dissent by a priest or minister could merit harsh punishment. This was known as **the alliance of throne and altar**. There was no separation of church and state. Governments did not tolerate people who were not members of the official church or at most granted them limited rights. Many absolutist kings believed (or said they believed) that God himself had made them king. Therefore they were only answerable to God, and an attack or insult on the monarch was an attack on God. This was called the **divine right of kings**. Priests and ministers promoted this to Christian worshipers, further bolstering the power of the king.

The fifteenth and sixteenth centuries saw the establishment of powerful regimes in England, France, Spain, Turkey, Russia, China, Northern India, and Japan. In the seventeenth century, however, all these regimes saw popular uprisings that taught the kings that they had to move cautiously. The people would only surrender a certain portion of their blood and treasure for the absolutist rulers.

These four basic attributes dominated most of the world, but areas had developed in different ways and had different problems and priorities in the eighteenth century.

# Western and Central Europe

The most important regimes (England, France, Spain) were distinguished by a high degree of national feeling for the time. They had common languages with the king sitting atop the heap as the shining model of the nation. Royal succession was recognized as passing from father to the oldest son.

This nationalism had developed in the Late Middle Ages from 1250 to 1500. Kings had convened representative assemblies to achieve national goals. In particular, the assemblies such as the **Parliament** in England and the **Estates-General** in France gave the king important tax privileges. In the late fifteenth century, monarchs in these nations exploited tax rights, reformed their administrations, and either built large armies or banned private armies. Wars among nations sharpened their national identities. The alliance of throne and altar used religion as a unifying force.

When the English king **Charles I** (ruled 1625–1649) tried to increase his taxing authority without the consent of Parliament, it raised an army, defeated the King's forces, captured Charles, and cut off his head. The **English Civil War** (1642–1649) began as a protest by the English House of Commons against the growing power of the King, but it was infused with a strong religious element, which grew as the war progressed.

The confusion of the War allowed small revolutionary groups to grow. The **Levellers** were made up of a number of soldiers who put forward a written social contract, "the Agreement of the People," to give people control over the government. There should be elections to the Parliament every year in districts with equal populations. The state should pay salaries to members of Parliament so all could participate. This immediately led to a discussion of property rights since those with more property inevitably had more influence. The Levellers grudgingly accepted that property owners represented the entire country, not just their own selfish interests. The Levellers' plans did not extend the vote to the lower classes. Some talked of limiting landed wealth. The state would pay administrators but would move them around so that permanent parties did not form.

A more radical group started by calling itself the "True Levellers" and drew inspiration from the Bible's Book of Acts: "And the multitude of them that believed were of one heart and soul: and not one of them said that aught of the things which he possessed was his own; but they had all things common." The group changed its name to the **Diggers** when it put its communistic plans into action and dug and planted on common land. Their leader **Gerrard Winstanley** urged the confiscation of property and placing the common treasury under "overseers" who would have sweeping powers of punishment.

Although the execution of King Charles was a revolutionary act, the Levellers and Diggers were crushed thereafter. A military dictator, Oliver Cromwell, put an end to any revolutionary ideas. Most came to hate Cromwell's dictatorship, so Charles' son was soon invited back if he would behave himself. By 1688, the British Parliament had asserted its supremacy over the kings.

In France, the **Fronde** of 1648 was a rebellion by peasants and certain nobles against the boy-king Louis XIV (ruled 1643–1715) and his chief minister, who was trying to raise taxes. Fifty years later, Louis pushed through a major tax increase during wartime, but it was revoked upon his death.

Internal revolts and external wars weakened Spain. Portugal regained its independence in 1648 after a revolt. Catalonia rebelled but was not able to break from Spain.

Central and Southern Europe were divided into large numbers of smaller countries ruled by princes who wished to emulate the absolutist empires, but most did not have the resources to do so. Two German-speaking states, Prussia and Austria, increased in size and their absolutist rulers built strong administrations. By 1770, these two states dominated Central Europe.

# Russia

## The Rise of Russian Power

This empire had a European core, but its vague eastern boundary had pushed well into Central Asia since the sixteenth century and its vague southern boundary was pushing toward the Black Sea. Ivan IV (The Terrible) (ruled 1533–1584) grew up under the authority of the great nobles. He greatly resented them and began reforms to reduce their power. He killed the most troublesome. After his wife's death in 1560, Ivan went mad. He would fly into rages. He finally killed his son in one of these rages. He forced the nobles to render more and more service, and they in turn squeezed their peasants. Many peasants fled the area of Ivan's control and formed loose bands of Cossacks. Ivan was the first **tsar** (emperor).

After Ivan's death, Russia began to fall into the "Time of Troubles" where the succession was disputed and a number of nobles vied for the tsar's crown. Other countries intervened to grab parts of Russia. Finally, Russians from all classes banded together to elect Michael Romanov (ruled 1613–1645) as tsar. Michael's son Alexis (ruled 1645–1676) forged real ties to the West even as the peasants were finally enserfed by law; they were forbidden to leave the land. Alexis took over Ukraine. Another fight broke out over religion when the Church brought Russian practices into line with the Greek Orthodox practice; this led to "Old Believers" who would not accept these changes. The Church turned to Alexis for help, and at this point the state gained total control and cemented the alliance of throne and altar. Alexis dismissed the Russian form of the Parliament, which was unpopular because every time it met, taxes went up. He fired the head of the Russian Orthodox church without suffering a backlash.

Russia did not develop revolutionary movements at this time, though the seeds were there. The Old Believers provided religious fervor, but many preferred to move to the distant areas of Russia rather than fight the tsar. The serfs deeply resented their near-slave conditions and regularly rebelled. In 1670, Stenka Razin led a massive serf rebellion that failed. A true Russian revolutionary movement would have combined the religious fervor of the Old Believer with the social grievances of the serfs to demand a political and social reordering, but no such mass movement appeared. Perhaps the memory of the Time of Troubles and fear that outside powers could carve up a weak Russia deterred this.

## Peter the Great (ruled 1689–1725)

When Peter took over Russia, it had almost no standing army, just a disloyal palace guard. Almost all of Peter's reforms were aimed at improving the military. Peter's first war was against the Turks. After much trouble, he took the port of Azov on the Black Sea in 1696. He faced a much tougher fight against the Swedes and had to reorganize the army. He increased service from the lower nobles as army officers. He also forced through conscription so that one out of every seventy-five serf households had to surrender a drafted soldier for a twenty-five-year term. By 1725, the army numbered 210,000 regulars plus 100,000 Cossacks. Russia defeated Sweden and took the Baltic Sea coast.

This army was tremendously expensive. Its cost doubled from 1701 to 1724. Peter imposed taxes on nearly everything, including beards and mustaches. Many households tried to flee. Peter also wanted a new city to be Russia's capital instead of Moscow. He built a beautiful city on the Baltic Sea, St. Petersburg, to signify greater contact with the west. Peter commissioned the exploration of Siberia's Pacific waters and ordered an expedition to Alaska.

Peter had built up the military but worsened the burden on the serfs. The gap between top and bottom in Russia widened. He had managed to create an absolutist government and indeed anticipated later developments in revolutionary France without any real degree of democratization or liberalization. By leaning on Westerners, he helped spur a Russian "inferiority complex" and continued to keep the most energetic people, the Old Believers, unreconciled and out of Russian life.

Peter was a revolutionary figure, but he was virtually alone. There was a backlash after Peter's death. The rulers were ineffective and gave away considerable lands to the nobles. The nobles reduced their service to the tsar as much as they could. Finally, the tsar abolished mandatory service by the nobles, while giving the serfs no relief at all. Indeed, landlords won the right at this time to transfer, buy and sell serfs and even exile them and/or recall them from Siberia.

# The Ottoman Empire

The Ottoman Turks had come out of Central Asia around 1300 and conquered the old Greek empire. They rolled through southeastern Europe and advanced up the Danube river. In 1526, they conquered Hungary and killed its king. In 1529, they reached Vienna, the capital of Austria, but failed to take that city. The Ottomans staged a series of wars against Egypt and Persia to take much of the Middle East. By 1566, the Turks had a great empire in the Middle East, southeastern Europe, and North Africa. The Turkish navy dominated the Eastern Mediterranean. The Turks preached tolerance and drew upon Muslims, Jews, Catholics, and Orthodox believers. Constantinople was bigger than the cities of Europe with half a million people. The cities were large, well lighted, and well drained with extensive schools and libraries. They had better mills, guns, lighthouses, and horses. Europe feared the elite **Janissaries**: tough soldiers who had been taken as boys from Christian families and trained as dedicated troops.

The medieval Islamic world had been splendid and grown rich off the trade of silk and spices across Eurasia. This surplus money allowed the Arabic/Muslim civilization to support a strong intellectual base. After the year 1000, the united caliphate had disintegrated. The less-educated groups had come in waves: the Seljuk Turks and later the Ottoman Turks from Central Asia, the Berbers from the North African mountains. These peoples displaced the ruling Arabs and valued learning and knowledge less than their predecessors. In 1258, the Mongols had destroyed Baghdad, a shining center of the Muslim world. Then in the fifteenth and sixteenth centuries the Muslims lost one of their leading areas in intellectual activity, Spain. They also lost trade in western Africa as that region fell into chaos and European ships linked Africa with India, the Spice Islands, and China.

The Ottoman Empire grew too large. Europeans in the west worked with Persians in the east even as the split between Sunni and Shi'ite Muslims debilitated the Empire. Power was concentrated in the sultan and there was no set succession. After the death of Suleiman the Magnificent in 1566, the Empire suffered thirteen incompetent sultans. When expansion stopped after 1550, the Janissaries began looting the Empire to benefit their families. A revolt by Janissaries in 1648 killed the Sultan. The Empire subjected merchants to heavy taxes. Officials often accepted bribes.

These policies allowed the Europeans to surpass them in military technology. The Turks built no oceangoing ships that could challenge the European traders. The last blaze of glory came in 1683 when Turkish troops advanced to the gates of Vienna, but better guns and help from Poland drove them off and the Austrian counterattack drove the Turks down the Danube and freed Hungary in 1699.

# South Asia

The Indian subcontinent had experienced a number of invasions from the north and west throughout its history. In 1504, Babur (ruled 1483–1530), a central Asian ruler leading Turks and Afghans, captured Kabul and then swept south, capturing Delhi and Agra. Babur's grandson Akbar (ruled 1556–1605) consolidated his hold over northern India by integrating Hindus into the Muslim-dominated state and married two Hindu women. "Mughal" is a corruption of the word "Mongol," but Babur's people were largely Persian in culture. The state of Babur and Akbar became known as the Mughal Empire.

Succession was a big problem. Akbar's son rebelled and poisoned his father. The Empire mixed Indian, Persian, and Central Asian elements. Over time, the Indian element became more dominant, and Muslim obedience became mere lip service. Akbar's grandson Shah Jahan (ruled 1628–1658) began his reign in bloody fashion by killing his nearest relatives, but ruled over an artistically splendid time. He ordered the construction of the magnificent Taj Mahal and the jewel-encrusted Peacock Throne. Expenses caused him to increase taxes to one-half of all the crops; south Asia had a trade surplus mainly from the handcrafted cotton textile industry.

Shah Jahan suffered a stroke, which triggered a new civil war. His son **Aurangzeb** (ruled 1658–1707) emerged triumphant. Aurangzeb was the most pious and ruthless of the Mughals. He polarized the Empire and undid much of Akbar's work by outlawing Hinduism. When crowds gathered to protest the high taxes, Aurangzeb sent imperial elephants to crush them. The Sikhs rebelled in Punjab and were blown to pieces by the Mughal's artillery, leaving great anti-Muslim hatred in Punjab. Aurangzeb conquered the Deccan plateau in bloody fashion and left only the southern tip of India free. He ruled more of the subcontinent than anyone before or since. The Mughals distrusted any innovations the largely Hindu cities might come up with.

After Aurangzeb's death came a series of civil wars that saw the Deccan plateau, the Marathra region north along the Narmoda and Mahanadi rivers, and the Sikh Punjab break away. In 1738 and 1739, the Persians invaded Afghanistan, took Kabul and Kandahar, crossed the Indus, and sacked the Mughal capital of Delhi. When they left, they took the Peacock Throne with them back to Persia.

# East Asia

## China and Korea

The Chinese had thrown off Mongol rule in 1368 with the establishment of the Ming Dynasty, which came to dominate Korea. From 1405 to 1433, Emperor Yongle sent out major maritime voyages under the Muslim eunuch Zheng He that traveled to Aden and down the east African coast. But the voyages were tremendously expensive and did not seem to yield much except spectacle. They had no goal except getting more tributaries. Yongle moved the capital from Nanjing to isolated Beijing and lived in the "Forbidden City" in great luxury, which further drained the treasury. He ordered the building of the beautiful Porcelain Pagoda in Nanjing. The government paid for the voyages, the move of the capital, and the rebuilding of the Grand Canal by printing paper money which ended up losing 99.9% of its value. China returned to silver coinage. A backlash and fear of foreign influence set in. Jealous bureaucrats destroyed the records of Zheng He's voyages. China had pioneered gunpowder, the magnetic compass, the blast furnace, and fine porcelain. Its armies kept Mongol power disorganized north of China. The Mings extended and strengthened the Great Wall.

After 1450, the government wanted extensive control of the economy and kept most foreigners (Japanese, Koreans, Vietnamese) out. Trade and industry were considered morally questionable by Confucian teachings so an edict of 1433 banned all large ships. Another decree banned maritime trade by Chinese subjects. The bureaucracy grew excessive, and harem and eunuch intrigues consumed political life. One had to pass an examination to enter the civil service, which encouraged conformity and a precise knowledge of classics. To gain promotion required passing other exams. The Mongols had tried to put in changes, which gave change a bad reputation in Chinese eyes.

The Ming dynasty took giant steps to feed its people, especially in southern China, which was dependent on rice. It introduced Champa rice from Cambodia, which grows faster (up to two harvests a year) but has somewhat less nutrition. Farmers used fish in the rice fields to fertilize the soil and eat mosquitoes that carried disease. The population grew from 70 million to 130 million. Occupations were hereditary: peasants, soldiers, and artisans. The Emperor in theory wielded total authority.

Despite the luxury and inefficiency of the government, China prospered because of its huge trade surplus with the West. This grew rapidly after direct contact was established in 1513. Europe had very little that interested the Chinese, and few Chinese had the money to buy imported goods, while

Europeans bought tons of silk and porcelain and tea. Perhaps one-third of all the silver from the New World ended up in China. Chinese entrepreneurs tended to invest profits in land or education rather than reinvest the money in business.

The Ming rulers faced a grave threat from the Tungusic **Manchus** after 1600. China expanded its army and raised taxes. This provoked riots in the commercial centers of Suzhou, Beijing, and Hangzhou. Neglect had caused Hangzhou's harbor in the lower Yangtze delta to silt up. Factions tore apart the bureaucracy. Emperor Wanli (ruled 1573–1619) became increasingly frustrated by the bureaucracy's opposition. Finally, he gave up, refused to make decisions, and devoted himself to hobbies. He lavished money on his elaborate tomb instead of paying soldiers, who turned outlaw and often joined the Manchus. Entire provinces revolted.

Chinese bandits and rebels captured Beijing in 1644. The main Ming general preferred to surrender to the Manchus. This event marked the beginning of the Manchu (or **Qing**) Dynasty. The new dynasty reinvigorated China and borrowed from Manchu, Chinese, and Western traditions, although it was not strongly innovative. The Manchus stayed aloof, did not marry Chinese, and stayed out of trade and commerce.

The Chinese community abroad grew steadily. Chinese worked as miners in Malaya and laborers in the Philippines. Despite anti-Chinese riots, neighborhoods in Manilla and Batavia were repopulated. Some niche trade routes, such as Batavia to southeast Asia, fell under Chinese control.

Wanli had intervened in Korea to help that country defeat an invasion from Japan. The defense of Korea took troops from the northern borders and opened the door to the Manchus. Korea had been tributary to Ming China. It copied China's examination system and students had to learn Confucian and other Chinese classics. In 1636, Korea changed allegiance from the Ming to the Qing. The central government was weakened by the development of factions. This gave an opening to merchants who collected a grain tribute and sold it for a profit. Private craftsmen began their own businesses. In the 1700s, coinage became more common and credit developed in the main city of Seoul, where about 200,000 of the seven million Koreans lived. Slavery dwindled.

## Indochina

Vietnam lies at the meeting point of Indian and Chinese cultures, hence it has been called Indochina. It had never achieved the same degree of ethnic and social homogeneity as China, Korea, or Japan. Its old center of power, population, and production was around the Hanoi delta in the north. The Vietnamese empire of Annam had gradually moved south along the narrow strip of farmland and taken Hué by 1400. However, the empire was hard to govern and practical power was divided between princes of the **Trinh** family ruling from Hanoi and the **Nguyen** family ruling from Hué. The Nguyens built two massive walls around the 17th parallel to keep out the northerners. By 1700, the Nguyens had conquered the Saigon area in the south and in 1757 they took the Mekong delta. The Nguyens were more welcoming to the Europeans because they wanted trade and weapons. The French in particular became involved in Vietnam and supported missionary work to convert the Vietnamese to Catholicism.

## Japan

Around 1450, there were 250 warlords holding power in small areas. By 1600, there were only twelve. Guns came into Japan after 1540 and made foot soldiers more important than the mounted nobles. **Oda Nobunaga** (d.1582) had the ambition of uniting Japan. Nobunaga captured the imperial area of Kyoto, where the powerless emperor lived, in 1568 and broke the power of the Buddhist monks in 1571. He unified much of Japan but was murdered. The work of the unification was completed by Nobunaga's former general, Toyotomi Hideyoshi (d.1598), who carried out an early form of census for tax purposes. **Tokugawa Ieyasu** (d.1616), the warlord of Edo (later Tokyo) seized power. Tokugawa gained from the emperor the title of **Shogun**, or supreme warlord. In 1615, Tokugawa captured Osaka Castle from Hideyoshi's son and cemented his power. Tokugawa ordered the great nobles to establish a part-time residence at Edo and leave their wives and sons there as hostages. He established a succession system: the shogun would retire before death and pass the title to a chosen son. The shogun directly controlled one-quarter of all land. The other warlords controlled the rest under his direction. The shogun determined noble marriages and maintained a spy system. Taxes took between 30 and 40 percent of the rice crop. There was a stratification of the social classes: warrior-bureaucrats, peasants, artisans, and merchants. The rice economy slowly gave way to a money economy, as warlords had to grow money-producing goods in order to maintain residences locally and at Edo, which later approached a population of one million. Money helped spur the economy and general living standards grew. There was a relatively high level of literacy. The shogun completely controlled the emperor. Even though the shogun did not have the title of emperor, he ruled over a country as absolutist as France or Russia.

In the 1500s, Japan had been more receptive to European ideas and innovations than China. Among these ideas was Christianity, which claimed up to 300,000 Japanese converts out of 22 million people. Japanese leaders had been eager to attract European trade but did not like the missionaries.

In 1612, Tokugawa banned all missionary activity. Persecution of Christians increased. In 1616, the government limited European trade. The English gave up trade with Japan, while the shogun expelled the Spanish. In 1637, 20,000 Christian peasants revolted against high taxes. The government slaughtered them and drove Christianity underground. The shogunate forbade Japanese to leave Japan under penalty of death. In 1639, it expelled the Portuguese. The Dutch were the last Europeans allowed to trade with Japan and were restricted to Nagasaki. While Tokugawa Japan experienced a cultural flowering, it fell behind the rest of the world technologically.

# Western Africa

A series of large kingdoms grew rich trading gold and slaves from the coast to North Africa for salt from that region. With trade came Islam. The Kingdom of Mali dominated western Africa from about 1200 to 1450. When **Mansa Musa** (ruled Mali 1312–1337) made a pilgrimage to Mecca in 1324, he spent so much gold in Egypt that its price fell for twenty years. His entrance into Cairo was preceded by five hundred slaves each carrying a six-pound staff of gold; his huge retinue included a hundred elephants with one hundred pounds of gold each and several hundred camels to supply the pilgrimage. That is more than $180 million in gold!

As the gold supply dried up and new mines opened further to the east, power shifted again and the Songhai Empire ruled from 1468 to 1591. Then the Moroccans marched south through the Sahara Desert, overthrew Songhai, but could not keep it. The collapse led to chaos in western Africa, and the slave trade flourished in the constant wars. Only **Benin** maintained a strong city-state on the coast.

# Eastern Africa

Since ancient times, eastern Africa was part of a trading economy with the Red Sea and Indian Ocean. Much of this trade was with the Arabs, and many along the east African coast converted to Islam. East Africa traded raw materials such as leopard skins, gold, ivory, and tortoise shell for finished products from India and Arabia. Arab slavers also traded east African slaves to India and all the way to China. By 1500, a large number of city-states dotted eastern Africa.

# Southern Africa

The expansion of the Bantu was the most important development in southern Africa. The Bantu cultures originated at the bend of Africa in the Benue river valley along the border of present-day Nigeria and Cameroon. This cultural group spread south and southeast into the Congo river basin's rain forest. We can mark their progress because they used iron tools and weapons. From the area southwest of Lake Tanganyika, Bantu speakers began to fan out and differentiate. Iron farm implements enhanced productivity and Bantu numbers grew rapidly. Population pressure kept tribes on the move, and they gradually expanded southward at the expense of the native San and Khoikhoi peoples.

We have few records, but the effects must have been devastating when a tribe would have to move. Very small tribes with high degrees of military organization could absorb captives culturally and politically. They reached the Zambezi River around 400 and the Limpopo around 1100. By 1600, they reached the Transkei. To the east between the coast and the Drakensburg Mountains lay a fertile valley. By 1700, a Bantu-speaking people, the Nguni, had reached the Fish river and were in contact with the Dutch settlers.

The tsetse fly carries sleeping sickness and makes domestication of many animals impossible. This slowed technological progress in central Africa. The presence of many other diseases, the difficulty of navigating rivers, and poor soil in most of Africa hindered development. Near the equator heavy warm rains leached the soil of nutrients. There were deserts north and south of the tropical zone. Most "breadbaskets" around the world lie between 35° and 50° of latitude, but Africa cuts off at 35° South. The difficulty of growing sufficient food had hindered development and caused sub-Saharan Africa to lag behind parts of Asia and Europe.

# Australia and the Pacific

Australia remained almost unchanged from the days of its Old Stone Age settlement thirty thousand years before. Society was still in the hunting-gathering phase, and seas isolated Australia from the rest of Asia. In 1788, there were between five hundred and a thousand tribes linked by language and complex family ties. They lacked writing, sails, the bow and arrow, and woven cloth.

Starting from the South China Sea in about 2000 BC, the Polynesians had expanded great distances across the Pacific. They reached Samoa by 1200 BC, the Marquesas by the year 0, Hawaii and Easter Island by AD 500, and New Zealand around AD 1000. The Polynesians overwhelmed many of the native Pacific cultures except for areas such as New Guinea where farming had built up both population density and a disease pool. The Polynesians' social, political, and economic organization changed according to the environment of the particular islands.

The Dutch explored the north and south coasts of Australia from 1613 to 1627, while the English captain **James Cook** explored the east coast from 1768 to 1771 and would open the European phase of Australian history. A Dutch captain named Abel Tasman found New Zealand in 1642. Cook circumnavigated the islands in 1769 and found them occupied by about 100,000 Neolithic **Maoris** of Polynesian descent.

# TIMELINE

| | |
|---|---|
| 1324 | Mansa Musa's pilgrimage to Mecca |
| 1415 | John Huss burned |
| 1433 | China bans all large ships |
| 1504 | Babur establishes Mughal Empire |
| 1532–1535 | Melchiorites in Münster |
| 1566 | Death of Ottoman Sultan Suleiman the Magnificent |
| 1591 | Moroccans overthrow the Songhai Empire |
| 1603 | Tokugawa establishes shogunate in Japan |
| 1637 | Of Europeans, only Dutch allowed to trade with Japan |
| 1642–1649 | English Civil War |
| 1643–1715 | Louis XIV rules France |
| 1644 | Manchu (Qing) Dynasty established in China |
| 1658–1707 | Aurangzeb rules Mughal Empire |
| 1689–1725 | Peter the Great rules Russia |
| 1700 | The Bantu peoples make contact with Dutch settlers in Southern Africa |
| 1739 | Persians take Peacock Throne from Mughals |
| 1757 | Nguyens conquer the Mekong Delta of Vietnam |
| 1768 | Cook reaches Australia |
| 1769 | Cook circumnavigates New Zealand |

# KEY TERMS

John Huss
Absolutism
The alliance of throne and altar
English Civil War
Peter the Great
Janissaries
Aurangzeb
Tokugawa Ieyasu
Shogun
Mansa Musa
Bantu-speaking peoples

# PRIMARY SOURCE DOCUMENTS

**Bishop Jacques Bossuet**, Political Treatise, http://history.hanover.edu/texts/bossuet.html

**Levellers**, Agreement of the People, http://www.constitution.org/eng/conpur081.htm

**Gerrard Winstanley**, http://ebooks.gutenberg.us/Renascence_Editions/digger.html

**Peter the Great's reforms**, http://www.fordham.edu/Halsall/mod/petergreat.asp

**The Janissaries**, http://www.fordham.edu/Halsall/islam/1493janissaries.asp

**François Bernier**, Travels in the Mogul Empire, 1656–68, http://chnm.gmu.edu/wwh/modules/lesson5/lesson5.php?s=1

**Tokugawa Iemitsu**, Closed Country Edict of 1635, http://www.wfu.edu/watts/w03_Japancl.html

**Al-Umari**, Musa's Visit to Cairo, http://www.bu.edu/africa/outreach/resources/k_o_mali

**Tonga and New Zealand**, http://www.captaincooksociety.com/home/detail/articleid/33/cook-was-visiting-tonga-and-new-zealand

# THE RISE OF EUROPEAN CAPITALISM

The economic world of today is dominated by the **Capitalist** economic system. Like everything, capitalism started and grew at a particular time. It began in Western Europe during the historical period called **the Middle Ages** (roughly 500–1500).

## Definitions of Capitalism

Many people have different definitions of capitalism. It has been identified with market structures, social structures, and even political systems. Marxists identified capitalism with an industrial economy. Some identify it with free trade though capitalism has often existed and prospered under restricted trade. I will offer three related definitions:

1.An economic system where the person who puts the money into an enterprise receives a share of the profit, rather than people directly involved in enterprise.

2.An economic system where individuals or groups of individuals place capital at risk with an expectation of receiving back a profit equal to the risk. A clear relationship between risk and return is at the heart of capitalism. When the relationship becomes unclear, there is a crisis of capitalism.

3.An economic system where production is primarily for profit rather than consumption.

# The Pre-Conditions for Capitalism

Western Europe after the fall of the ancient Roman empire was a unique society for a number of reasons. Never before had a society with a heritage of civilization and a high level of social organization been based in the countryside. Also, there was a relative shortage of labor and a surplus of resources. In every previous world society labor had always been the cheapest commodity so that there was no incentive to increase labor efficiency and productivity because it would lead to mass unemployment. Slaves were common in those civilizations. From the high point of the Roman Empire around the year 150, Western Europe lost more than three-fourths of its population starting with the plague of Marcus Aurelius' time, the collapse of the Western Empire, the Byzantine-Ostrogothic-Lombard Wars, the plague of Justinian's time, the Muslim invasion, and the crisis of the ninth century. The extreme example is the city of Rome's population falling from one million or 750,000 to 20,000 by the year 800; that is a 97 percent decline. At the same time, the tighter integration of Ireland and the zone between the Rhine and Elbe rivers increased the value of capital substantially. Economic activity increased in Scandinavia and Eastern Europe. Northwest Europe has good soil, forests, mountains, navigable rivers, seas, and rainfall. About 26 percent of the land in today's European Union is good farm land, while the world average is 11 percent. Markets collapsed; England seems to have reverted materially to pre-Roman status. Now labor was very valuable and these societies needed a capital-intensive system. The West had no way to take advantage of this, however, as long as fear and uncertainty kept trade routes effectively closed and it lacked enough **hard money** (gold and silver). After 1000, the Western Europeans had subdued the Vikings and driven the Muslims from Sardinia, Corsica, and Sicily. Early pioneers in building regular trade routes included Jews, who were not bound by Christian restrictions and as second-class citizens in both Christian and Muslim societies engaged in trade rather than farming. Flanders in the north and northern Italy in the Mediterranean began to flourish as trade centers. To this day, if you draw lines from Flanders to northern Italy, the resulting area of land is the core of Europe, and the major institutions of the European Union are all located in the cities of this "power corridor": Brussels, Strasbourg, Frankfurt.

# Building Blocks of Capitalism

## Metal, Coins, and Currency

For the next 150 years from 1100 to 1250, the Western Europeans built the machinery and structure of a capitalist system. Coins are important in a modern economy because they allow for more and easier trades. The ancient world's money economy had collapsed during the late Roman Empire. The Romans did not possess the technology or the desire to invent the technology that would deepen and pump water out of their gold and silver mines. After the year 600, coins slowly returned to areas where they had ceased to be made (such as England) and spread to areas where they had not been made before such as Germany and Scandinavia. The economy needed new sources of precious metal. Silver came from areas unknown in ancient times. By 1100, silver coins had replaced barter or payments in kind throughout most of Europe. Western Europeans opened new silver mines in the 1160s from England to Italy. Gold coins appeared, especially after 1252 when Genoa and Florence minted gold coins on a large scale. Gold came from trade with sub-Saharan Africa via North Africa. Coins circulated briskly and stimulated commerce. There were few standards, and counterfeiting was a constant problem. In the 1400s, there was a vast expansion in silver and the money supply because of new silver extraction methods.

## Growth of Trade

When the Crusades got underway after 1096, anti-Semitism rose considerably. Heightened religious fervor labeled Jews as heathens almost as bad as Muslims. The new middle class, deeply in debt to Jewish moneylenders, would take advantage to erase their debts violently. This Christian middle class also wanted to take over a great deal of merchant activity from the Jews. By 1100, Christians had forced most Jews into ghettos and prohibited them from most professions.

Merchants in twelfth-century Italy set up a new kind of shipping business, the **Commenda**. A private investor or a group of investors would lend money to a traveling party expected to invest in a commercial operation for the duration of a round-trip voyage. The lenders assumed the risks and would get three-quarters of the profits. These contracts made long-distance trade much more efficient and many early ones specified what goods would be sold, to whom, and at what price. By one estimate, trade with the Italian city of Genoa increased fourfold from 1274 to 1293. Families of merchants diversified among a home office, carriers, and branches. They pressed for and gained better and more secure roads, bridges, and passes through the Alps

Mountains. The growth of trade enabled the Europeans of the Middle Ages to transform farm surpluses into usable money in a way the ancients never had. This is a form of **monetizing national assets**. It soon led to a new form of business as port cities of Italy dominated marine insurance that had developed by 1318.

## Banking

The banking system also grew in the thirteenth century: pawnbrokers who would lend money in exchange for holding collateral; deposit bankers to protect money and keep accounts; and merchant bankers to foster investment in commercial ventures. Deposit and merchant bankers had grown out of the money changers who transferred credits and changed currencies in accounts of clients. The word "bank" comes from the French for "bench" where the moneychangers sat at the fair. The pioneers in this field were the Knights Templar, a crusading order that became fabulously wealthy by setting up banking centers in Paris, Jerusalem, and other major cities. A crusader could deposit his plunder with the Templars in Jerusalem, receive a letter of credit, and draw upon his loot in France. The fourteenth-century debt of Florence grew from 50,000 florins to three million using overdrafts and credits. Bankers developed the idea of **fractional banking**. This means that at any given time, the bankers only have to hold a fraction of the deposits and invest the rest because it is very unlikely that all the depositors will want their money at the same time. Fractional banking created the possibility of overcoming the limits of precious metal and creating additional credit to stimulate the economy. Deposit bankers gave favored customers overdraft privileges, which meant a short-term loan.

Jews and Lombards (people of northern Italy) formed banking communities. "Lombard Street" became a synonym for banking. Problems came in relations with the state because kings would often borrow money for wars and then repudiate the debt, bankrupting the bank. In 1342, Edward III of England defaulted on his loans and bankrupted the Italian Bardi and Peruzzi companies. Philip IV of France killed the Templars and took their wealth. The state taxed Jews and Lombards regularly and persecuted and expelled them periodically. In the sixteenth century, the Fugger family of bankers lent 55 percent of their assets to the Habsburg emperor Charles V and went broke when he defaulted. To get something out of the government, the bankers charged high rates of interest, even above 40 percent a year. They hoped that the government would pay interest for a year or two before repudiating the debt—that is, refusing to pay. You could not sue an absolutist king. These high interest rates meant that affordable credit was scarce for everyone.

## Accounting

Arabic numerals (actually originating in South Asia) replaced Roman numerals after the Italian mathematician Fibonacci popularized them in 1202. It is far easier to do both simple and complex operations with Arabic numerals, and Roman numerals have pretty much disappeared except for the Super Bowl. The fourteenth century saw the invention of **double-entry bookkeeping**. An accountant kept credits and debits in separate columns and the profits made or lost from a transaction. Single-entry bookkeeping had only recorded the debts owed and the proprietor would not know until the end of the year whether there was a profit or a loss. Single-entry bookkeeping cost less but did not distinguish between capital and revenue and made the concealment of fraud easy. Accountants had noticed that receipt of cash involved two entries: a discharge in the account of the debtor and a charge in the record of the cashier. This was a rational way of dealing with money and keeping accounts.

## Joint-Stock Companies

The harnessing of waterpower in water mills was a crucial part of medieval development. By the mid-twelfth century, areas saw dozens of mills being built. Local nobles controlled and financed some of these. The eleventh century also saw the first primitive joint-stock ventures. A number of partners would buy shares in a project, usually a wheat mill, employ laborers to construct the mill, and would share in the profits according to the percentage owned. The Societé du Bazacle of Toulouse financed the mills of the Garonne River in southwest France. The problem was that the partnerships were short-lived and the partners tried to squeeze as much money out as quickly as possible. The *commenda* was a form of joint-stock agreement but only existed for individual trips and not continuing businesses.

## An Ideology for Capitalism

By 1250, capitalism was running into the prohibition on usury and the prevailing Christian ethic that condemned wealth. Jesus had thrown the moneychangers out of the temple and had said it was as easy for a rich man to get into heaven as for a camel to pass through the eye of a needle. In the early middle ages, the rich had lent money to free peasants at interest rates up to 50 percent a year. When the peasants could not pay, the rich took away their land.

By 1139, the Church had officially banned **usury**, which it defined as lending money at any interest rate. Only Jews, not bound by the Christian rules, could make these loans. It is a measure of religious intensity in the Middle Ages that there were few unscrupulous Christians who defied the ban and risked hell. But this prohibition threatened development by cutting off all credit. The interest rates of Jewish moneylenders could be as high as 33 percent. An unscrupulous Christian offered a loan at 20 percent in 1161.

A prominent Christian scholar named **Thomas Aquinas** solved the crisis. He identified the difference between usury and investment: the element of risk. In Aquinas' view, it is usury only if you know you are going to get your money back. If you get a peasant in your debt and can take his land, that is usury; if you invest in shipping and commerce, you run the risk of the ship being lost to a storm or pirates. You would then lose your entire investment. In the mid-fourteenth century, the Catholic Church formally modified its prohibition on usury to accept Aquinas' changes. By the sixteenth century, deposit bankers regularly paid 5 to 12 percent interest annually.

Aquinas provided an ideological basis for investment and capitalism by making money respectable. After Aquinas, there was a great surge of civic pride. People were proud of their wealth and showed it off by giving lavishly to the Church. The age from 1250 to 1350 is the high point for the construction of Gothic cathedrals that still stand today.

# THE AGE OF EXPLORATION

## Background

The European Age of Exploration marked the culmination of trends in nationalism and capitalism. Only capitalistic means, long-term planning, and investment could finance it. Nationalistic competition spurred nations to invest this money, sustain the effort, and occupy new areas. Europe had long had irregular contact with Asia and sub-Saharan Africa. The Romans had reached China via the Red Sea. The Mongols maintained the valuable "silk road" during the High Middle Ages though it was more expensive than the Muslim-controlled overseas route.

The Europeans had tried some early colonial ventures during the Middle Ages. The Vikings had colonized Iceland, Greenland, and tried a colony in North America. The North American colony failed almost immediately: while Vikings had the wheel and iron and the Indians did not, that was not enough to keep Vikings ahead. Viking expeditions were small and infrequent. Compare a maximum Viking migration of 165 to the 1,500 brought by Christopher Columbus to the West Indies on his second voyage to America. The Vikings lacked an agricultural surplus, capital, and population surplus. They also came into conflict with Indians by murdering eight of the first nine they met. The Vikings had not achieved sufficient population density to nurture a disease pool and make a good part of their people resistant to disease. The **Little Ice Age** (1250–1850) forced the abandonment of Greenland. Viking navigational techniques remained primitive. They could only hold Iceland because it was uninhabited by natives. The Crusades had been another failed venture. The Europeans lacked ships that could transport armies or large numbers of colonists to hold the areas. The Muslims united against them. Weather and disease (especially malaria) also worked against the Crusaders. They lost their last fortress in 1291.

# The Portuguese in the East

## The Motives

Mansa Musa's pilgrimage impressed the Europeans and gave them a sense of how much wealth was in western Africa. It directly inspired the kingdom of Portugal to establish contact with the gold sources. Europe suffered from a shortage of silver starting in the 1340s. In 1346, a Spanish sailing ship was shipwrecked looking for the sea route to Mali. Portugal had scanty natural resources and a population of one million at most. They begged, borrowed, and stole money to finance these voyages.

Better shipbuilding, sail manipulation, and the introduction of the compass from China freed the Europeans from hugging the coast in the 1400s. With methodical research and development, they studied Arab vessels on the Indian Ocean and learned of the lateen sail which was small and triangular. They put together the lateen sail with multiple masts and sternpost rudders from the Chinese to make the **caravel** ship. They started with a fifty-ton caravel in the 1440s. (That meant that the ship could carry fifty tons of cargo). By 1500, the Portuguese were building 200-ton caravels with a third mast and a combination of triangular and square sails that could move in almost any wind. These heavy ships could carry cannons and were highly maneuverable. Sometime after 1180, European sailors equipped themselves with the **magnetic compass** from China, which told them direction, and the **astrolabe** from the Arab world, which told them how far north or south they were.

## Atlantic Exploration

The Portuguese slowly made their way down the west African coast and discovered islands off the coast. They carefully made ever-better maps, sea charts, and logs with descriptions. They kept these very secret. The Portuguese settled the Madeiras in the 1420s and then dedicated the islands to raising sugar cane. The Portuguese enslaved the first four men they met on the Senegal River in 1441 and began a new phase of the slave trade. The Canary Islands became a major source of slaves until the Europeans exterminated the natives entirely. From 1450 to 1500, the Europeans enslaved 150,000 Africans. Sugar production from slave plantations expanded rapidly with the Portuguese conquest of the Cape Verde islands in the 1460s. Sugar plantations began in the Canary Islands in 1484. By 1490, the price of sugar had fallen by two-thirds. Madeira was a big producer at a thousand tons a year and Antwerp in the Netherlands had emerged as a major sugar refining center. The European demand for sugar kept growing and growing, especially as new delights such as coffee, chocolate, and tea could be used with sugar.

In the 1450s, the Portuguese pushed up the Gambia River and found that the Songhai Empire had shattered Mali. They finally reached the "Gold Coast" of Africa (present-day Ghana) and set up a gold-trading post at Elmina in 1482. Over the next fifty years, the Portuguese gained about seventeen tons of gold in trade. They could not venture into the interior because of disease and had to rely on middlemen traders. In 1483, they reached the mouth of the Congo River. The king of Portugal sent a group of eight into Africa; only one survived. On the coast, the Portuguese set up colonies and sugar plantations worked by slaves. After 1530, they had gained most of the gold they could, and slave trading became more lucrative. The initial plan of direct trade with the gold kingdoms had failed, but the Portuguese had set a greater goal.

## On to the Indies

By the late fifteenth century, reaching India had become the priority of the Portuguese. They wanted to outflank the Muslims who controlled the rich spice trade with southern and southeast Asia. The European diet was very bland, relying on bread, gruel, cabbage, turnips, peas, lentils, and onions. Spices could help preserve food or cover taste if it rotted a little. Hot spices in hot countries retard rot when put into sauces. The main spices—pepper, cinnamon, cloves, ginger, and nutmeg—came through the Middle East to Beirut and Alexandria. It had taken the Portuguese more than a hundred years to get to the mouth of the Congo River, but only four years later, their mastery of the seas had grown so much that they reached the Cape of Good Hope, the southern tip of Africa. The Portuguese slowly raised money for the next trip that would bring them into the Indian Ocean, and they sent spies to Persia and India to scout ahead. The Fugger bank refused to finance a new voyage. In 1498 **Vasco da Gama** reached India on behalf of Portugal. Da Gama's large vessels and cannon made him master of the Indian Ocean. He landed in Malindi on the East African coast (present-day Kenya) and secured the services of an expert on Indian Ocean currents and winds. The Indians realized that he was disrupting trade and drove him out. Da Gama came back to Portugal with only one ship and his crew suffering from scurvy. Two years later, Pedro Cabral lost seven ships of twelve that he brought to India, but came back with seven hundred tons of cinnamon. Da Gama went to India with twenty ships and troops in 1502. The Portuguese devastated the Indian cities and mutilated people in revenge. He returned in triumph to Portugal with thirteen ships and spices equal to a year's supply. This 1502 trip made a profit of 3,000 percent. The Portuguese soon discovered the law of supply and demand: Da Gama's pepper flooded the market and caused the price to fall 90 percent. At the 1509 **Battle of Diu** off the Indian coast the Portuguese defeated a Muslim fleet. They soon reached the Strait of Malacca near Singapore and made contact with the Spice Islands. They opened trade with Japan in 1542. The Portuguese sacked many cities and set up a chain of forts at Macao, Goa, Aden, Hormuz, Mombasa, Cape Verde, Luanda, Sofala, and Mozambique.

# Columbus, Spain, and the Americas

The announcement that Portugal had reached the southern tip of Africa in 1487 pushed its neighbor Spain into action. It financed the unlikely voyage of Christopher Columbus in hope that he could reach eastern Asia ahead of the Portuguese. Columbus was wrong: he stated that Portugal is 2,760 miles east of Japan, but it is actually 12,000. Instead of dying at sea, he got lucky and found an unexpected continent.

# The Establishment of Latin America

A succession of civilizations had existed in central Mexico. The last group was the **Aztec** civilization, which began expanding in 1428. The Aztecs ruled by terror and mass human sacrifice. To the south in present-day Peru, Andes civilization had existed for many centuries. Its agriculture was based on potatoes and corn, crops unknown in Old World. The **Incas** (1438–1530) had a high level of state organization and involvement in the everyday affairs of their people. Because it required less labor to raise potatoes and corn than many other food crops, the surplus labor constructed massive structures.

**Hernando Cortes** made contact with the Aztecs in Mexico and their enemies. Aided by the Aztecs' foes and measles that ravaged the Indians, he was able to take over the area in 1519. Twelve years later, **Francisco Pizarro** with a handful of troops overthrew the Incan empire in Peru. In a short period of time, the Spanish had organized Peru and Mexico into viceroyalties and set up operations. 200,000 Spaniards arrived. Measles and smallpox had killed the natives off at an astonishing rate, doing much more harm than the Spanish weapons. The Spanish grabbed those that remained and forced them to work in the gold and silver mines. Most of the Spanish who came to America at this time were men and many of them took Indian women for wives. The conditions for lasting European colonization were that land and climate had to be similar to Europe and the lands had to be remote where the people had been isolated from disease and technology. Europeans were generally unable to take over tropical zones; some gained mixed societies such as the Caribbean, Brazil, and Mexico. The areas that had the greatest density of Indians (Peru, Mexico, and Guatemala) have retained an Indian identity down to the present. The Church had followed the *conquistadors* and determined that the Indians should not be exploited. It set up missions and employed Indians to keep them out of the mining companies' hands. The companies, especially in Portuguese Brazil, turned to a new source of labor: slaves from Africa. At first slaving raids in Africa had been run-and-grab affairs but as the Africans learned to avoid the Portuguese ships, a new tack was tried. The Portuguese and Spanish made contact with powerful tribes that were willing to sell prisoners of war from other tribes into slavery. In this way, they gained access to the interior of western Africa that they never could have gained themselves. In the 1570s, the Portuguese began to plant sugar in Brazil.

Vast amounts of gold and silver came from the mines. The Americas prospered with universities established in Lima and Mexico City in the 1550s. Discoveries of huge amounts of silver combined with better extraction techniques meant that a flood of silver came into Europe. The mines yielded 35 million pounds of silver and 407,000 pounds of gold, more than ten times what Portugal had gained from the African Gold Coast. Portugal and Spain, and the Dutch ports through which the silver flowed, became the center of the world.

Having established colonies in Mexico (New Spain) and Peru, the Spanish continued to explore and set up new colonies. In 1567, they founded Caracas as the center of New Grenada. They founded Buenos Aires in 1580 as the center of the new colony of La Plata. By 1530, the Spanish had taken over the islands of the Caribbean and introduced slaves, mining, and agriculture. A rigid class and racial system grew in Spanish America. At the top were high-level Spanish officials born in Europe (*peninsulares*). Then came *creoles* (Spanish born abroad) and upper class Spanish immigrants. At the third rank were lower-class *creoles* and Spanish immigrants, high rank *mestizos* (the Spanish/Indian mix), and noble Indians. At the fourth rank were most *mestizos* and *mulattoes* (the European/African mix). Fifth were *zambos* (the Indian/African mix) and most Indians. At the bottom of society were the African slaves.

# Temperate America

North American Indians practiced extensive agriculture after corn arrived from Mexico, but they did not establish cities despite a major trade in copper in the Great Lakes region. They never got beyond copper in industrial metals. Cahokia near St. Louis may have been a city around 1150, but the Indians abandoned the great mounds of the Mississippi by 1600. There were ten different cultural groups comprising dozens of tribes with very different traditions. European exploration was slow because there was no obvious wealth as there had been in Mexico and Peru. In the sixteenth century, the Spanish explored the American southwest, while the French and British mapped the Atlantic coast and rivers. The Spanish attempts to colonize Florida and the southeast failed several times due to disease and the hostility of natives. In 1565, they founded St. Augustine, Florida. It took a long time to secure Florida and they did not expand northwards. They did not occupy Texas until 1720.

In the seventeenth century, Europeans established settlements along the Atlantic coast, starting with Newfoundland in 1583 as the first British area, followed by Virginia in 1584. The private London Company founded **Jamestown colony**, Virginia, in 1607, but its charter was revoked in 1624 and Virginia became a Crown colony. **Plymouth colony** in Massachusetts Bay began in 1620 followed by Connecticut, Rhode Island, and Maryland. North America produced a number of cash crops, starting with tobacco. Slaves first came to Virginia in 1619 to work on the large tobacco plantations. Meanwhile, the fur trade spurred the exploration of the interior. In the late seventeenth century, Louis Hennepin and Daniel du Luth explored the upper reaches of the Mississippi River. Pierre de Varennes, Sieur de Verendrye explored Canada west of Lake Winnipeg and stayed with the Mandan Indians from 1727 to 1743. But in 1770 much of North America west of the Missouri River was quite unknown to the Europeans.

# THE ESTABLISHMENT OF NATIONAL FINANCE

## Financial Changes and the Need for Cash

In 1564/5, the Spanish found a fast route from the Philippines to North America via Japan. Through a series of marriages, the Spanish rulers gained control of Portugal and the "Low Countries" (present day Belgium and the Netherlands). They brought in even more money for the crown of Spain than the silver and gold mines of the Americas, but Spain mismanaged them and faced revolts. The Netherlands gained control of much of the Spice Islands and many trading bases. After breaking free from Spain, the Dutch discovered a fast route to the Spice Islands by sailing far south of Africa and using the winds of the "roaring forties." Huge 600-ton ships plied the trade route. To handle their new trade empire, the Dutch set up the **East India Company** in 1602. It was designed to be the first immortal corporation. Each partner had a number of shares, but when the partner (shareholder) died, the partnership would not dissolve. Instead the shares would be sold or inherited or reassigned. After 1612, the shares became negotiable and the company encouraged their sale. It soon became common practice for shareholders to buy and sell and swap shares even while alive, and a **Stock Exchange** began to grow. This fostered an interest in long-term development and future profits, rather than quick riches.

Coinage and banking remained problems. The Dutch had fourteen mints with all sorts of coins and there were thousands of different European coins floating around. The Dutch government chartered the **Bank of Amsterdam** in 1609. It fixed exchange rates for European coins and minted gold florins that were universally accepted (and all that traded with the Dutch had to accept them for large trades). Investment capital flooded into Amsterdam. Merchants could borrow money from the Bank of Amsterdam at half the interest rate charged in Britain or France. It allowed the government of the Netherlands to borrow considerable amounts at reasonable interest rates. By 1700, the Dutch government's debt was 250 million florins while its annual income was only 13 million.

### Establishment of the Bank of England (1694)

Because England had a smaller economy and population than France, it found the costs of war more difficult to bear. England had run deeply into debt, and its creditors were worried. The first step in paying this debt was to raise taxes on land and many consumer goods in 1692. The government announced an official national debt in 1693. It had issued **bonds**, which mean "promises," but governments around Europe had often broken these promises. In 1694, some of its leading creditors, instead of being repaid, were given a charter to operate the Bank of England. The creditors raised more than £1 million from the public and lent it to the government at 8 percent interest.

This bank would issue banknotes and hold government accounts. The profit was considerable, so the creditors gained much more than if the government had simply repaid its bonds. As England continued to fight and win wars, it kept borrowing more money. England (which absorbed Scotland and Ireland and became Great Britain) finally reached a period of peace in 1713. The terms of the peace treaty gave Britain the right to administer the slave trade to the Spanish American colonies, and the government chartered the **South Sea Company** to run this. Naturally, leading creditors jumped at the offer to exchange their bonds for shares of Company stock. For a while, the price of shares rocketed up, far beyond the value of the company. This formed a **bubble** (that is, mostly made of air), and in 1719 the bubble burst. The Company's shares lost most of their value. Those who had held bonds and traded them for shares asked the British government for relief, and (amazingly) the government paid them for the value of their bonds. This created tremendous investor confidence in the British government. Creditors to the government were assured of payment. The government would not have to worry so much about debt. This gave tremendous fiscal backing to Britain that France did not have. Britain would have very deep pockets to draw on in times of war. By 1740, Britain could borrow four times as much as it had in the 1690s. Low risk meant a steady fall in interest rates, which encouraged business expansion. This also had the effect of monetizing production from the economy.

## France

France tried to follow Britain in modern finance. It chartered the Banque Royale in 1716 in imitation of the Bank of England. Like Britain, it swapped government bonds from the war for shares of a new **Mississippi Company** that would draw on the imagined profits of that river. A bubble also grew as the value of shares grew thirty times in value. The Mississippi Bubble burst in 1719, but the French government refused to compensate the shareholders. In fury, they attacked the Banque Royale physically and financially and caused its collapse. French investors now tended to put their money into land instead of paper securities. Investors influenced and at times controlled England, but not France. Unlike Britain, France's tax system remained confused and decentralized. British and Dutch borrowers enjoyed interest rates half that of France in the eighteenth century.

# MERCANTILISM AT ITS PEAK

**Mercantilism** was an early form of national economic planning. Leaders of European nations believed that the wealth of a nation depended on how much gold or silver it had. The way to increase this was to run a **trade surplus**, which means selling to other nations more than it buys from them. If a country buys more from other nations than it sells, it is running a **trade deficit**. Since measuring economic activity was very difficult, governments had trouble judging the effects of their policies. Governments fostered or subsidized industries they deemed important, imposed high tariffs, rigidly regulated prices and qualities of manufactured goods, sponsored royal monopolies, and encouraged colonial expansion as a way of getting more raw materials without having to import them from another country and to create a market for manufactured goods. England passed **Navigation Acts** (1651 and 1660) stating that goods had to be carried in British ships if traveling between England and its colonies. "British" meant the owner, master, and three-fourths of the crew must be British. Manufactured goods from foreign countries had to stop in Britain before going to British colonies. Raw materials from the colonies had to stop in Britain first. England seized New Amsterdam from the Dutch in 1664 and renamed it New York. Home countries tried to ban manufacturing in colonies to force them to buy goods made in the home country. This caused tremendous resentment in the colonies, and smuggling was common. The British **Calico Act** (1701) prohibited the import of printed cloth from India in an attempt to stop people from buying these imports.

The Dutch, British, and French controlled most merchant routes. In the eighteenth century, many other nations tried to found companies to compete but lacked capital or strong diplomatic, military, and naval support. Free cities, small republics or kingdoms, and Austria all tried and failed. The three big commercial countries stayed on top by hook or by crook. By the 1780s, the French and British led in foreign trade volume. The British traded more with the Americas and Asia, while the French led trade with Europe and Near East.

# THE "TRIANGLE TRADE"

Most foreign European trade was linked with the Americas and Africa. The key was sugar, grown in the Madeiras and Canary Islands early on, then planted abundantly in the West Indies of the Caribbean. From 1713 to 1792, Britain imported £162 million in goods from the Americas and £104 million from India and China. The sugar economy was based on plantations owned by absentee British or French landlords, managed indirectly, and worked by slaves. The richest single sugar colony was Saint-Domingue (present-day Haiti), owned by France. After 1650, the slave trade to the Americas was very substantial: the British brought 610,000 slaves to Jamaica from 1700 until 1786. The slave trade kept growing because sugar-growing was hot, backbreaking, and often deadly work. The average life expectancy for a slave out in the fields was seven years but many others died or were maimed from the sugar-processing machinery and the boiling pots used to make sugar syrup. By 1790, slave-produced goods (tobacco, cotton, sugar) accounted for one-fourth of the British imports. Sugar would be manufactured into rum. The Europeans brought it and other spirits to Africa along with gunpowder, flints, and textiles to trade for slaves, thus the name "Triangle Trade."

From 1600 to 1800, the Europeans brought some 9.5 million slaves from Africa to the Americas; it is estimated that an additional million died during the brutal passage across the Atlantic where slaves were chained together in tight quarters. If disease broke out, it could kill nearly everyone aboard. Records were not carefully kept and some estimates range to 13 million captured or killed. About three million slaves went from Angola to the sugar plantations of Brazil. Other slaves went from western Africa to the sugar islands of the Indies, where death rates were very high, or to the tobacco plantations in the south of what would become the United States. Europeans would either establish factory-forts or invite African dealers out to ships. Slavery spread in African societies as rulers were eager to make money. Some non-Europeans did well in the global economy: the tribal chiefs in Africa who sold slaves, Chinese and Indian merchants who sold porcelain, textiles, tea, silk, and spices. The lion's share of the profits went to the Europeans who supplied capital and technical and organizing abilities. While Vasco da Gama had gone around Africa in 1498, no Chinese ship came back the other way until 1851. Profits piled up especially in Britain, France, and the Netherlands. The wealthiest did quite well. The middle class became more comfortable, larger, and more literate. The lower classes tended to be worse off in Europe.

By 1770, economic links tied the world together closely and ideas and events could move great distances. When the ideas of the Enlightenment appeared in Europe, they spread across the Atlantic. When America put together the revolutionary idea, revolutions would spread around the world.

# TIMELINE

| | |
|---|---|
| 1268 | Aquinas redefines usury |
| 1324 | Mansa Musa's pilgrimage to Mecca |

| 1420s | Portuguese begin to settle Madeiras |
| 1487 | Portuguese captain rounds Africa |
| 1492 | Columbus reaches America on behalf of Spain |
| 1498 | Vasco da Gama reaches India on behalf of Portugal |
| 1567 | The Netherlands begin revolt against Spain |
| 1588 | Portuguese pepper fleet destroyed as part of Spanish Armada |
| 1602 | Dutch East India Company founded |
| 1609 | Bank of Amsterdam founded |
| 1694 | Bank of England founded |
| 1713–1740 | Peace between Britain and France |
| 1719 | South Sea and Mississippi Bubbles |

# KEY TERMS

Hard Money
*Commenda*
Vasco da Gama
Battle of Diu
Jamestown colony
Dutch East India Company
Bank of Amsterdam
Bank of England
South Sea and Mississippi Bubbles
Mercantilism
"Triangle Trade"

# PRIMARY SOURCE DOCUMENTS

**Thomas Aquinas on usury**, http://www.fordham.edu/halsall/sources/aquinas-usury.html

**Vasco da Gama**, http://www.fordham.edu/halsall/mod/1497deGama.asp

**Christopher Columbus**, http://www.fordham.edu/halsall/source/columbus1.asp

**Hernando Cortes**, http://www.fordham.edu/halsall/mod/1520cortes.asp

**William Bradford**, History of Plymouth Plantation, http://www.fordham.edu/halsall/mod/1650bradford.asp

**South Sea Bubble**, http://people.virgina.edu/~rwm3n/webdoc1.html

**Thomas Mun**, http://www.digitalhistory.uh.edu/disp_textbook.cfm?smtID=3&psid=82

**Olaudah Eqiuano,** http://history.hanover.edu/texts/equiano/equiano_contents.html

# Chapter 3

# AN AGE OF ENLIGHTENMENT

# BACKGROUND: THE SCIENTIFIC REVOLUTION

## The Centrality of Science

To paraphrase the historians R.R. Palmer and Joel Colton, science is important first of all because it affects practical life including health, wealth, and happiness. The population of Europe increased after 1650 largely because of the introduction of new crops and scientific farming. Scientific discoveries led to breakthroughs in manufacturing and transportation that would lift many out of poverty. Medical science brought life to billions and allowed them to live fuller lives. Misuse of science could also lead to mass destruction and death. Secondly, science affects modern thought. Seventeenth-century changes upheld the view of an orderly universe, the ability of human reason, and led to the intellectual movement known as the Enlightenment. Like European technology, European science borrowed from many traditions and civilizations. In the **Early Modern Period** (1500–1789), it combined the rigor of ancient Greek logic with pragmatism and experimentation from the Middle Ages.

# Scientific Method

It was necessary first to establish a regular scientific method. There had been a big gap between "natural philosophers," who ran experiments to discover basic principles, and practical inventors and tinkerers, who invented or improved existing devices and practices. The philosophers paid little attention to the inventors (who were generally trying to get rich), and the inventors did not consult with the philosophers for help. Communication is vital for scientific advance so that everyone knows about the experiments that succeed and fail. This prevents a waste of time and effort duplicating what has already been done.

Two writers led the way in creating scientific method: the Englishman **Francis Bacon** (1561–1626) and the Frenchman **René Descartes** (1596–1650). Starting in the 1620s, they outlined a program that started from scratch to prove basic principles. They understood that investigation led to physical laws. Using scientific method, you do not start off with a belief and then try to find some examples to back this up. You start with all the examples you can discover and see if you can derive general principles. Bacon criticized the ancient Greeks for their insufficient experimentation. Bacon strongly believed that the only science worth exploring was that which affected everyday life. He therefore helped unite science and technology. Descartes was a great mathematician and ensured that most science would be expressed in numbers and equations. Descartes completely separated matter from spirit, so matter could be studied in its completely mechanical form. They agreed that once people understood nature, they could manipulate it to build a perfect society.

Scientific method, which can be applied in a wide variety of fields from biology to baseball, works as follows. You start with a particular problem. You gather as large a group as possible to investigate the problem because there are always random variations and the smaller the group the larger the possibility that something can happen by pure chance. After carefully noting and measuring all conceivable aspects of the group relating to the problem, the scholar should notice some patterns. He may then form a **hypothesis**: a possible explanation. He will then test the hypothesis: does it hold up in all or at least most cases? Most hypotheses have to be discarded or modified, no matter how much this disappoints the scholar. If some conclusion remains, it may be presented as a **theory**. Others can then test the theories to see if they hold up or must be further modified. A scientific theory such as evolution of species or climate change is not just "some guy's opinion." It has been tested thousands of times and has held up with modifications. The scholar should publish results of the investigation, no matter the outcome, so others may learn. **Laws** of science refer to things happening the same way all the time under the same circumstances.

Governments founded institutions to foster research such as the Royal Society of London in 1662 and the French Royal Academy of Sciences in 1666. These societies and others held conferences, published journals on all subjects, and sent the journals to scholars across Europe. A scientific community could grow and build on members' work.

# Isaac Newton (1642–1727)

Astronomy and physics led the way in the seventeenth century because they could apply a wave of math advances including the use of decimal fractions, the standardization of algebra, the invention of logarithms, the development of coordinate geometry (by Descartes), and finally calculus by Newton and Gottfried Leibniz. **Johannes Kepler** had developed the theory that planets go around the sun in elliptical orbits in 1609, but no one knew why the orbits worked. Why did the planets not fly off into space? To measure the movement more precisely, Newton invented the reflecting telescope in 1671; this could see further. He also developed calculus to describe movement along an arc at any moment. Newton came up with three basic laws of physics: **The Inertial Law** (a body at rest or in motion at a constant velocity along a straight line remains in that state of rest or motion unless acted upon by a net outside force), **The Force Law** (the change in a body's velocity due to an applied new force is in the same direction as the force and proportional to it but is inversely proportional to the body's mass), and **The Reaction Law** (for every applied force, a force of equal size and opposite direction arises). With these laws, Newton determined the **Law of Gravitation**: every body in the universe attracts every other body; this force (gravity) depends on the distance between the bodies and their mass. Newton published these findings in his 1687 book *Mathematical Principles of Natural Philosophy*. In 1704, Newton followed this up with his book *Opticks*, which explored the properties of light and colors. Both of these books contained many equations, and the books were hard reads even for other scientists. While many grasped that Newton had proved important and even revolutionary ideas, it was hard for them to absorb the details.

# Consequences

Sailors had always understood that the gravitational pulls of the earth, moon, and sun affected the tides. Now gravity allowed a precise mathematical measurement and could be predicted far in advance, aiding sailing and trade. Calculus curves and trajectories led to more accurate use of artillery. Better guns made it easier to subdue rebels and the eighteenth century saw fewer revolts in the countryside. Modern revolutions would be based in the narrow twisting streets of cities where gun trajectories were useless. Scientific achievements thrilled many. The Europeans had answered many questions that had existed for thousands of years. Scientific method might solve the world's problems and lead to a perfect society, as Bacon hoped. But science frightened others. Newton proved that the sky's color in an optical illusion. Even Newton's improved telescope found no sign of God in the heavens.

## New Ideas and Questions

European expansion had led to contact with very different cultures and civilizations. The Europeans found new medicines, diseases, foods, and manufactures. So many different systems made Europeans wonder if their system was right. Jesuits often "went native" and had to be disciplined. Other religions seemed acceptable.

A desire grew among professional teachers and lawyers to apply the breakthroughs of the Scientific Revolution to social studies and law. Reforms in English law placed more emphasis on concrete evidence and less on character witnesses. Many trials had been little more than popularity contests amounting to which side could line up a greater number of influential persons to testify. This helped end the witch-hunts, such as those carried out in Salem, Massachusetts, in 1693.

Foreign cultures made reexamination of Christianity inevitable. Richard Simon wrote a critical work on the Old Testament. **Baruch Spinoza** (1632–1677) claimed that God was present in everything, denied organized religion and its tenets, and outlined an intellectual non-religious ethical code. God was the ultimate expression of reason. Later readers saw Spinoza as an atheist.

## Natural Right and Natural Law

The Italian political writer Niccolo Machiavelli around 1500 had been the first to say that all previous political philosophy, including Aristotle, was insufficient. He had separated politics from morality. Jean Bodin (c.1530–1596), a French political writer, believed that an absolute monarchic sovereignty was necessary, restrained only by the laws of God and nature.

**Natural Law** refers to the belief that some laws are basic and fundamental to human nature and are discoverable by human reason without reference to specific legislative enactments or judicial decisions. Ancient Roman law had recognized a common code regulating the conduct of all peoples. Aquinas had agreed that Natural Law is common to Christian and non-Christian peoples alike. **Hugo Grotius** (1583-1645), a Dutch writer who had supported decentralized authority, said that natural law prescribes conduct for nations as well as individuals. Law is based on human reason alone. Religion drives out reason. Natural Law was something that even God could not change.

Grotius and Althusius (1557–1638) agreed that sovereign authority must exist to give laws to the state. **Sovereignty** was lawmaking authority, bound by natural law. It represented a contract among individuals. People could not rebel but the intermediate bodies (assemblies, town councils and local officials) could, because the people had ceded power to these intermediate bodies, and those bodies had made (an unwritten) contract with sovereign power. But since the sixteenth-century Reformation, a flaw had developed: all contracts in the Middle Ages hinged on a third power: the Roman Catholic Church. Did the contract give full power to the sovereign or limit him? **Edward Coke** (1552–1634) suggested that there should be basic laws that no power, king or parliament, could break. He told King James I that he was subject to the law. Coke did not elaborate exactly what these laws were or should be, but there was a germ of constitutionalism here.

# HOBBES, LOCKE, AND ENGLISH POLITICAL THEORY

The rise of scientific method and political turbulence in seventeenth-century England made that area fertile ground for new ideas of politics that either supported absolutism without the divine right of kings or challenged absolute kings. The rulers of England had growing financial problems after 1600. Tax rates were low, and the absolutist kings had to share power with the powerful landowners who controlled the English Parliament. These landowners refused to grant the large permanent taxes that the king of France enjoyed because that king then ruled without calling the French Estates-General (the equivalent of the Parliament). In 1629, King **Charles I** (ruled 1625–1649) tried to rule without Parliament. Eleven years later, he was out of money and had to recall the angry Parliament. Relations worsened and the **English Civil War** (1642–1649) broke out with the king's army losing to a new army raised by Parliament. The winners then cut the king's head off.

## Thomas Hobbes, *Leviathan* (1651)

Thomas Hobbes (1588–1679) was materialistic and atheistic. He had opposed Parliament in the civil war and fled to France to tutor Charles II, the son of the dead king. The Parliament's victory did not last long. The general of its army, **Oliver Cromwell** (1599–1658), sent Parliament home in 1653 and ruled as a military dictator. Hobbes was friendly with scientists such as Bacon, Descartes, and the Italian Galileo Galilei. He wanted to apply scientific principles to human society and politics, just as Galileo and Descartes had worked on astronomy and math. In his book *Leviathan*, he wanted to separate absolutism from God and religion. He began with a low opinion of humans. People are nearly equal in mind or body so that whatever one holds, another can hope to acquire. The weak can kill the strongest if they use some brains. Without power to overawe them, "notions of right and wrong, justice and injustice have no place." In the state of nature, life is "nasty, brutish, and short." To escape the chaos, people surrendered their freedom of action and natural rights to an absolute ruler who maintained order. The ruler is the source of morality, property and perquisites. Hobbes emphasized that all absolutist actions should be for the public good; the state cannot kill. People have no right to revolt against the state unless they are threatened by death, or the ruler has failed to protect them. Absolute power can belong to a king or a parliament. Hobbes advocated using the church to pound the idea of the state's supremacy into people's heads. The state should ensure peace and the contentment of the people. This is why Hobbes was so upset at the Parliament's rebellion. It threatened to bring back the state of nature, which was worse than the most bloody despot. The publication of *Leviathan* angered the exiled royalists because it denied that God made kings.

Hobbes promoted a philosophy for the emerging nation-state. His Leviathan had geographical limits, it was not universal, as Christendom wanted to be. He was the first thinker to conceive of social groups making contracts. Unlike medieval feudalism, power is concentrated in the sovereign. He saw natural law as subject to the ruler's will. Hobbes was not popular with conservatives because he did not believe in a God-given monarchy and generally showed contempt for religion. Parliamentary liberals did not like his promotion of the king or his denial of people's rights. Totalitarians such as communists or fascists dislike contract theory, the limits of the state to the political sphere, the lack of leadership principle, and Hobbes' distaste for war.

# John Locke (1632–1704)

Oliver Cromwell died in 1658. His government had become much hated as it had waged more wars while imposing a rigid moral code on the English people. He banned public dancing and card playing, among other things. Charles I did not look so bad. Parliament returned and offered the crown to **Charles II** (ruled 1660–1685) if he would behave himself. Once he was king, Charles II did not talk about divine right of kings but did rebuild much of the absolutist system. He was much more clever than his father, and the opposition remained small and divided.

John Locke opposed the return to absolutism and fled to the Netherlands in 1683 because he feared arrest. Charles II died in 1685 and was succeeded by his younger brother **James II** (ruled 1685–1688). James was more like his father: he promoted divine right, reduced the Parliament, and abused the law. Although England was a Protestant nation, James had converted to Roman Catholicism, which alarmed strong religious elements. In 1688, some in Parliament combined with the Dutch ruler **William III** (ruled 1688–1702) to throw James out of England. Parliament became the main political force in England, sharing power with the monarch. This was not democracy since most people were not allowed to vote. It was called the **Glorious Revolution** because not as many people died as in the civil war of the 1640s.

Locke returned to England and published the book he had written earlier. This was the *Two Treatises of Government*. He saw Nature as benign and rational and people as basically good. The natural state is peace. There is no need for a massive "Leviathan state," but since there will always be disputes, society needs judges. The government makes laws and protects the natural rights of life, liberty and property. People have not consented to being enslaved (although Locke justified the enslavement of Africans), having their property seized, or handing over power to others. The executive (king) defends and carries out the law. The legislative branch (parliament) is supreme and makes the law. The Parliament has two houses: the House of Commons and the House of Lords (those who inherited a title or were appointed by the King). Locke believed that the Commons was the people's house although rich landowners controlled it just like the House of Lords. Hobbes had said that people only have a right to rebel if the government directly threatens their lives. Althusius had said only intermediate bodies had the right to revolt. Locke said people have the right to revolt if government breaks the contract with them. People would have the good sense to use this right very rarely.

Locke published a second book on a very different topic. This was an attempt to apply science to learning. In *An Essay Concerning the Human Understanding* (1690), Locke wrote that everyone was born with a blank slate (*tabula rasa*) for a mind. Knowledge grew from experience; in this, he followed Bacon and rejected Descartes who believed that people were born with certain ideas. Education and mental discipline could improve people. One needs all three aspects to learn: experience, education, and mental discipline. Locke made an important breakthrough by stating that almost everyone was capable of learning. If you believed that people were born smart or stupid, then trying to teach the stupid was a waste of time.

Out of Locke would spring the Enlightenment and the ideas of liberalism. His radical ideas that governments are responsible to their people and that everyone could learn would lead to democracy and the proposal that everyone should learn at government expense. The German-speaking state of Prussia would take the lead by making elementary education mandatory in 1717.

# THE WORLD OF THE *PHILOSOPHES*

"Enlightenment" refers to a common program of intellectuals in France, the Netherlands, Germany, Italy, Scotland, and elsewhere that lasted from about 1713, the end of a round of European and colonial wars, until 1789, the beginning of the French Revolution. There were many different currents and disagreements, but most Enlightenment writers shared the following ideas:

1. Universal principles exist governing humanity, nature, and society.
2. Human reason, given enough time, will discover all of these principles.
3. A belief in the perfectibility and progress of humanity.
4. A hostility to supernatural revelation as they attacked all based on revelation. This often brought conflict with religious leaders.

Before 1713, rich patrons commonly supported writers. These patrons could be members of the king's family, nobles, church leaders, or rich merchants. The emergence of a global economy had changed things. The middle classes had grown richer and larger in France and England and were the main consumers of Enlightenment literature and new novels. French colonial trade grew from 25 million *livres* in 1716 to 263 million (952%) in 1789, while British colonial trade grew from £10 million to £40 million (300%) in the same period. Catholic parish schools educated enough people for the French literacy rates to double in the eighteenth century. Perhaps half the men and one-quarter of the women in France could sign their names. In England, around 60 percent of the men and 40 percent of the women were literate. In 1713, there were 2.5 million newspapers sold in England; this rose to 16 million by 1801.The Enlightenment saw the beginning of modern publishing businesses, newspapers, the bestselling book, libraries, and all the things that go with a reading public. Half the books published in 1700 had a religious theme; in 1780, only 10 percent had a religious theme.

*Philosophes* were free-lance writers. The reading public had grown, and the middle and upper classes wanted to keep up with progress. Britain had ended censorship in the 1740s, but the rest of Europe censored books in various ways or banned them entirely. The *philosophes* had to use the abstract or face punishment. However, readers prized banned books. The authorities would imprison writers but breaking into the houses of nobles and other wealthy families was not a good idea since the taxes and loans from these families paid for the government.

The early years from 1713 to 1748 were largely spent popularizing the complex ideas of the Scientific Revolution. One of the early popular writers was a Frenchman who took the name **Voltaire** (1694–1778) in order to write more freely. He had been born Francis Arouet but began to call himself a nobleman (Francis d'Arouet) falsely. The real noble families beat him viciously. Voltaire hated the nobles and the Church for the rest of his life. His early works explained the meaning of Newton, Bacon, and Locke in simple language. Voltaire wrote *Candide* (1759), one of the most popular works of the time. This was the story of a simple young man who wanders Europe and America having various comic adventures. Most of the jokes were at the expense of the Church and thinly-disguised rulers and government officials of the time. The Enlightenment reached the height of its power from 1748 to 1776. Most of the important works of the Enlightenment were published in this era. We cannot go into all of them in a survey such as this, but we will discuss a few influential ones in this chapter and in later chapters two from 1776: Adam Smith's *Wealth of Nations* and Thomas Jefferson's "Declaration of American Independence." Denis Diderot enlisted Enlightenment writers from around Europe for a massive project that would summarize all the knowledge: the *Encyclopedia* (1751).

Although revolutions used many of the arguments of the Enlightenment writers, the emotional quasi-religious fervor of the revolutionaries did not fit comfortably with Enlightenment rationality. Most see 1789 as the end of the Enlightenment. One of the last *philosophes*, the Marquis de Condorçet, a scholar of mathematical probability, died in the Reign of Terror.

## Cesare Beccaria

The Italian Beccaria applied the scientific method to the criminal justice system. In his *Essay on Crimes and Punishments* (1764), he called for abolishing torture and all cruel punishments, along with capital punishment; the punishment should fit the crime. At that time, hundreds of laws could result in death or long sentences. For example, in 1744 Britain hanged a man named John Burton for stealing two wool caps. Governments should emphasize prevention, not punishment. Punishment should be severe enough that a rational person learns that crime does not pay, but the state should treat prisoners humanely. Crime was an injury to society. These ideas slowly had an effect. The U.S.

Constitution banned cruel and unusual punishment. While the number of death sentences rose in London and surrounding Middlesex county, the actual number of executions fell. British juries unilaterally revalued stolen goods so they would fall below the worth that merited hanging. Since Britain had insufficient prisons, it warehoused convicts in leaky ships and considered how to get rid of them.

# Montesquieu

**Baron Charles de Montesquieu** (1689–1755) was a noble and sat in one of the French regional courts as a judge. In *The Spirit of the Laws* (1748), he asserted that the climate, size, population, religion, and social customs determined the type of government. He opposed centralization and royal absolutism. He called for a **separation and balance of powers** among the king, legislature, and judiciary, and national, provincial, and local levels. There would be **checks and balances** among a variety of groups, so no one would be very powerful. Montesquieu tried to develop what we would call today comparative political science. He said there were three basic types of government:

DESPOTISM—One man rules by whim with no fixed law
    Courtiers or eunuchs have considerable influence
    His examples included Ottoman Turkey and China
    Note: *Montesquieu had never been to Turkey or China and this is not really how those nations were ruled.*

MONARCHY—One man rules
    There is a known and regular system of laws
    Knowledgeable counselors advise the Monarch
    Judicial tribunals register laws
    A good system for large territorial states

REPUBLIC—People govern themselves and make the laws
    1)Aristocratic
        Less than half of the population makes or carries out the laws
    2)Democratic
        More than half participate
        Exists only in small states
        Requires no great discrepancy in wealth and power

Britain did not fit the three models. Montesquieu called it a "moderate government" between a monarchy and a republic. It consists of three units of government: the executive enforces the law, the legislative makes the law, the judiciary oversees the law. *Montesquieu was wrong in this description.* The judicial branch has never been an equal, and no British judge would ever dare to strike down an act of Parliament. Montesquieu wanted to limit the power of absolutist kings and increase the power of nobles like himself. It has lasting influence because it helped inspire the frame of the United States Constitution.

# Jean-Jacques Rousseau (1712–1778)

Rousseau lived during the Enlightenment and is always included among the great Enlightenment thinkers, but he did not fit in very well. Most *philosophes* came from a noble or middle-class background, but Rousseau's father was a watchmaker who abandoned him at the age of ten. He ran away from Geneva at the age of sixteen and arrived virtually penniless in Paris when he was thirty. He fathered five children with a common-law wife and left them at orphanages. He attacked society, reason (a false guide when followed alone), civilization, and progress. He praised the best traits in humanity: kindness, unselfishness, honesty, and true understanding. His most popular work was an autobiographical novel of unrequited love, *La nouvelle Héloise* (1761). He had doubts about whether humanity had made any progress at all and found pure reason untrustworthy. Feelings and emotions were at least as important, and impulsive judgments were often the best. Had he written forty years later, he would have fit comfortably into the Romantic movement.

After laboring in obscurity for years, Rousseau suddenly gained attention when he won a prize for *Discourse on the Origin of Inequality among Men* in 1755. He agreed with Locke that the state of nature was good. Like earlier writers he praised the "noble savage" that he imagined lived in the Americas and Asia. People became overly sophisticated and lost touch with their basic nature. As population grew, the idea of communal property faded; men competed for resources, especially land. The real problems began with private property; this was a sharp break with Locke, who thought property was a fundamental right. Property caused people to move closer to Hobbes' view of the state of nature. In the present day, even if society were destroyed, there could be no return to the state of nature.

Rousseau's *Social Contract* of 1762 tried to describe the ideal state since people could never return to the state of nature. People should give up their power to the **"General Will"**: the common interest of all. Men must be educated to learn their common interests. He moved beyond Locke and urged that government pay for public schools for all so people would learn their self-interest. Everyone must be equal under the law without special privileges for nobles or discrimination against religious minorities. Rousseau wanted direct democracy, not representative democracy or intermediaries such as nobles. This vision was in direct opposition to Montesquieu's ideal. The people should never turn the "General Will" over to an agent. It is not quite "majority rule" but rather the "true will" of each citizen if they were truly informed of proper interests; we might call it a consensus. How would this start? There should be a supremely wise legislator to write the laws and then step aside. Citizens would approve further laws in referenda. This would be the best state because it would give everyone a stake and they would contribute more blood (as soldiers) and treasure (as taxpayers) than people in an absolutist state who had no say in government. Given the state of transportation and communication in his time, Rousseau believed that this kind of system could only exist in small states, with no great wealth or power divergences, just as Montesquieu had said for democratic republics. For Rousseau, the state was much more than just a guarantor of life, liberty, and property that Locke had described. It must enforce a high degree of economic equality among its citizens, control private morals, determine the education received, and must if possible be supported by a state religion that preached patriotism and civic virtue. Rousseau was well aware of contradictions in his thought ("man must be forced to be free") and tried endlessly to wrestle with them. The government of France ordered the burning of *Social Contract*.

When he was asked to suggest a model constitution for the dying nation of Poland in 1772, Rousseau wrote quite a conservative document. It maintained serfdom and denied most people political rights. Rousseau recognized that you could not go from the old way to a democratic republic, especially when most people could not even read or write. "Never forget, as you dream of what you could gain, what you might lose." Even though he had strong romantic tendencies, Rousseau could be realistic when needed. Many inspired by Rousseau would not be able to say the same.

# Enlightenment Society

## Religion

Even as the *philosophes* preached reason, there was a counter-movement. The early eighteenth century saw a religious revival that was known as the "Great Awakening" in the British North American colonies. Even as the most learned in Europe scorned religion, the common folk clung more closely to God. The Protestant churches, closely identified with the government, were especially challenged by new mystical movements. In the alliance of throne and altar, the governments increasingly appointed the leaders of the church for political reasons. Some called for giving up many theological ideas, such as the **Unitarians** who rejected the Trinity, and **Deists** who believed in a distant God who did not intervene in day-to-day human affairs. In England, there were new nonconforming sects including the Baptists and Congregationalists. The **Quakers** urged pacifism, church self-government, a strict separation from the state, and a lay ministry elected by members. The fastest-growing new religion was **Methodism** of **John Wesley** (1703–1791). Wesley started as a conventional Anglican minister but was influenced by Pietism, a German movement that emphasized meditation, prayer, Bible reading, Christian ethics, and a personal relationship with Jesus. Wesley emphasized the value of individual souls and, when denied the chance to preach in regular churches, set up tents in open fields. Wesley did not believe that salvation was pre-destined. Anyone who tried hard enough could be saved. Many of these nonconforming Protestant groups of the Anglo-American world revived the revolutionary ideas of the radical Reformation that had been crushed in the sixteenth century.

### The Culture of the *Salon*

Wealthy women arranged *salons*, which became the favored place of the *philosophes* to show off their ideas and writings. Writers and their patrons would meet in a private house and discuss the great matters of the day. Other matters besides political philosophy were discussed. The modern novel developed in Britain with Samuel Richardson's *Pamela* (1740) and Henry Fielding's *Tom Jones* (1743). Emotional fads and fashions also were common. Mesmerism, a form of mass hypnotism, took Europe by storm. It claimed that a miraculous "universal fluid" could cure anything. Beliefs in astrology and alchemy grew despite scientific advances. By the 1780s, the Enlightenment was dying, even in Paris.

# REVOLUTION FROM ABOVE: ENLIGHTENED DESPOTISM

The upper- and middle-class *philosophes* did not believe in mass movements for radical political and social change until Rousseau at the end. They supported central absolute rulers as bringers of reform and liberties.

# Meaning

The Enlightened Despots were a group of rulers in the middle-eighteenth century who continued earlier absolutist principles and practices while trying to show a greater degree of interest in the people and especially in the culture and philosophy of the Enlightenment. They did not claim that God had ordained them. They favored religious toleration, and often expelled the Jesuits from their countries until the Pope dissolved the order in 1773, only to revive it in 1814. Some despots were more "enlightened" than others.

The Enlightened Despots had some features in common: 1) they separated the prince's personal budget from the national treasury; 2) they introduced new legal codes and reforms on the basis of evidence; 3) they supported education, especially higher education; 4)they promoted institutions of poverty relief such as old age homes, asylums, orphanages, and hospitals; 5) they tolerated at least some religious minorities, modifying the alliance of throne and altar. Others went further. The main limit on the despots was that they made no attempt to change the social structure: king, nobles, and peasants or serfs, with a small middle class. They increased government administration. The countries did not have true Enlightened Despots (such as Britain under George III, France under Louis XV, and Austria under Maria Theresa) still increased their tax revenue and centralized their regimes.

# Maria Theresa (Archduchess of Austria/ Queen of Hungary 1740–1780)

Following their victories over the Turks and the loss of the Spanish Empire, the Habsburgs were left with a very diverse empire: Germans, Hungarians, Czechs, Slovaks, Romanians, Italians in the lands of central Europe, along with the Austrian Netherlands (Belgium today). Maria Theresa used advisers who belonged to different ethnic groups. She centralized authority and took over all taxes but allowed a separate Hungarian Diet to keep the second largest ethnic group in her empire happy. Nobles and clergy had to pay some taxes by 1760. She introduced a new law code in 1770.

Bohemia, Moravia, and Austria formed a customs union in 1775 but many internal barriers remained. Maria Theresa tried to rein in the nobles by asserting that Austrian serfs had rights and actually gave some rights to those serfs who lived on crown lands. Maria Theresa is not considered an Enlightened Despot because she was devoutly religious and despised Voltaire and others she felt were opposed to religion. She did not reject the scientific spirit, however, allowing for her large family to be vaccinated against smallpox. Maria Theresa's morals police were the first secret police in Austria.

# Joseph II (1780–1790)

Maria Theresa's son was one of the most advanced Enlightened Despots. He tried to accomplish much in his short reign and stirred up anger among the elite. He refused to make concessions to the Hungarians and transferred their government to the Austrian capital of Vienna. He attempted to Germanize Belgium and Lombardy as well as the Czech and Polish areas. He got into a fight with the Pope over control of the Austrian clergy. He confiscated monasteries and made them into hospitals. He reformed the legal code to create equal punishment regardless of class. He ordered the toleration of all religions. He tried to build overseas trade and commerce through Trieste, but Britain blocked him. He increased the bureaucracy and set up another secret police force to inspect the civil service. Finally, he tried to free all of the serfs and convert their labor dues into monetary payments which the serfs could not pay. The Austrian Netherlands and Hungary rose in revolt right before Joseph's death.

His brother **Leopold II** (1790–1792) supported many of Joseph's reforms but had to pull back in the face of opposition. He restored serfdom, which lasted until 1848. After Leopold's death, a very conservative and reactionary group took over in Austria.

# Frederick the Great (1740–1786) in Prussia

Frederick was perhaps the most successful of the Enlightened Despots. He was the son of the harsh "soldier-king" Frederick William I. Revolting against his father, Frederick had tried to run off with another soldier and friend to England. The two young men were caught, and Frederick was briefly imprisoned and had to witness his friend's execution. This left Frederick with a bitter and cynical view of the world. As king, Frederick simplified the law and used the government to work for people. He improved agriculture and industry. Frederick lived the life of a true Enlightened Despot and actually had Voltaire in residence in Berlin for a time. Frederick worked on poetry, played the violin, inspected the troops, took care of state business, looked after palace affairs, and met with visitors. He was no idealist like Joseph. Everything he did was to build up Prussian power. Bureaucrats earned their jobs by merit.

He expanded Danzig as a port to export Polish-grown grain. He encouraged immigration and took over part of Poland. By 1786, 20 percent of the Prussian people were non-Germans. He placed some limits on the serfs' labor but feared reaction. The *Junkers* (Prussian landowning nobles who lived east of the Elbe river) consolidated their lands and forced more peasants into serfdom. Frederick forbade the *Junkers* from selling any portion of their estates to pay off debts. This had the effect of keeping the huge estates together. Nobles in some provinces had to pay taxes, but the rest were exempt.

## Catherine the Great (1762–1796) in Russia

Peter III succeeded to the Russian throne in 1762. He was a great admirer of Frederick the Great and dreamed of being an Enlightened Despot. When he hinted at reforming Russian society and easing the burden of serfdom, the Russian nobles conspired with his wife Catherine. After only six months, Peter III was killed. Catherine had been born a German princess but had converted to the Russian Orthodox church when she married. She admired Voltaire, wrote letters to him, and had Diderot live in St. Petersburg for several years. French became the court language. Catherine called a national Legislative Commission in 1767 to try to understand what troubles existed. She reformed the law, restricted the use of torture, allowed some religious toleration, and expanded the administration. In 1773, a serf who claimed to be the slain Peter III led the **Pugachev Revolt**. Many serfs and Cossacks followed his lead. The authorities drove out Pugachev's rebels in 1773, but they returned in 1774, took Novgorod, and drove down the Volga river valley in a path of destruction. The government finally captured Pugachev and had horses rip his body to pieces. Catherine reorganized the government to allow some more local rule but would not touch serfdom. She encouraged education and founded the first girls' school in Russia.

In several wars against the Turks, Catherine secured the coast of the Black Sea and other lands. Her ultimate goal was to destroy the Turkish empire. She named a grandson Constantine in expectation that he would rule a revived Greek empire. The Polish Partition of 1772 marked the first time in centuries that Russia had to deal with large number of Jews; they had been forbidden since 1505. Catherine put the Jews into a "pale" of settlement that they could not leave without permission. She allowed them to keep their communal structure.

## Carlos III in Spain and Spanish America

Philip V, the grandson of Louis XIV, had strengthened absolutism as king of Spain. Philip sent his son Carlos to Naples to rule as king in that area, and

Carlos gained a reputation as an enlightened ruler over a very depressed area. When Carlos returned to Spain to rule after nearly twenty-five years away, he was shocked at the backward conditions. He increased central power and broke the power of the sheep grazers who had ruined considerable farmland. He instituted irrigation projects, built better roads and canals, and created uniform weights and measures, postal service, and coinage. But these projects cost money, and Spain teetered on the edge of bankruptcy. Fiscal reform was impossible without social reform. The nobles controlled most of the land in Spain, and the Church held 20 percent. Carlos abandoned the notorious Spanish Inquisition but avoided the issue of transforming society.

Carlos hoped that he could gain the needed revenue by squeezing the Spanish colonies in the Americas and by allowing free trade. He put them under closer control and took power from native-born *creoles*. In 1778, Carlos issued a **Decree of Free Trade**, one of the first moves toward the Enlightened doctrines promoted by Adam Smith. The twenty-four ports of Spanish America could trade with each other or any port in Spain (not just Cádiz and Seville). The Crown would get revenue from once-smuggled goods; Buenos Aires boomed. A visitor sent by Madrid streamlined Mexican finances. Mexico and Peru became more self-sufficient. In 1786, Carlos decreed new forms of taxing and intendant authority and that estates would be divided among heirs. These were all aimed at the *creole* elite. While, the move toward free trade hurt infant industries, volume may have grown 700 percent from 1778 to 1788. The Crown seized the lands of the Jesuits and sold them off. However, expenses also rose in the Americas. Mexico had only 3,000 troops strung out in presidios along the Indian frontier. Britain humiliated Spain in 1762 when it captured Havana. The Crown had to rely on the creole militia.

## The Limits of Enlightened Despotism

By 1790, the despots had gone as far as they could. Without an increase in nationalist fervor, they could not control more land or claim more taxes. The nations could only increase this nationalism by making concessions to the people and changing the social structure. In short, they would have to become true revolutionaries.

# TIMELINE

| | |
|---|---|
| 1605 | Bacon, *The Advancement of Learning* |
| 1609 | Kepler, *The New Astronomy* |

| | |
|---|---|
| 1627 | Bacon, *The New Atlantis* |
| 1637 | Descartes, *Discourse on Method* |
| 1642–1649 | English Civil War; ends with execution of King |
| 1651 | Hobbes, *Leviathan* |
| 1660 | Charles II returns to England as King |
| 1687 | Newton, *Mathematical Principles of Natural Philosophy* |
| 1688–1689 | "Glorious Revolution" ousts King James II of England |
| 1690 | Locke, *Two Treatises of Government* |
| | Locke, *An Essay concerning Human Understanding* |
| 1704 | Newton, *Opticks* |
| 1713 | Peace treaty between England and France |
| | Enlightenment begins |
| 1733 | Voltaire, *Elements of the Philosophy of Newton* |
| 1736 | John Wesley sets up evangelical Christian societies |
| 1740 | Richardson, *Pamela* |
| 1740–1780 | Maria Theresa in Austria |
| 1740–1786 | Frederick the Great in Prussia |
| 1748 | Montesquieu, *The Spirit of the Laws* |
| 1755 | Rousseau, *Discourse on Origin of Inequality among Men* |
| 1759 | Voltaire, *Candide* |
| 1759–1788 | Carlos III of Spain |
| 1762 | Rousseau, *Social Contract* |
| 1762–1796 | Catherine the Great in Russia |
| 1764 | Beccaria, *Essay on Crimes and Punishments* |
| 1776 | Smith, *Wealth of Nations* |
| | Jefferson, "Declaration of American Independence" |
| 1780–1790 | Joseph II in Austria |
| 1787 | United States Constitution |
| 1789 | Enlightenment ends |

# KEY TERMS

Francis Bacon
René Descartes
Isaac Newton

Law of Gravitation
Natural Law
Thomas Hobbes
John Locke
Voltaire
Baron Charles de Montesquieu
Jean-Jacques Rousseau
Joseph II
Frederick the Great
Catherine the Great
Carlos III

# PRIMARY SOURCE DOCUMENTS

**John Locke**, http://libertyonline.hypermall.com/Locke/second/second-8.html

**Thomas Hobbes**, http://www.fordham.edu/halsall/mod/hobbes-lev13.html

**Voltaire**, http://www.fordham.edu/halsall/mod/1778voltaire-lettres.html

**Montesquieu**, http://www.fordham.edu/halsall/mod/montesquieu-spirit.html

**Jean-Jacques Rousseau**, http://www.fordham.edu/halsall/mod/Rousseau-inequality2.html

# THE WORLD WAR OF THE MID-EIGHTEENTH CENTURY

Wars among the European powers had increasingly been reflected in their colonies and on the seas. The war from 1740 to 1763 was the first time that there was real coordination among the conflicts. These wars often involved more maneuvering than fighting. Soldiers were expensive and took a long time to train, so the commanders did not want to waste them. There was no draft in most countries and hired soldiers (mercenaries) were often of a different nationality from the army commanders. Wars usually ended when one side ran out of money.

## The First Phase: The War of the Austrian Succession/King George's War

### Europe

After a long stretch of peace from 1713 to 1740, Europe was getting restless. Unlike Western Europe, Central Europe had been divided among a large number of weak and mostly small states. By 1700, two German-speaking states had emerged as the most powerful: Prussia (run by the Hohenzollern family) and Austria (run by the Habsburg family). It was perhaps inevitable that these two would fight for supremacy in Central Europe. The Austrian succession was thrown into doubt when the Emperor had no sons, only a daughter, Maria Theresa, who we met in the previous chapter. When her father died in 1740, everyone tried to carve up the Habsburg lands. Frederick the Great, the young king of Prussia, led the attack by grabbing the province of Silesia. This gave Prussia a dominant position in the German-speaking lands. France joined with Frederick because it wanted the Austrian Netherlands and bore a longtime grudge against the Habsburgs. The British joined Frederick to oppose the French. In the War of the Austrian Succession (1740–1748), the succession was not really disputed. Maria Theresa rallied the Hungarian nobility to elect her as Queen of Hungary and kept the rest of her lands.

## The Seas and North America

It was a different story outside of the continent. The British blockaded the French West Indies and cost the French revenue from sugar. They drove the French ships from the seas.

The American phase of the war was called King George's War. The key event was an expedition of American colonists and British officers to the Cape Breton Island fortress of Louisburg, which they surrounded and captured in 1745. In 1740 and 1741, British officers commanded a mainly American force to attack Cartagena in Colombia and Guantanamo in Cuba. The attacks failed with great loss of life, and the Americans felt the British treated them badly. The British governor of Virginia tried fruitlessly to organize an American force to fight in the war, but the Virginians did not see any threat to their interests.

## India

In 1619, the British signed their first trade agreements with the Mughal empire. They bribed southern Indian leaders and set up twenty-seven trading forts. The Portuguese gave the city of Bombay over to the English in 1668. This marked the effective end of Portuguese power in India. The British traded silver, copper, zinc, lead, and fabrics for cotton, silk, pepper, spices, and sugar. As unrest grew in India, the British settlements became places of refuge and they began to exercise political influence. The British East India Company's profitability rose after 1700 when trade began with China. Contrary to mercantilist hopes, it was Europe that wanted Indian and Chinese manufactured goods, while Asians had little interest in European manufactured goods.

After Aurangzeb, the Mughal Empire fell into decay and governors became powers in their own right. Political and religious differences began to tear India apart. Local European colonial agents were ambitious to increase their power. They used some European troops, but also began to drill Indian troops in European tactics. The French started to cultivate Indian princes as clients. The British founded Calcutta in 1700 as their fort in Bengal where the Ganges river flows into the Indian Ocean. The French presence was centered at Pondicherry south of Madras. Joseph François Dupleix, the president of the French East India Company, captured the fort of Madras, then fought off 10,000 Indian troops with 230 French and 700 native troops. Dupleix now dominated southern India with his military and generous bribes.

## Interlude

The first phase of the war ended with the Treaty of Aix-la-Chapelle (1748). Frederick kept Silesia, but the treaty restored all the colonial possessions.

Conflict continued in the Ohio Valley as the British colonists pressed claims against the French and Indians. The French extended their claims south to the Ohio River, founding a fort at the site of Pittsburgh. A British Virginian force, with George Washington as its second-in-command, tried in 1754 to force the French to withdraw. The French and Indians defeated this force and a stronger attack of 1755. Now Britain sent a large army to America to press its claim. The French held more land, but there were more British American colonists.

# The Diplomatic Revolution (1756)

Meanwhile in Europe, Maria Theresa was determined to win back Silesia. She decided that it was time to end Austria's old rivalry with France and make an alliance. As part of this deal, Maria Theresa's teenaged daughter, Marie Antoinette, was sent to France to marry the French king's grandson. Russia also joined against Prussia. Frederick had named three dogs after Maria Theresa, Empress Elizabeth of Russia, and the French king's mistress. Now these three women had created what seemed to be an unbeatable combination against him. Britain had sided with Austria in the first phase but since colonial interests and the rivalry with the French were priorities, it allied with Prussia. This became known as the Diplomatic Revolution because Britain and France had switched sides. For three hundred years, France and Austria had been on the opposite sides of nearly every conflict.

# The Second Phase: The French and Indian War

Britain concentrated on naval and colonial warfare and gave money to Frederick instead of soldiers. In 1758, the British took Pittsburgh and Louisburg. A British force captured Quebec City in 1759 and made French resistance in Canada impossible. Britain then took the French sugar islands. In an attempt to mollify the Indians, the British promised that their land expansion from the Atlantic coast would cease.

# The Second Phase: Colonial Conflict in India

**Robert Clive** (1725–1774) of the British East India Company had been captured at Madras by the French in the previous conflict. He used the lessons learned from Dupleix. He trained his own force and used the military and bribes to put his favorites into power in the southern Indian principalities. The French recalled Dupleix in 1754. In 1756, the Nawab (ruler) of Bengal overran British Calcutta. He threw sixty-four prisoners into the fort's dungeon, which was only fourteen by eighteen feet large. When the doors were opened twelve hours later, only twenty-one were left alive in the "Black Hole of Calcutta." Clive took Bengal with 800 European troops and 2,000 natives by bribing the Nawab's generals to desert. The money came from Hindu bankers whom the Nawab had repeatedly fleeced. British naval power transported Clive's forces to drive the French out of India. Clive himself became fabulously wealthy. This was a vital shift of territory. In 1730, fully half the value of Dutch Asian imports had come from Bengal.

# The Second Phase: The Seven Years' War in Europe

Frederick did not wait to be attacked. He invaded his neighbor Saxony. He looted that land to serve as a military and supply base. Frederick led his Prussian troops personally and won some brilliant battles, but the Russians got to the outskirts of his capital Berlin. Just when all seemed lost, Elizabeth died and was succeeded by Peter III, the ill-fated tsar who admired Frederick and immediately called off the Russian attack. The war ended in a stalemate and when the dust cleared, Frederick still held Silesia.

# The Treaty of Paris (1763)

France lost all of its Canadian lands, but regained its sugar islands. It considered this to be a good deal. The French had to dismantle their forts in India but regained Pondicherry. Prussia kept Silesia. The war had left both the British and French deeply in debt. On a per person basis, the British debt was four times that of the French.

# THE GROWTH OF BRITISH PARLIAMENTARY POWER

The events of 1688 had enhanced the power of the Commons, but the rulers still largely determined the cabinets from their favorites. In 1714, the crown passed to the German cousin George I (1714–1727). He spoke no English and was content to let experts run the system; neither he nor his son George II (1727–1760) attended many cabinet meetings.

## Robert Walpole (Prime Minister 1721–1742)

George I at first relied on the German advisers he had brought over but finally fell back on Whigs backed by a small group of London merchants and seventy landed families. The king still picked the ministers. Walpole emerged as the first real Prime Minister in Britain after the collapse of the South Sea bubble. At first Walpole only controlled finances, but by 1730 he was running foreign affairs as well. Walpole desired prosperity, hated war, and helped keep the peace that lasted in Europe from 1713 to 1740. Walpole established the principle that the ministers were not just responsible to the king but also to the Prime Minister.

A glory-seeking war party led by Henry Pelham (Prime Minister 1744–1754), his brother the Duke of Newcastle (Prime Minister 1754–1756), and **William Pitt** (Prime Minister 1756–1761) ousted Walpole and enmeshed Britain in the prolonged world war. Newcastle put together a patronage system, rewarding friends and punishing enemies for their votes. Though the King did not like the Pelhams, he could not find another man who could command a majority in the House of Commons.

## George III's Enlightened Ambitions

King George III of Britain (ruled 1760–1820) dreamed of being an Enlightened Despot. Under the settlement of 1688, the king still had sweeping power, especially handing out jobs and monetary honors, and George was determined to use it. In the middle of the Seven Years' War against France, George dismissed Pitt and replaced him with his personal tutor. George copied the Newcastle system and maintained his own group in the House of Commons with payments and government honors. This group was called "the **King's Friends**." They let France have an easy peace in 1763. The king tried to increase his control over the thirty-one governments in the British Empire (the North American colonies all had separate governments). The only exception to this centralization was that the King gave more power to Protestant landowners in the Irish Parliament. Eventually, however, Ireland rebelled with the help of French troops and its Parliament was abolished in 1801. To run an empire, George had to take account of the needs of West Indian sugar planters, American Indians, French Canadians, and British taxpayers, not just North American colonists.

## Calls for Political Reform

Calls grew for political reform on two fronts: fixing the way of election and ending corruption. Most members of Commons were elected from **boroughs** (towns); many of these boroughs had few electors ("rotten boroughs") or were under the control of the local notable ("pocket boroughs"). Robert Clive, for example, bought a number of rotten borough seats to control. There had been no **reapportionment** (division to match how many people lived there) since 1688. There were only eight members of the House of Commons to represent the eight million people living around London, while forty-two members represented 100,000 people in Cornwall. Fifty-one English and Welsh boroughs with fewer than 1,500 voters total chose 100 members, about one-fifth of the House of Commons. The opponents of reform said that it was unnecessary and unwise. The British system, unlike today's American system, rests on the idea of **virtual representation**. Members of the House of Commons do not represent the district that elected them but all British possessions and people. There was no need for British workers or peasants or women to vote because the wise rich landowners of Britain already provided them with a fair representative.

## The Wilkes Affair

**John Wilkes** (1725–1797) was a reformist member of Parliament who wrote critical articles about the king and the peace with France. The government charged Wilkes with libel. The "King's Friends" expelled him from the House of Commons in 1764, although Wilkes had won his court case. Wilkes reprinted the article, was outlawed, and fled to France. When he returned in 1768, he was arrested. Demonstrators filled the streets chanting "no justice, no peace." Troops fired on the unarmed crowd, driving it into a frenzy. Wilkes was released from prison and elected to the Commons. The Commons refused to accept the result or let Wilkes take his seat. This happened three times. Then the Commons proclaimed the election loser as winner. Nevertheless, slow change began. In 1771, there was full press publicity of debates so the Parliament could no longer operate in secret. In 1774, Wilkes once again won election to the House of Commons. This time, with uneasiness about the King growing, he was allowed to take his seat. He immediately introduced a reform bill.

# NORTH AMERICAN PROBLEMS

George III's biggest headache came with North America. Since the 1680s, Britain had allowed these colonies to govern themselves and had not taxed them. It governed through colonial assemblies, some of which were quite democratic; 80 percent of adult white men got to vote in Massachusetts, for example. During the Seven Years' War, London struck down laws in Virginia and South Carolina and tightened royal control of the colonial courts. The British taxpayer had borne the entire cost of the war, and the British army had done most of the fighting. The population of the British colonies had grown from 250,000 in 1710 to 2.5 million by the 1770s. In the 1760s alone, the population of New York grew by 40 percent while Virginia's nearly doubled. Many of these were young people from England who had not found work, and oppressed people from Highland Scotland, the Scottish islands, and Ireland who bore grievances against the Crown. Starting in 1717, Britain had transported 30,000 convicts from England and 10,000 convicts from Ireland to North America.

## Pontiac's Rebellion and the Tax Acts

The Treaty of Paris had not ended the fighting in North America. After the war, the British settlers began to squeeze the Indians' territory. **Pontiac's Rebellion** erupted in 1763. This Ottawa chief formed an alliance with other Great Lakes tribes and attacked Fort Detroit. The British government decided to maintain 6,000 troops as a border force and forbade colonists from settling west of the Appalachian Mountains, lest it cause more Indian wars. This would also give London direct control over the lucrative French and Indian fur trade. That angered the colonists. Britain also worried that emigration was depleting the supply of British farm labor.

Britain was determined to get its money back through a series of increased taxes. At one time, the Land Tax of 1692 had paid 20 percent of revenue, but there had been no reassessment as the landowners controlled the House of Commons, and other taxes from sales and trade filled the gap. Britain had to pay £2 million a year interest on the money borrowed for the Seven Years' War plus another £3.5 million to defend the empire. The Revenue Act of 1764 (called the **Stamp Act**) effectively doubled taxes from one to two shillings per American while British residents paid twenty-six shillings per person. It would only raise £150,000 per year.

The largest colonies of Virginia and Massachusetts protested against the Stamp Act. Virginia delegate Patrick Henry proclaimed that there could be "no taxation without representation." This was a direct challenge to Virtual Representation. If King George yielded and gave the North American colonists a few representatives, it would encourage Wilkes and the reformers to demand their proper representation. Thus, the King was in a difficult position. Mob violence began to spread in Boston, the capital of Massachusetts. Radical thought had more influence in British America than Britain. *Cato's Letters* (1720–23) denounced the Walpole system as corrupt and armies as instruments of tyranny. The *Letters* sought a republic with no king, which was unthinkable for most Britons. Nine colonies met in a Stamp Act Congress (New Hampshire, Georgia, North Carolina, Virginia, and the Canadian colonies were not present). Parliament repealed the Act in 1766. The British tax situation grew worse as Parliament, against King George's wishes, reduced Land Tax enforcement.

# The Century of Revolution Begins

The repeal of the Stamp Act and the reduction of Land Tax enforcement led to the **Townshend Acts** (1767) on imported paint, glass, lead and tea. Under mercantilism, the American colonies had run a trade deficit of £2 million and had to balance it with illegal trade. Britain's Sugar Act of 1764 cracked down on smugglers. A merchant named Isaac Sears had created a mob in New York City to protest the Stamp Act. In January 1770, Sears and his mob clashed with British troops in the "Battle of Golden Hill." One New Yorker died of a stab wound. This was the first American blood spilled in a protest against British policies. New England had outgrown its food supply and felt the burden of mercantilism most keenly. Illicit trade with the Caribbean provided New England with the necessary money to buy manufactured goods from Britain. Boston tried to refuse imports, and violence culminated in the **Boston Massacre** (March 1770) where British troops who had been redeployed from the frontier killed five Americans. **Lord North** had just become Prime Minister of Britain. North was young at thirty-eight (the same age as George Washington and only two years older than King George) and had been a leader of the King's Friends. He had been a major force in expelling John Wilkes from the House of Commons and keeping him out. North now repealed all the Townshend Acts except for a symbolic tea tax. Parliament kept this just to show that it had the right to tax the American colonies.

# The Boston Tea Party

The tea issue became critical when the British East India Company, which had borne most of the costs for the Indian theater of the Seven Years' War, pleaded for help and was given a monopoly over the American tea trade; this would force a payment of tax. In December 1773, Bostonians destroyed the tea by throwing it into the harbor. A few months later, Sears and his New York mob boarded a ship and destroyed its tea. North now put through **Coercive Acts** to close the port of Boston and revise the Massachusetts colonial charter. He also extended Quebec's borders to the south to cut off more western territory.

# The Continental Congress

Some leading men in Massachusetts called for a meeting of the colonies to discuss a common response; all but Georgia and the Canadian colonies sent delegates to Philadelphia. It condemned all the acts since 1763. While **John Jay** claimed they were asserting rights as Englishmen, the radical Patrick Henry said that the contract of government in a Lockean sense had been dissolved and there was now a state of nature. Using the Enlightenment language of Montesquieu and Beccaria, the Congress sent letters to the Canadian colonies and to the colonies of East and West Florida asking for help, but got little. The Parliament dominated by the King's Friends declared the New England colonies in rebellion in February 1775. Radicals and others called for a reconciliation but lost in the Parliament by a vote of 270 to 78. The revolution began in April 1775 as local militia in Massachusetts fired on British troops at **Lexington and Concord**. The Continental Congress formed a defensive army of 20,000 and put it under the command of **George Washington** (1732–1799), an American officer from the Seven Years' War. This army expelled the British from Boston in 1776.

# Declaration of Independence

Authority became an issue as royal assemblies were overthrown, and chaos swept away government and tax collection. Sears briefly became the boss of New York City. The recently-arrived English radical **Thomas Paine** (1737–1809) and his pamphlet *Common Sense* (1775) whipped up public enthusiasm. The American literacy rate was one of the highest in the world: about 70 percent of men and 40 percent of women could read. *Common Sense* sold 150,000 copies from January to July 1776. About 6 percent of the whole populace bought the book over a seven-month period. **Thomas Jefferson** (1743–1826) of Virginia took the lead in drafting a Declaration of Independence (July 4, 1776) that used the terms of Locke and Enlightenment to bring a bill of charges against the King and state the reasons for a separation of the thirteen colonies from Britain. This included a condemnation of the slave trade, but Congress removed it from the final document. Nine state assemblies followed up on the Declaration by drafting new state charters. Six states solicited authority from the voters in advance; two submitted drafts for popular ratification. These charters varied widely: North Carolina reserved voting rights for the wealthy, while Pennsylvania extended voting rights for all male taxpayers over age twenty-one with annual elections. In Massachusetts about one-quarter of the free adult men participated in voting.

# Defeat of the British

Washington tried to avoid set battles with the British and their German mercenaries. As was common, much of the war depended on maneuver. Washington's defense of New York City in 1776 collapsed when the British got through Jamaica Pass at night and outflanked him. He beat a hasty retreat to New Jersey. A year later, the British forced the Congress to flee Philadelphia temporarily. Away from the coast and naval support, the British army ran into problems, losing the Battle of Saratoga for example.

In 1775, John Wilkes, now Lord Mayor of London, served as an intermediary between the American agent Arthur Lee and the French playwright Pierre de Beaumarchais. France shipped massive quantities of arms to the rebels but did not intervene until it thought the rebels had a chance to win after 1777. Spain entered the war in 1779, the Netherlands in 1780. France sent troops and ships. Learning from earlier lessons, the French had invested in a much better navy since 1763. The French sent a navy to the Indian Ocean that inflicted a series of defeats on the British. The British bungled an attack on the Dutch colony at the Cape of Good Hope, and the French reinforced that defense point.

The British shifted the conflict to the more loyal southern colonies in 1780, but this enmeshed them in complex local vendettas. The British impressed slaves as laborers for their army or to work for their loyalist planters. Meanwhile Massachusetts raised black battalions while Virginia and Maryland allowed slaves to serve in their armies in place of whites. Southern colonists turned against the British as their fear grew that Britain might free the slaves. The British had paid for 37 percent of the cost of the Seven Years' War with loans. They had to borrow 40 percent of the cost of the American War of Independence. The Dutch held more than 40 percent of the British debt and when they cut off further loans, it threatened the entire British debt structure. In 1781, the French navy won control of Chesapeake Bay even as a Franco-American force hemmed in the main British army at **Yorktown**. The British had to surrender. The Commons overturned the resolution fixing the election against Wilkes. In 1782, the reformers in the House of Commons invented a new device: they asked the members to state that they had confidence in Lord North and his government. Although North survived this **vote of no-confidence**, it was so close that he had to resign. The British debt in 1783 was nearly double what it had been in 1763, and the British government was paying an unsustainable 66 percent of its annual revenue just to cover interest on the debt.

The **Peace of Paris** (1783, not to be confused with the treaty of twenty years earlier) won U.S. independence, and Spain gained Florida and Minorca in the Mediterranean. It limited the French and British to an equal number of warships in the Indian Ocean. The United States would be the area between the Atlantic Ocean and the Mississippi River. Many Americans who had supported the British lost their land. Three to 5 percent of the total population left the United States forever. In both private land confiscation and emigration, the American Revolution was far more radical than the later French Revolution as 2,200 Loyalist estates were taken.

# AFTER THE WAR

The Congress continued to run affairs, but unlike Parliament, it had no taxing authority. The states contributed $6 million, and Congress borrowed more than $7 million. Congress also issued paper money. Some northern state constitutions provided for the gradual freeing of slaves: Pennsylvania began the process in 1780, New Jersey in 1804. New York had a gradual emancipation from 1799 to 1827. As late as 1830, there were still 3,500 slaves in the North. The northern states plus Maryland, Delaware, and Virginia all banned the African slave trade.

The soldiers presented a thorny problem. Congress had promised grants of 100 acres once the war was over but would not meet the demand of lifetime pensions at half pay. The soldiers wound up selling many of their land warrant certificates to speculators for a fraction of the value. After the peace treaty, some soldiers talked about forcing Congress to meet their demands, but Washington took a hard line against any action and strongly supported the demobilizing of the army. Despite the violence, North America would not be militarized as other revolutionary societies would be.

In March 1781 the states ratified the **Articles of Confederation**. The Union was a "league of friendship," and each state had one vote. Problems soon rose over debt payment by states, paper money, and the general postwar recession. The Articles could only be amended unanimously. Washington and a New York lawyer, **Alexander Hamilton** (1755–1804), called for a meeting in Philadelphia to correct the defects in the Articles.

# The U.S. Constitution

The Constitutional Convention of 1787 wrote a constitution and carefully separated powers among executive (the President), legislative (the Congress), and judicial branches. It was heavily influenced by the radical reformers in Britain, the Enlightenment (especially Montesquieu), and the ideas of ancient republics. In a radical departure, there would be no king or possibility of absolutism. As Locke would have wanted, the legislature would be supreme. The Constitutional Convention modeled the two houses of Congress on those of the British Parliament but since there were no nobles in the U.S. and the Constitution forbade the creation of a nobility, state legislatures would choose U.S. Senators. The House of Representatives would be elected under voting rights that differed from state to state. Equal districts for the House meant no rotten boroughs or pocket boroughs. There would be no property or religious qualification for any office, unlike Britain where only members of the Church of England could serve in Parliament. Many of the leaders of the revolution such as Washington and Jefferson were not Christians but **Deists**: they believed that God had created the universe but then left it alone and did not intervene in human affairs. When Hamilton was asked why Jesus' name was nowhere in the Constitution, he joked "We forgot!" In 1788, half of the states provided for popular election of presidential electors; not until 1828 did this become the general rule. The federal government gained the power to levy taxes and regulate interstate and foreign commerce, while the Constitution forbade states from diplomacy or taxing imports and exports.

As state conventions considered the Constitution, several demanded a **Bill of Rights**. The first ten amendments guaranteed various rights to all people under American authority (not just U.S. citizens), including freedom of the press, freedom of religion, the right to a jury trial, and no imprisonment without charge. Inspired by Beccaria, the Bill of Rights banned cruel and unusual punishments. Lester Langley has suggested that one of the main reasons that the states did not fragment like the South American states was that there was a strong danger that the trans-Appalachian West could be taken by the British, French, Spanish, and/or Indians. Access to the West had been a major cause of the revolutionary war, and more than 50,000 Americans had crossed the mountains to settle even when the British had banned it. During the war, American forces had roamed west to secure the Ohio river valley. The British abandoned their Indian allies in 1783, but low-level fighting continued for another ten years. Fragmentation would have handed the West to a foreign element and this threat kept pushing the thirteen states toward each other. The old ideas of federalism, limited government, and constitutionalism had been associated with reactionaries and nobles trying to fight the power of the king. Now these ideas became progressive.

# IMPACT OF THE AMERICAN REVOLUTION

The American Revolution and the Constitution showed the *philosophes* that their ideas could be put into practice. In 1778, American revolutionary leader Benjamin Franklin embraced the aged Voltaire to symbolize how the Enlightenment inspired the United States. Jefferson followed Franklin as Ambassador to France while John Adams was in the Netherlands. The Revolution inspired action as far away as the Comoros Islands in the Indian Ocean, where people rose up against Arab domination and claimed inspiration from America.

## Impact on the British Isles

An Anglican elite had long governed Ireland. Just 10 percent of the population owned 83 percent of the land. Absentee landlords were common. George III had put in some reforms such as holding elections every eight years, not just at the king's death. Ireland got a resident viceroy. The American Revolution caused a trade disaster in Ireland. The British feared a French invasion and armed "volunteers," but after Yorktown these volunteers pressed demands. Lord North granted more independence for the Irish Parliament and allowed Ireland to export more items, relaxing the mercantilist stranglehold that was destroying the Irish textile industry. The Irish Parliament allowed Catholics to buy land starting in 1782 and a few to vote starting in 1793. A reformist attempt to abolish rotten boroughs in Ireland failed.

The American catastrophe caused the fall of the King's Friends and the rise of a new generation led by **Charles James Fox**, who had supported the American rebels and the Irish volunteers, and **William Pitt the Younger**.

Pitt introduced an electoral reform bill that was defeated by a vote of 161 to 141. In 1785, as Prime Minister, Pitt tried to abolish the thirty-two most depopulated boroughs. After this failed, Pitt's interest in reform waned and he became North's successor as King George's trusted minister. Fox was his great opponent. Parliament voted down attempts to allow non-Anglican Protestants to hold civil, military, or town office.

# The Netherlands

The population was small (less than two million) but it held 40 percent of British debt and in 1796 all of the U.S. debt. The regents, hereditary aristocrats who controlled town councils, clashed with the Stadholder (a hereditary Dutch noble who controlled the army) over American relations. In 1786, "Patriot" regents got control of Holland, the largest state in the Netherlands, and two other states. This broke into civil war in 1787 with Britain and France arming the two sides. The German state of Prussia intervened with British backing to drive out the Patriots.

To the south were the Austrian Netherlands. Their leaders rebelled against Emperor Joseph II in 1789 when he tried to tighten his control as King George had tried in North America. They passed a Declaration of Independence and then an Act of Union based on the American Articles of Confederation. The Church and the nobles rallied the peasants against the rebels, and Austria regained control in 1790.

# Conclusion

The French were moving in all parts of the world against the British. They concluded an alliance with the Nertherlands in 1785. They encouraged the Dutch Patriots in 1786 to send thousands more troops to the Cape Colony and to Ceylon to reinforce these depots against the British. The Cape served as a major base for private captains ("privateers") to attack and plunder passing British merchant ships. In 1784, the French gained the right to build a naval base in Göteborg, Sweden, that would allow its navy to harass and block the timber transports in the Baltic Sea that Britain desperately needed. Pitt worried about the potent combination of Dutch bases and French ships and the threat to British India. The French set up their own East India Company in 1785 in anticipation of plucking that British fruit.

It became impossible to disguise the American Revolution as a restoration of ancient liberties. By the time of the Declaration, the Americans admitted that they were doing something new and moving forward. The refusal to have a king and nobility confirmed a total break with the norms of absolutism.

The Constitution had taken older ideas promoted by Montesquieu but utterly transformed them into progressive policies by including many of the demands of Wilkes and the radical reformers. The revolutionaries regularly employed Enlightenment language to justify their actions. The events in America left the conservatives aghast and made the United States the beacon of freedom and liberty for the next seventy years. The people, not an intermediate body as allowed by Grotius and Althusius, had carried out the revolution. *Common Sense* had been the turning point for popular opinion.

# TIMELINE

| | |
|---|---|
| 1763 | End of Seven Years' War between France and Britain leave both deeply in debt |
| 1763–64 | Pontiac's Rebellion in North America |
| 1764 | House of Commons expels John Wilkes |
| | Stamp Act |
| 1767 | Townshend Acts |
| 1770 | Battle of Golden Hill and Boston Massacre |
| 1773 | Boston Tea Party |
| 1775 | American Revolution begins |
| 1776 | Declaration of Independence |
| 1781 | French and Americans defeat British at Yorktown |
| 1782 | First vote of no-confidence in British House of Commons |
| 1783 | Peace of Paris ends American war |
| 1787 | United States Constitution |
| | Civil War in the Netherlands |
| 1789 | U.S. Bill of Rights |

# KEY TERMS

Robert Clive
John Wilkes
Boston Tea Party
U.S. Declaration of Independence
The U.S. Constitution

# PRIMARY SOURCE DOCUMENTS

**Robert Clive**, http://www.fordham.edu/halsall/mod/1757plassey.asp

**John Wilkes**, http://18thcenturyreadingroom.blogspot.com/2006/03/item-of-day-john-wilkes-north-briton.html

**Patrick Henry**, http://www.law.ou.edu/ushistory/henry.shtml

**Thomas Paine**, http://www.fordham.edu/halsall/mod/paine-common.asp

**Thomas Jefferson, Declaration of Independence**, http://avalon.law.yale.edu/18th_century/declare.asp

**Ebenezer Denny**, http://www.let.rug.nl/usa/documents/1776-1785/ebenezer-denny-1781-describing-the-surrender-of-cornwallis-at-yorktown.php

**U.S. Constitution and Bill of Rights**, http://avalon.law.yale.edu/18th_century/usconst.asp

# ATTEMPTS AT REFORM

France was a rich country. On average, its people had about two-thirds of the wealth of the average English or Dutch resident, but the French were far better off than the people in Spain, China, Mexico, or the Italian lands. Because many more people lived in France, its economy was perhaps one-third or one-half larger than Britain's and was the biggest in Europe. The Seven Years' War compelled King Louis XV of France (ruled 1715–1774) to take strong measures. He imposed a 5 percent tax on net landed revenue in 1749, which he raised to 10 percent in 1756, and 15 percent in 1760. He tried to take offices from corrupt officeholders. The nobles had gotten out of hand. They imprisoned royal governors and military commanders who tried to carry out the King's commands. In 1771, he stripped much of the power from the noble court of Paris and exiled the judges.

## The Aristocratic Reaction

### Failure of Reform

King Louis XV contracted smallpox and died. His grandson, **Louis XVI** (ruled 1774–1793) wanted to be loved by all at the beginning of his reign and repealed the previous decrees. Nobles whipped up the mob of Paris to ensure there would be no reversal. Like George III, Louis XVI fancied himself an Enlightened Despot. He would not address the issue of taxing the nobles.

Before the government could deal with education or poor relief, the nobles forced even mild reforms to cease. There were some limited rights given to Protestants. France abolished its tax on Jews. The call for reform grew.

## Fiscal Crisis

French aid to American colonies during their revolution had put a heavy strain on the French Treasury. Instead of raising taxes, the Treasury under **Jacques Necker** borrowed a billion *livres* at interest rates as high as 10 percent from 1777 to 1781. By 1787, the monarchy was up against the wall: heavy debts, no way to raise taxes, no way to borrow more money. Finance Minister **Charles de Calonne** called for a new property tax and the abolition of internal grain tariffs to create free trade. When the nobles resisted, the government called an **Assembly of Notables** to discuss the problems of France. This upper-class group rejected the Calonne proposal and said that only the **Estates-General** could raise taxes. This was the French equivalent of the British Parliament and had not met in 175 years. The notables demanded that control be given to provincial assemblies, which they expected to control, in return for taxes.

## The Debt

The government debt was four billion *livres*. The French budget of 1787 would have 475 million *livres* in taxes and borrow 145 million. It spent 50 percent to service the debt, 27 percent on the military, and 6 percent to maintain the king and his palaces. This left only 17 percent for useful spending. France had only half of the equivalent debt of Britain and less than a fifth the per capita debt of the British. Since France had a much larger economy than Britain, there should not have been a problem, but unlike Britain, France did not have a solid banking and credit system.

# THE REVOLUTION OF 1789

## Calling of the Estates-General

The King tried to decree taxes, but the court of Paris refused to register them. The King banished the court but had to recall it after a month due to popular outcry. The court sensed blood and in January 1788, it presented a list of grievances. The King abolished it and called for the Estates-General. The nobles insisted that the Estates-General should meet as it had in 1614: three separate estates of clergy (First Estate), nobles (Second Estate), and everyone else (Third Estate). This would control the middle class. The public had seen the nobles as its only defense against the tax-hungry state but now grew angry at the naked power grab that would certainly raise the ordinary person's taxes. The middle class began to find its voice in the work of **Abbé Emmanuel Sieyès'** work *What is the Third Estate?* (1789) which said that the Third Estate is everyone. As such, the Third Estate should have 600 representatives as opposed to 300 each for the nobles and clergy. Sieyès claimed that he was a "patriot" (like the Dutch revolutionaries) and reformers took this label, identifying themselves with the nation. The royal council agreed and doubled the Third Estate. The nobles and clergy raised no objection because they believed that voting would be by chamber and they would always control two of the three chambers.

## The Nobility

To raise money, the government had opened more offices for sale in the eighteenth century. Men would pay for these offices because they conferred nobility. From 1715 to 1789 there were 6,500 new noble families; this made up 25 to 33 percent of all noble families, so the nobility was relatively new. Many rich town dwellers bought land, many nobles served as investors. Noble families comprised 400,000 persons (about 2 percent of the population) and owned about 25 percent of the land. The French nobles had largely avoided taxation and had other privileges: only they could carry a sword in public, sit in the first pew in Church, or be buried in a cathedral or its grounds. They walked in the front line of processions. Nobles could appoint judges in their area, could punish civil and minor criminal offenses, and could sell crops first to local merchants when the price was highest. They received payments made by peasants in the form of money, goods, and services. However, nobles constantly had to prove to the King's government that they had the money and drive to maintain their noble status. Louis XV's taxes enraged them not only because they infringed on their privileges but also threatened the status of some. Nevertheless, about one-third of the nobles in the Estates-General were "patriots."

## The Church

In France, there were about 240,000 clergy (1 percent of the population) during the Enlightenment. It held about 10 percent of the revenue-producing land. Most money in the church went to bishops, who were nobles. There were many non-noble priests who were unhappy with the rule of the nobles in the church. Parish priests were key figures in the villages: they were often the only literate men in the village and would announce new laws and had outside contacts. They were often the spokesmen for the village. A little under one-half of the clergy in the Estates-General were "patriots."

## The Commoners

The upper part of the Third Estate became influential as trade increased 500 percent from 1713 to 1789. The **bourgeoisie** (the upper class of the cities that was not a part of the nobility or the clergy) grew to about 8 percent of the total population of France. It resented noble privileges and felt shut out from government. Outside of the upper part, commoners were not well off compared with nobles. Price inflation rose 65 percent from 1730 to 1780, while wages rose only 22 percent. About half of the peasants owned land. Around one-sixth of the commoners elected to the Estates-General were conservatives; the rest were "patriots."

## The Election Process

There were several stages: primary assemblies chose regional assemblies of electors. The electors then chose deputies to the Estates-General. The assemblies also drew up grievance petitions at each level. The King decreed that all men over the age of twenty-five who had paid taxes equal to three days' wages could meet in the primary assembly. Most of the grass roots petitions complained about the high burden of taxes and the obligations to nobles. The regional and national petitions were more radical: an unequal tax system, a middle class excluded from politics (particularly from local politics), an inefficient government, and finally, the fiscal crisis. Paris had 30,000 voters eligible out of 500,000 residents; 12,000 (40 percent) showed up at sixty primary assemblies. Most of the 407 Paris electors chosen in this process were lawyers and government officials. The 1789 elections for the Third Estate were much more democratic than the British elections of the time. Only some American states were more generous in voting rights. A few women participated in the primary assemblies of the First and Second Estates. Not a single peasant or artisan was part of the Estates-General at the King's palace of Versailles outside Paris.

## The Tennis Court Oath and the National Assembly

The Estates-General opened on May 5, 1789. The King had recalled Necker as finance minister to try to win some reformist support. The "patriots" were not as radical as the Americans and wanted to keep a king as long as he was subject to a Constitution and the Estates-General. They also wanted a guarantee of liberties and liberal economic reforms such as eliminating internal trade barriers.

The Estates-General met in its three estates: clergy, nobility, and commoners. The commoners demanded a single assembly where all three would vote together. Otherwise, the commons would be overruled by the other two estates. The swing group was the clergy, divided between wealthy bishops and poorer parish priests. On June 13, a few clergymen went over to sit with the Third Estate. The clergy's first vote on sitting together failed by a vote of 133 to 114. King Louis' own family was divided: his brothers sat in the Estates-General as conservative nobles, but his cousin **Philippe, the Duke of Orléans (Philippe Égalité)**, joined the patriot nobles.

On June 17, 1789, the Third Estate declared itself a **National Assembly** and invited the other two estates to join it. The clergy now agreed to join, giving it legal authority. King Louis, never a strong personality, was distracted because his infant son had died a week before. The King closed the meeting hall to the National Assembly on June 20, so it met on a nearby tennis court, where it took the **Tennis Court Oath** not to disband until it had written a constitution for France. King Louis went back and forth: first he was conciliatory, then harsh. Eighteen thousand soldiers massed around Versailles at the end of June.

## The Great Fear

The winter of 1788/89 had been the coldest of the century. The bread price had doubled and was at its highest since 1715. Families had spent 50 percent of their budgets on bread in 1788, 80 percent in 1789. With food so expensive, many workers had lost their jobs and wandered the roads as beggars, thieves, and robbers. The harvest was poor. When the king dismissed Necker on July 11, the 407 electors of Paris met to form their own provisional government committee and arm themselves. Necker was popular in Paris because he had imported grain to feed the people. The mob raided prisons. On July 14, it grabbed cannon and 32,000 muskets from the Invalides, and then a mob of 8,000 men and women **stormed the fortress of the Bastille** to gain arms. Ninety-eight Parisians were killed. The mob killed the governor and put his head up on a pike and displayed it, just as government had done to so many criminals.

Louis immediately backed down as he believed the troops were unreliable. He recognized the citizens' committee as the city government of Paris. The **Marquis de Lafayette** (1757–1834), who had fought in the American Revolution, took over command of the guard. Lafayette sent the key to the Bastille to George Washington. The Paris leaders displayed a new **tricolor** flag: the red and blue colors of Paris with Bourbon (the king's family) white. Rumors swept the countryside that conservatives were gathering an army of beggars to reassert their privileges and ancient taxes. Revolts broke out in the countryside as peasants burned tax records and refused to honor feudal dues usually done in the summer. Mobs robbed or murdered grain dealers. Twenty thousand conservative nobles left France. Provisional governments took power in twenty-six of the thirty largest cities.

### The End of Privilege

On August 4, the nobles agreed to give up privileges (including their tax privileges) in exchange for an amount of money that was never paid. The peasants had won a great victory. On August 27, the National Assembly issued the **Declaration of the Rights of Man and Citizen**, a combination of British and American demands for rights: freedom of thought, freedom of religion, all equal under the law. Only citizens or their representatives could enact laws and taxes. The natural rights were "liberty, property, security, and resistance to oppression." The State could take property but only with fair compensation. The Assembly elected a patriot noble named **Honoré de Mirabeau** (1748– 1791) as its president and began to compose a constitution.

# THE LOWER CLASSES PROJECT POWER

## The Move to Paris

Rumors swept Paris that the King would not accept the reforms and that he would use troops. King Louis' brother-in-law was Joseph II, the Habsburg ruler of Austria. Perhaps the Austrians, already sour on the revolution in the Austrian Netherlands, would aid the King. False stories spread of members of the King's Bodyguard wearing Habsburg colors. On October 5, about 6,000 women walked the thirteen miles from Paris to Versailles to ask what was going on and demand relief from the high food prices. The men of the National Guard joined them the next day. The King was conciliatory, but a scuffle broke out in which one Parisian and two bodyguards were killed. The mob dragged the King back to Paris, along with his wife Marie Antoinette, their son, and wagons full of flour. The National Assembly followed. From this point on, the Paris mob was the dominant force; shouts from galleries would drown out speakers not liked by the mob. More conservatives began to go back to their estates or form a second wave of emigration.

## The Jacobin Clubs

During the debates over constitution in the fall of 1789, many men formed societies to debate constitutional issues. The most important was the Society of the Friends of the Constitution, known as the Club of St. James or **Jacobins** because they met in a former monastery. Dues were fairly expensive so only people from the middle class and upper middle class could join the Jacobin club as they tried to coordinate strategy among their few members.

## Constitutional Monarchy

The Assembly wrote a constitution allowing the king a veto for four years, and limited suffrage that gave 4.3 million Frenchmen full voting rights (about 16 percent of the total population and close to two-thirds of the adult male population). Men over age twenty-five who paid a small tax would vote for electors from a pool of 50,000 men who paid taxes equivalent to fifty-four days of labor. The electors would then vote for a legislative assembly. The constitution favored country districts over the towns and cities. The Assembly abolished internal tariffs, erased old provincial boundaries, and replaced them with eighty-three Departments of roughly equal size. These consisted of smaller districts and cantons. Municipal government became uniform. All local officials would be elected locally. It seemed that the revolution was over.

# CHURCH, STATE, AND *ASSIGNATS*

The upheaval did not solve the financial crisis that started the revolution. The call for "patriotic" loans fell upon deaf ears. Necker announced a budget deficit of 294 million *livres*, worse than ever. The Assembly took the radical step of confiscating all the lands of the Catholic Church and the monasteries in November 1789. This land was to be collateral for 400 million *livres'* worth of *assignats*, a 3 percent bond; by September 1790, another 800 million *livres* were being printed up in smaller denominations (fifty *livres*). The value of the land was more than 1,200 million *livres*, but people were hoarding hard money or taking it out of the country. Bad harvests had led to a trade deficit as France tried to buy wheat. When they gained power after August 1792, the Jacobins printed small-money notes, which they would exchange for *assignats*. The government then issued 100 million *livres* in five-*livre assignats*. This led to a spiral of inflation as the government printed more and more in smaller denominations. At the end of 1791, they were being accepted at 75 percent of face value; four months later, at 60 percent, as counterfeiters had a field day.

The government then sold church land in large, undivided blocks, so most peasants could not afford to buy it. Without its land, the Church officials had to be supported by the government as employees of the state. Under the **Civil Constitution of the Clergy** passed by the Assembly, priests and bishops would be chosen by the same electors who voted for the Assembly, including Protestants and Jews. In April 1791 Pope Pius VI condemned this arrangement and the entire Revolution. Half of all the priests in France resigned, and the new priests were not liked by the people. Only seven of 130 bishops were willing to swear the oath of loyalty to the constitution. An underground church with the old priests sprang up.

# POLARIZATION OF THE KING AND THE ASSEMBLY

Mirabeau's death in April 1791 weakened the moderates. Another wave of strikes by disgruntled workers swept through the cities. On June 20, 1791, the king and his family attempted to flee France, leaving a note behind repudiating the revolution. They were caught and dragged back. The "patriots" who dominated the Assembly were now stuck. They did not want an American-style republic and were saddled with an unpopular king. A growing number of people wanted a republic, and they took over the Jacobin clubs. In September 1791, the Assembly declared the constitution in effect and held the first elections under the new system. No one from the first National Assembly was allowed to run for another term so there would be no candidates with the advantage of incumbency. Participation in the election was disappointing: only 25 percent of active citizens (or about 4 percent of the total population) bothered voting. Even Paris, the center of the revolution, had a turnout of only 10 percent of voters. When the new National Assembly met October 1, 1791, the conservatives had vanished. The political groups were the old "patriots," trying to preserve a constitutional monarchy, squaring off against the Jacobins who favored a republic. Of 745 votes in the Assembly, neither side had 200 votes. The center, called the **Marsh** (because it was soft and squishy), voted with whatever minority it feared more.

International tensions grew. The Revolution inspired the lower classes in the German-speaking lands, the Austrian Netherlands, England, and Hungary. The British easily rigged juries in Scotland to convict Jacobin sympathizers. Businessmen wished they could dominate their governments as the French had. The Jacobins pushed the idea of seizing the papal land of

Avignon, a small independent area surrounded by French territory. Absolutist rulers grew more oppressive. French émigrés centered in the Austrian capital of Vienna lobbied Marie Antoinette's Habsburg brothers to attack France. The leaders of Prussia and Austria issued the Pillnitz Declaration on August 27, 1791, and declared that they would protect Louis as a brother monarch and go to war if all joined them. This was nonsense because they knew that financially-burdened Britain was completely opposed to another war with France.

# RIGHTS OF WOMEN

The *philosophes*, even Rousseau, had generally been silent or negative about the place of women in their progressive society. The language of the Anglo-American radicals began to change that. American women sewed uniforms, made gunpowder, ran farmsteads, fought and died promoting the idea of American freedom. In New Jersey, for a brief time, women even gained voting rights. Women played a key role with the transfer of the King to Paris. The Declaration of the Rights of Man overthrew privilege. **Olympe de Gouges** (d.1793) wrote a "Declaration of the Rights of Women and Female Citizen" in 1791. In December 1790, the Dutch baroness Etta Palm d'Aelders called for civil rights for women. The *philosophe* Marquis de Condorçet considered the "Admission of Women to Rights of Citizenship."

The Briton Edmund Burke bitterly condemned the French Revolution in his *Reflections on the Revolution in France* (1790). Britons Tom Paine (*The Rights of Man*) and **Mary Wollstonecraft** (1759–1797) (*A Vindication of the Rights of Man*) defended the Revolution. Wollstonecraft, who had founded a girls' school, then made the next step, *A Vindication of the Rights of Women* (1792). Anger in Britain forced both Paine and Wollstonecraft to flee to France. However, Jacobin leaders had no interest in women's rights; they soon dissolved the Society of Revolutionary Women and when the Terror was at its height, women were seen as the leading defenders of old religion. The Jacobins executed Gouges as a royalist.

# WAR WITH EUROPE AND THE "SECOND REVOLUTION"

## The Fall of the Monarchy

### The Move to War

A left-of-center group, the **Girondists**, controlled the Jacobin clubs and called for war. They believed that it would discredit King Louis, cause his fall, and allow the Jacobins to establish an American-style republic. They urged France to spread the revolution, and on April 20, 1792, the French National Assembly declared war on Austria, supposedly because of the Pillnitz declaration. Only seven deputies opposed the war. Patriot leaders such as Lafayette believed that appearing as a war leader would improve Louis XVI's damaged image. The King could then enforce the constitution and crush the radicals. Émigrés who had grown in number were happy, wanting to see revolution strangled. Prussia joined Austria as its general swore that he would restore Louis to his full absolutist power and punish Paris. Inflation was in high gear by the spring of 1792 as counterfeit *assignats* circulated and the market was breaking down. From 1790 to 1793, the price of bread rose by 27 percent, beef by 136 percent, and potatoes by 700 percent.

### War Hysteria Rules

To understand why France went berserk, one must always recall that there was war hysteria. Victory by the Austrians and émigré nobles would mean terrible retribution not only against the leaders of the revolution, but also the many peasants who had risen in the countryside. Some French nobles, including two brothers of the King, were helping the enemy. This spread the fear of a "hidden enemy" inside France. Winning was worth any price, and there was a terrible logic. Those who opposed the increasing pace of trials and executions might be secret enemies themselves. The government applied torture that only brought a flood of false accusations and more witch hunts. The war was at the root of the Terror.

The war went very badly. Only nobles had led the army before the revolution. Two-thirds of the army officers had fled. The army was disorganized, and many officers were inexperienced. The government could not afford mercenaries. The radical Jacobins claimed that King Louis was supporting the enemy. In June, Lafayette tried to raise the National Guard to crush the Jacobins. On August 1, 1792, the Assembly ordered the arming of all able-bodied men. Any man who volunteered for the army would gain voting rights.

## The Convention Takes Over

On August 10, 1792, the mob, swelled by provincial recruits, stormed the Tuileries Palace, killed six hundred Swiss Guards, and arrested the King. The radical Jacobins, led by **Georges Danton** (1759–1794), the deputy prosecutor of Paris, allied uneasily with the moderate Jacobins. Danton took command of a provisional government and suspended the constitution. Even though the constitution had only been in effect for a year, the Jacobins said a new one must be written in a Constitutional **Convention**. All men would be allowed to vote for the Convention, about 28 percent of the population. Turnout varied wildly depending on the area: between 10 and 50 percent of those eligible turned out for the election. Despite the wider electorate, there were only two workers in the Convention.

The old Patriots such as Lafayette had fled or retired from politics. All the leaders of the Convention belonged to Jacobin clubs, whose membership swelled as more and more joined. Tom Paine was one member of the Convention. The Girondists controlled about one-quarter of the seats as the right wing, representing mostly great provincial cities. They were opposed by **the Mountain**, drawn from Paris and controlling about 40 percent of the seats. Danton was the main figure, backed by the bloodthirsty failed doctor **Jean-Paul Marat** (1743–1793) and the lawyer **Maximilien Robespierre** (1758–1794). This group had opposed the war earlier but now was determined to spread revolutionary republicanism across Europe. The Mountain's supporters in Paris were known as *sans-culottes*, because they wore long trousers rather than the knee-length breeches common to the upper and middle classes. Fear led to summary executions of prisoners in the **September Massacres** in major cities, including between 1,100 and 1,400 persons in Paris. Good war news finally came in September when a French army beat the Prussians at the Battle of Valmy. The French moved into the Austrian Netherlands, Savoy, Mainz, and the left bank of the Rhine river.

## The Terror

The quasi-religious fervor that accompanies many revolutions was especially prominent after the Jacobin takeover. They proclaimed the Year 1 with a new revolutionary calendar named after weather events. Months included Brumaire (the cloudy month), Fructidor (the harvest month), and Thermidor (the hot month). They expanded education as Rousseau might have wanted but regimented it tightly. Dechristianization began: the government fostered cults of reason and the Supreme Being set up, although Robespierre tried to preach tolerance. Their equivalent of God's kingdom on earth was the "Republic of Virtue."

The September Massacres had polarized the situation. Debate centered over the trial of the King. The Convention found the king guilty of treason by an overwhelming vote. On punishment, 361, including the King's cousin Philippe Égalité, voted for death, 334 voted for some other punishment, thirty-four voted for death under certain conditions. The Mountain gained control of the Jacobin clubs by December 1792 and began to expel the Girondists. On January 21, 1793, Louis XVI was executed. His head was cut off by a new "humane" device called the **guillotine**. Its conceiver, Dr. Guillotin, had complained that axemen were too likely to miss their targets and need several chops to take the head off. His device fit the neck securely into a bracket. A heavy, sharp blade would then do the job every time with little awareness by the victim. It would become known as the "revolutionary razor." The government guillotined Queen Marie Antoinette in October.

The Convention then ordered a military draft to raise 300,000 new soldiers as it expanded the war and declared war on Britain, Holland and Spain. A royalist revolt in western France, supplied by the British, protested the draft and demanded the return of the Old Regime and the old priests. More men, including a general and Louis Philippe, the son of Philippe Égalité, went over to the Austrian side. There was a vast tax shortfall because of the chaos in the provinces; the government issued more *assignats* and sold the lands of the Church that were supposed to be collateral for the *assignats*. The Austrians and Prussians pushed into France. Mobs demanded that hoarders of food be killed and called for price controls. This led to charges of treason being thrown about. Marat was tried but acquitted. The government authorized trials without jury or appeal. It set up Revolutionary Committees in each section or town to look for traitors.

The Jacobins were in a difficult position. The French armies were again collapsing, and the entire power structure was lined up against them. Reactionary nobles controlled much of western France; Prussia and Austria were pressing on the eastern border. The underground church told its followers that the Jacobins were devils. If the reactionaries won, it would mean the restoration of the king and absolutism and certain death or exile for the revolutionary leaders. They were fighting for their vision of a better world but also fighting for their lives. There was no possibility for compromise once the King was under arrest. The Jacobins now "doubled down" on the Revolution, hoping that a much larger and inspired army could defeat the reactionaries internally and externally. They had no money for trained soldiers so they would have to draft young Frenchmen. Since they would be paid little, these young men would have to be given a cause, the cause of revolution and the future. The government would have to print money and deal with the debts after it gained peace. Printing money caused price inflation and the Jacobin government's only choice was to freeze prices and wages. To prevent the spread of rebellion or undermining of the war effort, only the harshest of penalties would suffice: death. Step by step, there was an awful logic to the Terror.

The Convention set up a **Committee of Public Safety** in April 1793. The name came from the English Civil War; it had the power to oversee the Executive Council and suspend its decrees. Philippe Égalité, Duke of Orléans, was suspected of trying to follow his cousin as king; the Committee arrested and executed him. The Convention wrote a new constitution establishing a liberal democratic republic, then suspended it immediately. Danton set up a Commission of Twelve to investigate treason. The sans-culottes accused the moderate Girondists of treason, and the first arrests came on May 31, 1793. The radical Mountain group led by Danton and Robespierre now took complete control.

The **Reign of Terror** (1793–1794) began. The arrest of the Girondists triggered waves of revolts, the crippling of the army, and the advance of the enemy. Robespierre was put on the Committee of Public Safety on July 27 and became its guiding force. The Committee temporarily stopped inflation by freezing prices and warned that it would regard any merchant breaking the price law as a traitor. The government replaced locally-elected officials with centrally-appointed administrators. On August 23, 1793, the desperate government ordered the *Levée en masse*: all unmarried Frenchmen aged eighteen to twenty-five had to join the army. Older and married men would engage in war work, women would work in hospitals and make tents and clothing; old men should engage in propaganda. The government confiscated gold and silver and foreign currency. The Committee imposed strict wage and price controls, punishable by death. Resistance and black markets sprang up. Peasants stored or destroyed goods. The government outlawed pastries and white bread, confiscated supplies and ordered production of items needed for the war. Orders made the army more mobile and filled it with revolutionary fervor. By the end of 1793, France's army topped 700,000 men. Nine months later, it was well over a million.

By end of 1793, Danton and others began to call for an end to the Terror. Robespierre in 1794, after military success, began to relax the economic controls. The most radical sect, led by Jacques Hébert, a writer and publisher, formed a conspiracy to redistribute all property and plotted to overthrow Robespierre. Instead Hébert was executed. Danton's allies criticized the Committee of Public Safety for abuses of civil rights and challenged the

Convention. The Committee arrested Danton and executed him April 5, 1794.

The Terror officially executed 17,000 and imprisoned 500,000 persons. Twenty thousand died in prison or were killed without a trial. Convention attendance was often below a hundred, for it had no power and no one would cross Robespierre. France was mobilizing its full strength and power for the war, and the world would tremble.

# The Thermidorian Reaction

The executions of Hébert and Danton led to the question: who's next? New laws speeded up executions tenfold and deprived the accused of the right to a defense attorney. On July 26 (8 Thermidor under the Revolutionary calendar), Robespierre spoke to the Convention and asked it to investigate a possible conspiracy, but the Convention referred it to a committee. The next day, he returned with specific accusations but found that his enemies controlled the mob in the galleries and shouted him down. The Convention moved before the Paris Commune or Jacobin clubs could organize themselves. On July 28, Robespierre was arrested and guillotined, ending the Terror.

The Convention stripped the committees of power, disbanded most revolutionary committees, and restored legal rights. There were fewer executions, and suspects were released. It abolished price controls in December 1794. Inflation returned: the *assignats* had fallen to 34 percent of face value by Thermidor, then 20 percent by winter 1794. They would fall to 8 percent by the spring of 1795, and 4 percent by the summer 1795. Bread prices rose 1,300 percent from March to May 1795. Beef prices rose 500 percent, pork and eggs more than 100 percent. In general, the cost of living rose 900 percent from 1790 to 1795, while wages did not keep pace. The government closed the Jacobin clubs in November 1794. The Convention recalled the Girondists in March 1795. Economic suffering was great but the most radical Paris leaders had died in the Terror, and the new government suppressed the mob of Paris when it imprisoned 1,200 after a demonstration on May 22, 1795. The Jacobins who had ousted Robespierre were themselves removed in the "White Terror." The government ordered the execution of the members of the revolutionary committee as the émigrés began to return. It granted toleration of the Church in February 1795; the underground priests began to resurface.

The Terror sputtered to an end, but its impact was felt for two centuries. For the next two hundred years, the rich and members of the power elite knew that if they went too far in oppressing the lower classes, there could be an upsurge of violence and they could all wind up hanging from lampposts or shaved by the revolutionary razor.

# The Directory

The Convention wrote yet another constitution. It limited voting rights to about 8 percent of the population and reduced the pool of electors to 30,000 from 50,000 in 1791. There would be two chambers, as in the United States. The Council of 500 initiated bills and passed them after three readings. One-third of the 500 had to retire each year. The Council of Ancients (all members were over forty years of age) could not initiate or amend but passed bills from the Council of 500. The Council of 500 chose five Directors, and one Director had to retire each year by random lot. The Convention automatically put two-thirds of its surviving members into these councils.

This constitution caused much discontent. Royalism began to grow. The son of Louis XVI and Marie Antoinette had died in prison in June 1795. His uncle proclaimed himself Louis XVIII and called for full reaction and to turn the clock back to 1789. In October 1795 a royalist mob outnumbered troops by four to one, but the troops had cannons and were led by a young general named Napoleon Bonaparte. The Government was becoming dependent upon the army. Bandits multiplied on roads. There were also conspiracies on the radical left. Gracchus Babeuf organized the "Conspiracy of Equals" in 1796 to abolish private property. The Directory smashed this conspiracy and executed Babeuf.

The Directory tried to repair the damaged economy. It oversaw the rationing of scarce resources, foreign exchange, and the stock market. Metal coinage began to return. It imposed high tariffs to protect industry and reduced spending. Most people were tired of the revolution. They were no longer seeking God's kingdom on earth or a Republic of Virtue. Many wanted the peace of the old days, including a king. The Directors were also tired of revolution but knew that if Louis XVI's brother returned, he would have their heads.

# The Revolution Expands outside of France

In December 1794, the French army moved into the Netherlands and proclaimed the **Batavian Republic** on the French model. France made peace with Prussia and Spain at the **Peace of Basel** in 1795. France gained much land west of the Rhine River and annexed the Austrian Netherlands (Belgium). The Belgians, Dutch, and Rhineland Germans had been dissatisfied with their rulers and did not rise against the French. In many areas, people welcomed the French as liberators. In Paris, revolutionaries from across Europe had gathered to work on revolutions in Ireland, Poland, Switzerland, the German lands, and the Italian lands.

## The Netherlands

The Republic resumed the Patriot movement of the 1780s that Britain and Prussia had stopped. Many leaders turned radical and revolutionary only under the circumstances. Between 4 and 12 percent of adult males had belonged to Dutch Jacobin clubs before the French invasion. The French reassured the moderates: all they wanted was the ouster of the English and the stadholder. There was no Reign of Terror. Once they were victorious, the French demanded some Dutch territory, the maintenance of a French army of occupation, a payment of indemnity, and for the Dutch to declare war on Britain. In exile, the stadholder authorized the British occupation of all Dutch colonies. The British also captured Dutch ships and suspended payment on their debt to the Dutch.

In February 1796 a Dutch Constitutional Convention was elected by all men except paupers. Too many compromises led the voters to reject the proposed constitution in August 1797. In January 1798, a coup drove the conservatives from the convention. This led to a new Constitution creating a unitary government, ending the long history of federalism. It gave more power to direct elections rather than electoral colleges and gave citizens the ability to initiate amendments. The voters approved this Constitution overwhelmingly, and it would survive the fall of the government.

## Italy

In 1796, a French army poured through northern Italy to attack the Austrian-held lands there. The governments were afraid to arm their own people lest they lead a revolution. After breaking up the Paris demonstration in 1795, Napoleon had received a command. With just 30,000 troops and outnumbered two to one, on May 10, 1796, Napoleon personally stormed across the bridge at **Lodi** in a hail of gunfire and led his troops in a rout of the Austrians. His army was intensely loyal. What had begun as just a diversion from the center and north became the breakthrough area. Napoleon lived on local requisitions in Italy and established his own foreign policy. The cities aided the French by rebelling against the old rulers and the Austrians. Napoleon established the **Cisalpine Republic** with Milan as its capital. Napoleon extorted funds from fearful cities and stole art treasures. The liberation of Italy echoed across the Atlantic: in 1798 the American Senator Andrew Jackson praised it and hoped that England would be next. Napoleon concluded the **Treaty of Campo Formio** in October 1797 with Austria: France kept Belgium and the left bank of the Rhine, and Austria recognized the Cisalpine Republic. Austria annexed Venice. Revolutionary activity, aided by Napoleon, swept through Italy in 1798 and 1799. Genoa changed into the **Ligurian Republic**. In Rome, the Pope lost his temporal power and a Republic was set up. Most of Italy was now divided into French-dominated republics. Only Britain was left at war. The British blockaded most of the French fleets and their Dutch and Spanish allies making a Channel invasion impossible.

## Ireland

The British government feared that Napoleon would next be sent to Ireland, but he was actually dispatched to Egypt, with major consequences that Chapter 9 will discuss. In 1791, the Anglican lawyer **Theobald Wolfe Tone** founded the Society of United Irishmen. It first called for parliamentary reform. In 1793, the British allowed a small number of wealthy Catholics to vote (but not serve) in the Irish Parliament. In 1794, the Society entered into secret correspondence with the French and desired independence. Tone went to the United States and then France. In 1796 the French landed in Bantry Bay, but the Irish were not ready and the fleet withdrew. The Dutch planned in 1797 to invade Scotland and Ulster after naval mutinies racked Britain, but the plan failed because of bad winds. In 1798 the United Irish rose in a bid for independence. 140,000 British soldiers under Cornwallis crushed the rebellion and killed 30,000 men, women, and children. A French force of several hundred, accompanied by Tone, landed too late on the west coast. The British captured and executed Tone. Over the next fifty years, Britain transported about 1,500 Irish political prisoners to the bleak shores of Australia. The 1801 **Act of Union** abolished the Irish Parliament, and until 1922 Irish voters would have to send representatives to London. The enemies of France were confused and divided: Prussia was out, Austria had been defeated, and Britain was torn by the antiwar, political reform group at home, and the Irish revolt.

# THE FRENCH IMPERIAL POSSESSIONS

The acceleration of slavery in the Caribbean depressed *philosophes* who believed in progress. The French West Indies in 1770 had 379,000 slaves in a population of 430,000 (88 percent). This increased after 1770 with 30,000 new slaves arriving each year from 1785 to 1790; even if half died, this still meant 75,000 young slaves. Africans in their twenties were the largest group in Saint-Domingue (Haiti). Between the whites and the Africans was a mixed-race group, known as people of color. Most free people were black or colored. In the United States, there had been relatively few free people of mixed race. Most lower-class whites, especially in the southern states with large African American populations, had accepted the leadership of the elite planters and merchants. In Latin America, whites had repeatedly rejected those of mixed race even when their political and economic interests coincided. The different mixture of race may have been the biggest factor in explaining why the revolutions in French and Spanish America took a different course than the one in British America.

This racial mix ensured that the American Revolution did not spread to the British West Indies. The planters would have had to arm their slaves if they were to fight the British crown. The goal of successful planters was the return to Europe and enjoy life there. The French armed people of color and even a few Africans in some attacks on the British. The French governors of Saint-Domingue sent about 500 people of color and Africans to fight in the American Revolution. They returned with the idealism of those battles. The slave population of Saint-Domingue was young and dynamic. The French West Indies were exporting far more than the British. On the eve of the French Revolution, Saint-Domingue's population was 88 percent slave, 7 percent white, and 5 percent free colored.

When news came of the storming of the Bastille, lower-class whites in Saint-Domingue broke out their revolutionary clothes. The colony split between the pro-independence south and the colonial north. Free people of color, who had generally supported slavery, now found their race was most important. Vincent Ogé led a revolt of 300 free people of color in the north in 1790. Another rebellion by people of color killed the governor after he refused to promulgate a French National Assembly decree allowing free people of color to vote. This disunity gave an opening to a massive slave uprising of 12,000 people in August 1791. By the end of 1791, whites and people of color were each arming slaves to use against the other. Some slaves actually brandished royalist symbols. Whites begged for someone to intervene.

In the spring of 1792 France recognized all free persons as citizens and sent 6,000 troops to unite the free groups and put down the slaves. When the king was overthrown, the radical commissioners deported the governor and replaced white colonial officials with free people of color. But when the Convention declared war on Spain in 1793, it gave the slave rebels a place to hide on the Spanish-controlled eastern part of the island. The Convention sent a new governor who clashed with the Commissioner in a new war. The Commissioner then appealed to the slaves and abolished slavery in August 1793. The Convention confirmed this in 1794. Former slave **Toussaint Brèda**, who took the name **L'ouverture** (the opening), had been a commander with the Spanish/slave forces and emerged as a leader.

These events convulsed the Caribbean basin. The British, with 300,000 slaves in Jamaica, were deeply upset, as were the southern states of the United States. The events in Haiti inspired slave revolts in the United States, culminating in **Gabriel's Rebellion** of 1800 where at least 2,000 slaves in Virginia organized an uprising. North Carolina barred all Haitian planters and slaves, lest they "infect" that state. In Guadaloupe, another radical French commissioner liberated the slaves. Martinique put down its slaves by asking for British protection. Britain and Spain invaded Saint-Domingue in 1793/94 and restored slavery. This was complicated by disease. To bolster their ranks the British organized African units by offering freedom to some. In May 1794, Toussaint turned against the Spanish and offered his services to the beleaguered republic. The war had ruined the economy. The Peace of 1795 temporarily drove the Spanish from the island. Five forces contended in the western third of the island. The British increased their force to 30,000, but disease struck down many. Toussaint's strategy was to be loyal to whatever government ruled Paris. By 1797, his army of 20,000 controlled most of the colony.

# TIMELINE

| | |
|---|---|
| May 5, 1789 | Estates-General convenes at Versailles |
| June 17, 1789 | Third Estate declares itself the National Assembly |
| June 20, 1789 | Oath of the Tennis Court |
| July 14, 1789 | Storming of the Bastille |
| July–August 1789 | The Great Fear in the countryside |
| August 4, 1789 | National Assembly abolishes feudal privileges |
| August 27, 1789 | National Assembly issues Declaration of the Rights of Man |
| October 5, 1789 | Parisian women march on Versailles and force royal family to return to Paris |
| November 1789 | National Assembly confiscates church lands |
| July 1790 | Civil Constitution of the Clergy establishes national church |
| | Louis XVI reluctantly agrees to accept a constitutional monarchy |

| June 25, 1791 | Arrest of the royal family while attempting to flee France |
| August 27, 1791 | Declaration of Pillnitz by Prussia and Austria |
| April 20, 1792 | French Assembly declares war on Austria |
| August 10, 1792 | Parisian mob attacks Tuileries palace and takes Louis XVI and family prisoner |
| September 1792 | September Massacres |
| | National convention declares France a republic and abolishes monarchy |
| January 21, 1793 | Execution of Louis XVI |
| February 1793 | France declares war on Britain, Holland, and Spain Assembly asks levy of 300,000 soldiers; revolts break out in provincial cities |
| April 1793 | General Dumouriez and Louis Philippe, son of Duke of Orléans, flee France |
| April 6, 1793 | Robespierre and the Mountain organize the Committee of Public Safety |
| May–June 1793 | Girondist leaders arrested by the Mountain and Commune of Paris |
| August 23, 1793 | *Levée en Masse*—all unmarried Frenchmen 18–25 called to the army |
| September 1793 | Price controls to aid the *sans-culottes* and mobilize war effort |
| 1793–1794 | Reign of Terror in Paris and the provinces |
| Spring 1794 | French armies victorious on all fronts |
| March 24, 1794 | Hébert executed |
| April 5, 1794 | Danton executed |
| July 27, 1794 | Execution of Robespierre; Thermidorian Reaction begins |
| November 12, 1794 | Jacobin Club in Paris ordered closed by the Convention |
| 1795–1799 | The Directory |
| April 14, 1795 | Ratification of Peace of Basel with Prussia: France gains west bank of the Rhine |
| May 20–22, 1795 | Radical rising in Paris by *sans-culottes* ends in arrest of 1,200; 6 condemned to death |

| October 3–5, 1795 | Royalist rising in Paris broken up by Generals Barras and Bonaparte |
| October 17, 1797 | Treaty of Campo Formio with Austria: Napoleon returns triumphant to Paris |
| 1798 | Austria, Great Britain, and Russia form the Second Coalition against France |
| | Napoleon's expedition to Egypt ends in disaster |
| | Toussaint makes peace with Britain |
| 1799 | French force lands in Ireland but is defeated |

# KEY TERMS

Estates-General
Storming of the Bastille
Declaration of the Rights of Man and Citizen
*assignats*
Georges Danton
Maximilien Robespierre
Committee of Public Safety
Reign of Terror
The Thermidorian Reaction
Toussaint L'ouverture

# PRIMARY SOURCE DOCUMENTS

**Arthur Young**, http://history.hanover.edu/texts/young.html

**French notebooks of complaints**, http://www.historyguide.org/intellect/cahiers.html

**Abbé Sieyès**, http://www.fordham.edu/halsall/mod/sieyes.html

**Tennis Court Oath**, http://www.historyguide.org/intellect/tennis_oath.html

**Declaration of the Rights of Man and Citizen**, http://avalon.law.yale.edu/18th_century/rightsof.asp

**Levée en Masse**, http://www.fordham.edu/halsall/mod/1793levee.html

**Olympe de Gouges**, http://www.fordham.edu/halsall/mod/1791degouge1. html

**Vincent Ogé**, http://www.historywiz.com/primarysources/assembly.htm

# Chapter 6

# NAPOLEON

## Napoleon's Background

Napoleon Bonaparte was born in 1769 to Corsican nobility. France had taken over the island the year before, so he was a French citizen. He went to military school where he mastered calculus and trajectories and joined the artillery corps. Even in school he had a reputation for brilliance, but because he was Corsican he had no chance of commanding a French army while the Old Regime lasted. He became a general during the Terror. Napoleon was brilliant, full of energy, and a master at manipulating people and events. He could work eighteen hours at a stretch and sleep at will. He was also a superb organizer.

As seen in the previous chapter, Napoleon aided the Directory, gained command of a French army, and overran northern Italy. The 1797 elections saw the royalists do well. The Directory asked Bonaparte to help them in annulling the elections. On September 4, 1797, the Directory and Chamber removed their royalist and Jacobin elements, including two of the five Directors.

## Egypt

In 1798, Napoleon invaded Egypt, alarming the British. The goal was to assure France a share of the decaying Ottoman Empire. With 23,000 men, he stormed Alexandria in the middle of a blazing summer. Near the pyramids, the French defeated an Egyptian army of about 60,000. That army was ill-equipped with a core of **Mamluks**, cavalrymen unsuited to fighting massed riflemen and modern artillery. Even as Napoleon's army advanced, the British cut his supply line by destroying the French fleet. The Ottoman overlords assembled an army in Syria and another gathered on Rhodes waiting to retake Egypt. Napoleon took the offensive by moving north into Syria, chased and defeated the Turkish Syrian army. The second Turkish army of 18,000 landed in Egypt. Napoleon's army weakened to 6,000, but he wheeled it south again and wiped out the Turkish force. Final victory was impossible. Napoleon left the rest of his army and broke through the British lines in a small speedy boat. In Paris he told a more favorable version of the story and preserved his reputation. His soldiers did not return to France for years.

# Napoleon's Coup of 1799

The 1798 elections would be difficult because with the purge of 1797, the Chamber would have to elect three of the five Directors. The Directory fixed the elections of 1798 to elect centrists, and the Chamber refused to seat 127 newly-elected deputies. The Directory tackled the financial problem in 1799. It repudiated two-thirds of the national debt, including the *assignats*. It established new indirect taxes. This settled the issue of French debt that had hung over the country for so long, but it had come at a heavy cost. Corruption filled the Directory as many members sold their votes and influence. To make matters worse, war resumed with Austria. France occupied Piedmont and built a friendly government called the **Parthenopean Republic** in Naples and southern Italy.

Emmanuel Sieyès had joined the Directory in 1799 and sought to strengthen the executive. Then the war turned bad. An Austro-Russian force pushed through Switzerland and northern Italy and rolled up the republics allied with France. The Councils ousted three Directors and chose three Jacobins to join Sieyès and Barras. Sieyès gave up on constitutional government. On November 9, 1799, Napoleon, Sieyès and another director staged a coup and set up **the Consulate**. Napoleon had a following among soldiers and the intellectual élite: in Egypt, he had talked of building a massive canal at Suez and antiquities. He was only thirty years old.

# Government under the Consulate

There would be three consuls with Napoleon as First Consul. An overwhelming vote of the people approved the new system. Napoleon wanted to combine the best of the Old Regime and the Revolution. He ended all feudalism and centralized administration and justice. Citizens would rise based on their merit. There would be no tax exemptions based on birth. The vote had shown that Rousseau's "General Will" was embodied in Napoleon. The people called for order and Napoleon answered. Napoleon used the secret police and administration to keep peace and put down marauders. He gave a general amnesty, and most of the émigrés from 1789 returned, except for the royal family and about 1,000 monarchists.

The Russians withdrew from the war, leaving the Austrians to fend for themselves. At the **Battle of Marengo** (June 14, 1800) Napoleon beat Austria. France occupied northern Italy and southern Germany. The **Treaty of Lunéville** (February 8, 1801) confirmed Campo Formio. Spain ceded Louisiana to France. Pitt the Younger's government fell over the issue of removing the civil disabilities of Irish Catholics. The new government was friendlier to Napoleon and signed the **Peace of Amiens** on March 25, 1802. The British gained the Cape Colony at the southern tip of Africa from the Dutch.

# The Haitian Revolution

Fox and the British opposition had embarrassed Pitt by denouncing the loss of perhaps 100,000 lives and £10 million in fighting the Saint-Domingue war. By March 1798, the British had made a truce. Now Saint-Domingue fell into another civil war between Toussaint and his remaining rival who commanded mulatto forces. By January 1801, Toussaint controlled the entire island. A new constitution declared Toussaint governor-general for life. Perhaps one-third of the population had died. Toussaint invited the white planters to return and did not declare independence from France. Haiti was now a military regime with compulsory labor. Former slaves would engage in a profit-sharing, getting one-quarter of the profits. Landowners would get another quarter, and the government would take the rest.

Napoleon's wife Josephine had grown up on Martinique and perhaps this gave him a false confidence that he understood the Caribbean and could retake Saint-Domingue. The mission became more urgent with the Peace of Lunéville and the gaining of Louisiana because he needed Saint-Domingue to anchor a planned American empire. At first, the French force of 20,000 was able to capture the ports in savage fighting, but then yellow fever took its toll and killed half the soldiers. The French trapped Toussaint and sent him to France where he died in April 1803. When word came that Napoleon would restore slavery, the rebels gathered strength. The French commander died of disease. **Jean Jacques Dessalines** broke with the French and fought the most atrocious war yet. But France's resumption of war with Britain in 1803 led to a blockade, and France could not supply its force. On January 1,

1804, Haiti became independent after the remaining French forces and white planters fled to Cuba. It was the first nation freed by a slave rebellion. When he could not regain Haiti, Napoleon sold the French territory of Louisiana to the United States.

# The Reforms of Bonaparte

The government concentrated its authority in paid agents. No one was above the law. The Minister of the Interior (Napoleon's brother Lucien) appointed prefects to control the regions. The government finally pacified areas such as Brittany and Vendée that had been in revolt for years. This meant they would pay taxes. Napoleon drew military officers and administrators from the élite of the nobles and the middle class. The professional tax collectors were much more honest than their royal predecessors, which greatly enhanced tax collection. Napoleon made France's first simple budget. He introduced a sound currency in 1803 by regulating the silver content in the **French franc** and fixed the value of silver to gold. Thanks to the Directory wiping out the *assignats*, the debt was secure. Taxes on consumption, such as salt and tobacco, contributed more and more to the revenue. The Bank of France was established in 1800. It would discount promissory notes, make loans to the treasury, and receive and manage some government assets. It issued 30,000 shares of 1,000 francs each. The biggest 200 shareholders could elect regents to govern the Bank.

Lawyers had toiled for years to overhaul the French legal system. Before the Revolution, it had been divided by province and marked by inequality based on the social class of the accused and the victim. The committees working on the law codes finished their work while Napoleon was in charge, so naturally he named it after himself. The **Napoleonic Code** included a civil code (1804), commercial code (1807), penal code (1808), and civil and criminal procedure (1806). The law was the same throughout France and privileged private enterprise by banning unions. It gave men rights over women. All the property of a wife would belong to the husband, and she could not testify in court. It favored the prosecution over the defense as the local prefect selected the jury, a majority was sufficient to convict, and the accused were presumed guilty until proved innocent.

Napoleon ended the fight with the Church in the **Concordat** (1801) which put all French bishops under the Pope's authority for the first time in four hundred years. It permitted seminaries. The Vatican in return dropped its demands on the confiscated land and Avignon. The treaty put all clergy, Catholic and Protestant, on the state payroll. France became the first European country to recognize Jews as full and equal citizens.

The Revolution was mostly over with the settlement. The Third Estate had gained most of its demands. France was at peace, and its borders reached to the Rhine. Many émigrés quietly regained their land. In May 1802 Napoleon created the Legion of Honor as a first step toward the establishment of a new nobility.

In 1802, a popular vote made Napoleon Consul for Life. It was not a secret ballot but taxes were lower than in 1791 and the draft had taken one-tenth the number of soldiers claimed at the height of the Directory. In December 1804, Napoleon crowned himself Emperor of the French, supported by a vote of 3,572,329 to 2,569. Napoleon could name his successor. It seemed the Bourbon dynasty had given way to the Bonaparte dynasty.

# Napoleonic Warfare

The first consideration was that the French often controlled larger numbers of troops than their opposition. Second, the army trained soldiers to be more mobile. Third, they had higher nationalistic morale. Early modern armies had consisted of soldiers from all language backgrounds of Europe, many of them simply there for pay or plunder. The French had not been able to afford mercenaries and had compensated by filling the soldiers with patriotic and revolutionary enthusiasm. Promotion was on the basis of ability. Of Napoleon's twenty-six marshals, none were nobles. Three had been sergeants in 1789, and three had been privates.

Large numbers meant new strategies. Columns would charge with fixed bayonets. Napoleon scored his greatest strategic triumphs at the battles of Marengo and Austerlitz when he was outnumbered. Napoleon had a basic strategy: maneuver the enemy to an unfavorable terrain, then force the main battle and a full commitment of force. At the key moment, he would use reserve troops on the enemy's flank or rear.

France had the largest population in Europe and 40 percent of its men were in their fighting prime. A strong economy supported the war effort. Army desertion and draft evasion remained problems. Communes were responsible for draft-dodgers and had to find substitutes for them. France asked more from what had been its eastern frontier and less from the unstable west and Rhine provinces. Napoleon called fewer men to the colors, but a greater percentage complied. The draft term was usually five years. From 1800 to 1814 France conscripted two million (7 percent of the total population). The wealthy could pay for substitutes and 5 to 10 percent of the draftees were actually substitutes. In World War I from 1914 to 1918, France would conscript close to 20 percent. In the early years, Napoleon only drafted 60,000 a year, but that gradually grew to 120,000 in 1810. There was no massive levy until after the Russian disaster. France drafted a million young men in 1813 and 1814. Supplies were spotty, contrary to Napoleon's philosophy of "an army travels on its stomach." It lived off the country in some areas but not in north Germany, Poland, or Russia, where careful staff work and supply trains kept the army provisioned for a while. Napoleon reorganized the army in 1800 and 1804 into seven separate corps with their own artillery, cavalry, and infantry. Napoleon had the ability to improvise and shift regiments among the corps and redefine the corps' roles. The battles killed more officers than the military academies could produce, so after 1808, 20 to 25 percent of the officers came from the ranks.

# Napoleon and the Spread of Revolution

In 1805, war broke out with the **Third Coalition**: Austria and Russia joined Britain. Napoleon planned to invade Britain, but the British smashed his combined French and Spanish fleet at the **Battle of Trafalgar** in October 1805. This battle assured the British of naval supremacy. Napoleon marched with 200,000 troops from the Channel to the Danube and routed Russia and Austria at the **Battle of Austerlitz** (December 2, 1805). Napoleon forced the **Treaty of Pressburg** (1806) on the Austrians: Bavaria and Württemberg became kingdoms, Baden a Grand Duchy in Germany with a puppet **Confederation of the Rhine** that included other small German states. The Treaty took Venetia from Austria and gave it to the Republic of Italy.

Napoleon's German policy pushed Prussia into war. At the **Battle of Jena** in October 1806, the French smashed the Prussian army. Napoleon then beat the Russians at the **Battle of Friedland** (June 1807). Tsar **Alexander I** (ruled 1801–1825) did not want to retreat into Russia because he feared that the lower classes might rise in revolution if the French soldiers crossed the border. At the **Treaty of Tilsit** (July 1807) Napoleon took much land from Prussia and Hanover (a German kingdom under Britain's control) and gave it to the new kingdom of Westphalia ruled by Napoleon's brother Jerome. In the battles of 1805 to 1807, Napoleon had lost 65,000 men of the original 210,000, but made it up with early draft call-ups and help from Switzerland, Holland, Spain, Poland, and Italy. He used loot and contributions to fund the army.

The British built a new overseas empire during these wars. They were eager to take over ports and islands around the globe that they could use as resupply stations. The British attitude on neutral ships changed with time. As long as there was a strong French fleet, Britain was careful to respect the rights of neutrals. After sinking the French fleet off of Egypt in 1798, the British turned harsher. They began to attack all ships bound for French harbors.

When Denmark, Sweden and Russia created a League of Armed Neutrality at the end of 1800, Britain seized all Danish and Norwegian ships in British harbors and West Indian colonies. The Danes retaliated by seizing British property in Germany, and the British responded by attacking the Danish fleet at Copenhagen and forcing a truce in April 1801.

In 1796, the British scooped up the settlements that would become Guyana along the South American coast. Napoleon had taken the Mediterranean island of Malta on his way to Egypt, but a rebellion soon broke out, and the British controlled the island by 1800. In 1809, the British conquered six of the main Ionian islands off the coast of Greece and got the seventh, Corfu, in 1815. The British navy also operated in the Indian Ocean and took the Seychelles islands from the French in 1794. Then it took the sugar island of Mauritius in 1810.

# The Continental System (1806)

Britain refused to negotiate peace even though its allies were beaten. Since Trafalgar, it was safe from invasion. The French emperor gathered all his allies and recently-defeated enemies and forced them to sign a treaty that built the Continental System. This was a tariff fortress to harm British trade and force them to make peace. The British made up the lost trade by turning to Latin America. Britain had won control of the slave trade from Africa to the Spanish colonies in 1713. It had expanded regular smuggling to get around Spanish mercantilism in the 1730s by going through its North American colonies, Portugal, and Brazil.

The British heard rumors that Denmark was about to close its ports to British trade and use its fleet to help Napoleon. In July 1807, Britain demanded that Denmark surrender its fleet and landed 30,000 troops to besiege Copenhagen. Up to 2,000 people were killed in the British bombardment, and there was a six-week occupation after Copenhagen surrendered. The British took the Danish fleet and £2 million worth of stores. Denmark now allied with Napoleon and joined the Continental System in 1807.

The system actually hurt Europe more, and the middle-class outside of France became disillusioned with Napoleon. In the Dutch port of Amsterdam, 1,350 ships had entered in 1806, but only 310 in 1809. Land transportation was too expensive. Other countries felt that France was benefiting at their expense. Dependent states paid heavily for "French defense."

# Napoleon at the Height of His Power

Britain continued to use Sweden as a trade route. Napoleon asked his allies Denmark and Russia to shut it down. The British captured the last major Danish warship and held 1,400 Danish ships and 7,000 Danish and Norwegian sailors captive. It took the Danish colonies in Africa, India, and the Caribbean. In 1808, Russia invaded Finland, which was part of Sweden. Sweden did not want to rely too much on British help and was beaten badly. By the end of 1808, the Swedes had abandoned Finland. The Finnish leaders gathered at the **Diet of Borgå** in 1809 and accepted the Russian annexation of Finland as long as the tsar ruled as Grand Duke of Finland and recognized Finnish laws, religion, and liberties. This defeat caused the Swedish Assembly to overthrow the king and installed his uncle, who was childless. As heir, the Assembly chose **Jean-Baptiste Bernadotte**, one of Napoleon's marshals.

Austria declared war on France in April 1809 but was turned back at the **Battle of Wagram** (July 6, 1809). Napoleon called up the draft classes of 1809 and 1810 early and mobilized troops from the Confederation of the Rhine, Italy, Holland, and Warsaw. Many of these soldiers eagerly joined the French not only because they hoped for victory and plunder but also because they supported the French Revolution. Poland had adopted a Rousseau-influenced constitution in 1791. Prussia, Austria, and Russia had then destroyed Poland and removed it from the map of Europe. In 1794, there had been a Polish uprising led by Tadeusz Kosciusko, a veteran of the American Revolution. Napoleon had restored part of Poland as the **Grand Duchy of Warsaw**. The Austrian empire, amazingly, sustained four defeats without a revolution or internal collapse. At the **Treaty of Schönbrunn** (1809) Napoleon increased the size of the Grand Duchy of Warsaw. Bavaria and Russia, now allies of Napoleon, gained land. The Treaty took Dalmatia, Slovenia, and Croatia from Austria and merged them into the French-run Illyrian Provinces. Napoleon divorced his wife Josephine, who had borne him no children, and married Marie Louise, the daughter of the Austrian emperor.

By 1810, Napoleon's empire consisted of France, Belgium and the Netherlands, the German coast to the West Baltic Sea, the left bank of the Rhine River, and the Italian coast down to Rome. The Swiss Confederation was republican. Napoleon's relatives sat on the thrones of Westphalia, Spain, and Naples. His stepson was viceroy for him in northern Italy. Prussia, Austria, Denmark, Russia, and Sweden had signed alliances binding them to Napoleon.

French domination went through three steps: conquest by the army, establishment of a satellite government, and the drafting of treaties and a constitution on the French model. Italy and Germany and Spain underwent the third stage and had a massive internal reorganization. Napoleon believed in one European civilization and one law for all and tried to promote this as an ideology to bring all together. All people were equal. He abolished noble privileges, but gave them compensation. He tried to free Polish serfs. Liberals welcomed Napoleon at first and saw him as a great hero. The German Goethe said: "Napoleon was the expression of all that was reasonable, legitimate and European in the revolutionary movement." There would be religious toleration for all. Most Catholic states followed the terms of Napoleon's Concordat: the church tax ended, the churches lost their land, and most monasteries closed. France introduced the decimal and metric systems and modernized taxes and finance. However, Napoleon refused to introduce representative assemblies. His model for European civilization was French civilization, his model for European law the Napoleonic Code. This would cause trouble down the road.

# NATIONALISM AND THE FALL OF NAPOLEON

## Nationalism in Germany and Italy

The German-speaking middle states were reasonably happy but Prussia and Austria smarted. German nationalism found its roots in J.G. Herder's book *Ideas on the Philosophy of the History of Mankind* (1784). Herder called for the separate development of cultures, based on the *volksgeist* (national spirit) of the common people, not the upper classes. Against the internationalism of Enlightenment, Herder emphasized differences among peoples. In 1808, J.G. Fichte, originally a supporter of the French Revolution and even the Terror, delivered *Addresses to the German Nation*, calling for a unified German state. This attracted many German patriots.

Italy did not revolt against Napoleon. The continental system did not hurt the Italian middle class. It welcomed religious toleration and the reduction of papal influence and the expulsion of Austrian domination. Italy had been rationalized and hopes grew for a possible Italian unification. The middle class enjoyed French manners and culture. In Italy, Poland, and France, Napoleon remained a hero long after his death.

### Reform in Prussia

The defeat at Jena severely shook the proud Prussian military. Big changes were needed. Prussia, although it was much smaller than France, would need a bigger army. That meant a military draft of peasants. They would not be fighting for high pay or for revolution. Prussia needed to give them something and so promised reforms and a better life. By freeing the peasants from the burdens of the nobles, it would give them a stake to fight for. It was their country as well as the King's. **Frederick William III** (ruled 1797–1840) set up a reform ministry under **Baron Karl Stein** and then **Karl von Hardenberg**. It abolished serfdom in 1807 and restored self-government in the cities. Townsmen could buy land and serve as army officers. Prussia remade and enlarged its army on the French model. Austria instituted the draft and promised freedom for serfs but did not fulfill its promise.

# The Occupation of Iberia

Carlos III died in 1788. His son Carlos IV (ruled 1788–1808) pulled back in a conservative direction. Spain fought revolutionary France from 1793 to 1795, then allied with France despite the opposition of Crown Prince Ferdinand. In October 1807, after beating the Prussians and Russians, Napoleon concluded a treaty with Carlos against Portugal, which was Britain's sole entry point for trade after the Continental System took effect. The next month, a joint force including 100,000 French troops captured Lisbon. The Portuguese royal family fled to Brazil, carried by the British. In March 1808, there was a brief uprising against Carlos and his ministers. Ferdinand briefly became king, but the French intervened and installed **Joseph Bonaparte**, brother of the French emperor.

Joseph put in a French-style Constitution. The great Spanish landowners despised land reform, and the clergy opposed tolerance of faiths other than Catholicism. In other areas, Napoleon and the French had appealed to middle-class reformers (Netherlands, Germany, Italy) or to nationalism (Poland). In Spain, there was no middle class to make a natural base of support for the Bonapartes. Provinces such as Andalusia, Catalonia, and Galicia were unhappy about French-style centralizing. Former Spanish soldiers and ordinary people organized attacks on French soldiers, installations, and supporters. They wore no uniform and after attacking would melt back into the general population. These new kinds of warriors were called *guerrillas*.

# The Spanish War of Liberation

After the *guerrilla* war broke out, Britain sent a force under Arthur Wellesley (later **Duke of Wellington**). A British army of 35,000 supplemented 125,000 Spanish regulars, levies, and irregulars. Napoleon came in with 194,000 troops and secured Spain by January 1809. The British force withdrew to Portugal and joined about 30,000 Spanish *guerrillas*. The French suffered

40,000 casualties each year from 1808 to 1813. In August 1812, Wellington took Madrid. By the end of 1813, the rebels and the British had cleared Spain of French troops.

In 1810, the free area around Cádiz chose a constituent assembly, which promulgated the Constitution of 1812. The leaders of this group called themselves **Liberals**, the first time this name was applied to a political movement. It called for progressive reforms, land reform, religious toleration, modernization, and a restoration of Ferdinand. The constitution called for a one-chamber parliament elected by all men. When Ferdinand VII (ruled 1814–1833) was restored, he promised to abide by this constitution.

# The American Early National Period

The exercise of power in the early years of the Republic was quite different from today. Congress was seen as supreme, as the Parliament was in Britain. The founders expected that in most presidential elections, the electors would fail to reach a majority and the House of Representatives would elect the President, thus ensuring Congressional control. The Congressional caucuses of the parties nominated candidates for the Presidency. The Cabinet was not provided for in the Constitution, but Washington established a system of calling department heads together. Although one of Washington's two vetoes was a policy matter, it was expected that a President (like the British King) would only veto a bill for constitutional reasons. From 1789 to 1829, the President only issued ten vetoes. Congress did not override a veto until 1845.

Democracy slowly grew. Vermont entered the Union in 1791 and allowed all free men to vote. Kentucky entered the Union the next year on the same terms. After 1812, states generally joined the United States allowing all free men to vote. By 1828, only two states still had presidential electors picked by the state legislatures, not by voters. The war in the west continued. Up to 1,500 American settlers died between the Peace of Paris and 1790. In the latter year, Washington sent a force against the formidable alliance led by the Miami chief Little Turtle. For three years, the Indians defended their lands and killed hundreds of U.S. soldiers. Little Turtle hoped that this demonstration would bring the British back into war against the United States. In 1793, a well-trained and equipped force of 3,000 marched against the Indian armies. Little Turtle attacked one of the new forts but realized that the American force was too strong. The Indians rejected Little Turtle's peace advice, chose another leader, and were slaughtered within sight of the British Fort Miami, which refused to open its gates to the Indians. The Americans sacked and burned their villages. The **Treaty of Fort Greenville** (1795) formally gave over Ohio and part of Indiana to the United States. Under Jay's Treaty (1795), the British gave up their remaining forts in Michigan, Ohio, and New York.

The French Revolution deeply divided American opinion. The original United States Senate chamber had large portraits of King Louis XVI and Queen Marie Antoinette. When the revolution overthrew the King, the United States did not consider the Convention to be the legitimate government of France. As the French West Indies flared in rebellion and the British attacked, France asked the United States to honor its commitment from the 1778 alliance to defend the islands. The United States refused. The French sent an agent to stir up American opinion. This irritated Washington. Both the French and British attacked American shipping. The faction dominant in government, led by Washington, Adams, Hamilton, and John Jay, leaned toward the British. Jefferson and his Congressional leaders James Madison and Aaron Burr were initially sympathetic to France and always suspicious of Britain. Jefferson also believed that Hamilton favored the rich and trading interests over farmers. This caused two factions to harden: Hamilton, Washington, and Adams as **Federalists**; Jefferson, Madison, and Burr in the **Democratic-Republican** party.

In 1798, the French tried to bribe U.S. officials, causing a sensation. The United States annulled the French alliance. Adams and the Federalists passed the Alien and Sedition Acts to give the President unilateral power to arrest and expel aliens in time of war and banned criticism of government officials. Hamilton dreamed of war across the Americas and taking over Canada, Mexico, and Latin America.

The Jefferson/Madison group soon reduced the Federalists to a regional party. The Jeffersonians did reluctantly accept some Federalist principles. The Federalists had used courts to prosecute "seditious" enemies, and Adams had created new federal judges after losing the election of 1800. One appointment had been the Federalist **John Marshall** as Chief Justice of the Supreme Court. Marshall claimed a sweeping right for the Court that no British court ever had: the power of constitutional review. Marshall struck down one of these Federalist appointments and part of the law that enabled the Supreme Court to order the Secretary of State to give a commission in the famous *Marbury vs. Madison* case of 1803. The implications were enormous, but it would be almost fifty years before the Court dared to strike down an entire Act of Congress.

The independence of Haiti and the end of Napoleon's hopes for an American empire led France to sell Louisiana territory in 1803 to the United States for $15 million. This accelerated the opening of the "West." Tennessee, Ohio, and Kentucky had already become states, and the West was becoming a region on an equal footing with the North and the South. The West's main interest tended to be Indian affairs, internal improvements, and land policy. The Shawnee chief **Tecumseh** had refused to sign the Fort Greenville Treaty. His father and brother had died fighting Americans. Tecumseh, a brilliant orator and strategist, teamed up with his brother Tenskwatawa the Prophet and founded a model community at the Wabash and Tippecanoe Rivers. In 1811, the Prophet led an unsuccessful attack on the territorial militia and Tecumseh's alliance unraveled.

# The War of 1812

The Continental System and a renewed British blockade angered Jefferson. From 1803 to 1812 the British impressed at least 5,000 sailors from American vessels. The U.S. responses were ineffective or backfired. Renewed battles with Indians and a lingering desire to conquer Canada led the western War Hawks in Congress to push the United States into the War of 1812 against the British. The British dominated the high seas and appointed Tecumseh as a brigadier general. Canadians and Indians repulsed American attacks and captured Detroit and Fort Dearborn (later known as Chicago). Again the British retreated in 1813 and left the Indians to take the brunt of the American attacks. Tecumseh was killed at the Battle of the Thames in October 1813.

# The Russian Disaster

At the end of 1810, Alexander I pulled out of the Continental System. He felt he had not gotten much out of the alliance with Napoleon except Finland: Napoleon did not help in Russia's war against Turkey, married an Austrian princess, and supported Poland. For his part, Napoleon saw a conflict with Russia as inevitable. He tried unsuccessfully to win peace with Britain. A Grand Army of 611,000 assembled by Napoleon, consisted of one-third French, one-third German, and one-seventh Polish soldiers; the rest were Italians, Swiss, and Dutch. The Russians had 160,000 soldiers. Napoleon invaded in June 1812, carrying only three weeks of supplies. He fought his way to Moscow, which was abandoned and burned by the Russians. Almost half of his Grand Army had deserted by this time. Napoleon hesitated for a month, could not make winter quarters in the ruined city, and began a retreat. Russian irregulars and army harried the Grand Army. The weather turned bad and bitterly cold early. Nearly 400,000 died of cold, disease, and the enemy. The Russians took 100,000 prisoners. Perhaps 100,000 survived; only 30,000 troops returned home.

# The End of the War

When things went sour, Napoleon abandoned his troops and rushed to Paris in thirteen days to raise another army. Things were falling apart. Bernadotte, the effective Swedish ruler, secretly decided that it would be easier to gain Norway from Denmark than Finland from Russia. This put him at odds with Napoleon. Sweden fought a phony war with England while smuggling continued but soon made peace and an alliance with Russia in 1812. As the Russians reached their border with Prussia, the latter proclaimed an alliance as well as a War of German Liberation from France. Britain poured in £32 million for subsidies. Austria joined in August 1813, creating a **Quadruple Alliance**. At the **Battle of Leipzig** (October 1813), armies from four nations with twice as many soldiers overwhelmed and defeated Napoleon.

Revolts now followed Napoleon's retreat across Germany. Austrian Chancellor Metternich offered Napoleon a chance to keep his crown and the Rhine frontiers, but Napoleon refused. The forces of the Quadruple Alliance followed him into France. Finally, on March 31, 1814, the Allies marched into Paris, ending the Napoleonic Empire. France desperately wanted peace and would not rally to Napoleon. At the **First Peace of Paris** in May 1814, 1) Louis XVIII returned as king and restored the Bourbon family; 2) France lost all its acquisitions since 1792; 3) Napoleon was exiled to the Italian island of Elba. Louis reserved the right under the treaty to reclaim Haiti if he could.

In America, the British went on the offensive against the United States. They sailed up the Potomac river and burned the capital city of Washington. Peace restored things to prewar status. After the peace, **Andrew Jackson** beat the British at New Orleans and established himself as a war hero.

# The End of the Slave Trade

The end of the European slave trade is one of the most curious events of the time. Economically, slave owners were making a profit and the volume of slave-produced goods—cotton, sugar, and coffee—was growing. Very few free workers would work under plantation conditions. The British plantations were thriving. Napoleon's takeover of Spain had the unintended consequence of opening the Cuban market to British ships. The anti-slave trade movement was both intellectual and political, sprang from the Enlightenment, and was centered in England. Montesquieu (slavery corrupts masters), Rousseau, and Adam Smith had condemned slavery. Quakers and nonconformist Protestants took up the call, giving it a strong religious flavor. In 1771, the Chief Justice had effectively ruled that there could be no slaves in Britain.

The belief grew that free labor was more productive than slave labor and that abolition would increase profits. In 1787, Britain paid a ship to take freed slaves to Sierra Leone in western Africa. Half of these settlers died in the first year, and some became slave dealers. In 1788, Parliament placed the first limits on the manner of carrying slaves. New Jersey, Pennsylvania, Connecticut, Rhode Island, and Massachusetts abolished the slave trade. The Haitian revolution magnified the urgency. In 1792 Denmark said it would abolish import of slaves as of 1803. In 1799, Parliament increased the space requirements for slaves on the ships. Urged by President Jefferson (himself a slaveowner), the United States abolished the import of slaves in 1807. In Britain abolitionists in the House of Commons led by William Wilberforce pressed step by step until the trade was outlawed starting January 1, 1808. The majority in the Cabinet, King George III, and his sons opposed abolition, but Pitt, Burke, and Fox had all supported Wilberforce. The new Irish members joining the British House of Commons bolstered the anti-slavery forces.

# THE CONGRESS OF VIENNA

## The Reconstruction of Europe

The Congress of Vienna began in October 1814. Czar Alexander I of Russia was a leading personality. **Lord Robert Castlereagh**, the British Foreign Secretary, sought a moderate peace but was willing to tolerate a reactionary mood. He came from the right wing of the Conservative Party and was disliked by those who saw themselves as more progressive, such as the Romantic poet Percy Bysshe Shelley.

*I met Murder on the way –*
*He had a mask like Castlereagh –*
*Very smooth he looked, yet grim;*
*Seven blood-hounds followed him:*

*All were fat; and well they might*
*Be in admirable plight,*
*For one by one, and two by two,*
*He tossed the human hearts to chew*
*Which from his wide cloak he drew.*
———From "The Mask of Anarchy"

**Klemens von Metternich**, the Austrian Chancellor, was the host and dominant influence at the Congress. His main goal was to restore a balance of power in Europe and to get Russian troops out of central Europe. He would become the main foe of liberal and revolutionary forces in Europe. More than anything, he hated nationalism because Austria was a multinational empire that would explode if nationalism prevailed. He also wanted to ensure Austrian supremacy in central Europe against Prussia, the other great German power. The King of Prussia, Frederick William III, wanted to annex Saxony, which had aided Napoleon. That would make Prussia the supreme German-speaking nation.

Frederick William and Alexander teamed up against Metternich. Poland had supported Napoleon to the end, and the great powers had agreed to wipe it off the map of Europe. Prussia was willing to give its parts of Poland to Russia if Russia would support Prussia taking all of Saxony. Metternich desperately turned to France for help at the Congress. Napoleon was gone, but King Louis XVIII had kept his foreign minister, the clever **Charles de Talleyrand**. Britain, France, and Austria allowed Prussia only a piece of Saxony. The rest remained an independent kingdom. Poland was theoretically separate from Russia but would have to accept Alexander as its king.

### Territorial changes of the Congress of Vienna:

1) Austria gave up Belgium and its southern German possessions in exchange for Lombardy and Venetia in northern Italy. It recovered its Polish parts and lands in Tyrol and Illyria. The result was that Austria was more centralized but less German.

2) Russia had taken Finland from Sweden and Moldova from Ottoman Turkey during the Napoleonic wars. By taking control of a puppet kingdom of Poland, Russia had moved its effective territorial boundary west.

3) Prussia got half of Saxony, but lost three-fifths of its Polish lands. It also received Swedish Pomerania and Rhineland as a buffer against France. The result was that Prussia became more powerful within Germany and more German.

4) The South and North Netherlands were united. The House of Orange had dominated the North before the French Revolution, and its leader became king of the united area. The Allies wanted to create another strong power on the French boundary. The result was that it proved unworkable quickly.

5) Germany was divided into thirty-nine states. The result was a group of stronger middle states. The chances of German unification were much better than before Napoleon.

6) In Italy, the king of Piedmont-Sardinia and the Pope enlarged their territories. The Bourbon family regained the Kingdom of Two Sicilies.

7) Other provisions included the assurance of Swiss neutrality. Denmark lost Norway to Sweden. Britain received strategic islands including Helgoland, Malta, and Ceylon. After the Congress of Vienna, only Spain (below 10° North) and Portugal (below the equator) remained as European slave traders. However, the slave trade was increasing across the Sahara Desert to North Africa and in East Africa.

## Waterloo

Just as they were finishing the agreement, Napoleon got loose from Elba. He had heard of the dispute over Poland and Saxony and hoped his enemies were split. Louis XVIII sent the army to capture Napoleon, but it went over to him instead, and it was King Louis who fled. Napoleon again wore the imperial crown. Europe trembled: Britain had borrowed huge amounts of money to finance the Quadruple Alliance and now owed twice as much as the entire country's Gross Domestic Product. If Napoleon could inflict one solid defeat on the British, they might go bankrupt and the French would rule again. The British and Prussians defeated the French at the Battle of Waterloo in June 1815. The **Second Peace of Paris** (November 20, 1815) exiled Napoleon to St. Helena in the south Atlantic as King Louis returned again. France lost some strategic posts and suffered an indemnity and an army of occupation for three years.

# THE CONCERT OF EUROPE

## The Concert

The five great powers of Europe would work together to uphold the international order. As long as no crisis required absolute commitment, the system could work. Henry Kissinger, a student of Metternichian diplomacy, in the 1970s also perceived five powers that could form a new concert: the United States, the Soviet bloc, Western Europe, China, and Japan. There was an idea that the great powers should hold regular meetings even during peacetime. At the **Congress of Aix-la-Chapelle** (1818), the four powers admitted France into the alliance and removed their army of occupation.

# TIMELINE

| | |
|---|---|
| 1798 | Napoleon invasion of Egypt ends in disaster |
| 1799 | Napoleon and Sieyès overthrow Directory; Consulate established |
| 1800 | Bank of France |
| 1801 | Thomas Jefferson becomes President, ending Federalist dominance |
| | French Concordat with Catholic Church |
| 1801–2 | Treaty of Lunéville and Peace of Amiens |
| 1803 | French franc established |
| | France sells Louisiana to the United States |
| 1804 | Haiti independent |
| | First parts of Napoleonic Code put out |
| 1805–7 | War of Third Coalition: France defeats Austria, Prussia, and Russia |
| 1806–13 | Confederation of the Rhine |
| | Continental System |
| 1808–13 | Guerrilla war in Spain |
| 1812–15 | War of 1812 between Britain and U.S. |
| 1812 | Napoleon invades Russia |
| 1813 | Battle of Leipzig |
| 1814 | Quadruple Alliance occupies Paris; fall of Napoleon |
| 1814–15 | Congress of Vienna |
| 1815 | Battle of Waterloo |
| 1818 | Congress of Aix-la-Chapelle adds France to Concert of Europe |

# KEY TERMS

Napoleonic Code
Battle of Trafalgar
Battle of Austerlitz
Confederation of the Rhine
Continental System
*guerrilla*
Quadruple Alliance
Battle of Leipzig
Klemens von Metternich
Congress of Vienna

# PRIMARY SOURCE DOCUMENTS

**Napoleon Speeches to Troops**, http://www.historyguide.org/intellect/
nap1796.html

**Remembrances of Napoleon**, http://www.fordham.edu/halsall/mod/
remusat-napoleon.html

**Fichte, Addresses to the German Nation**, http://www.fordham.edu/halsall/
mod/1806fichte.html

# Chapter 7

## LATIN AMERICAN REVOLUTIONS

## The American Revolution's Impact on Latin America

Of the 14 million persons living on the mainland of Iberoamerica, about one million were slaves, 9.5 million were Indians or of mixed race, and the remaining 3.5 million were Spaniards born in either Spain (*peninsulares*) or America (Creoles). Since the establishment of Spanish colonialism, the *peninsulares* had been dominant, much to the annoyance of the Creoles, who outnumbered them by a hundred to one.

Enlightenment reforms in Spain allowed Creoles into local governments. The Creoles formed a militia in Mexico. Discontented Creoles sought to thread a needle: they wanted to increase their opportunities against the ruling class while preserving their property rights against the lower classes. They looked to the radicals of the United States and Britain, not to the Spanish liberals who opened trade and imposed taxes. Spain raised liquor, tobacco, and sales taxes to pay for its colonies' defense while tax collecting became more efficient because of enlightened reforms. The defense burden was large because Latin America was so big and vulnerable to attack from many different directions. More than ever, the Spanish rulers needed the support of local notables. The Creole elite had read the Enlightenment works and was familiar with events in British North America. With their more efficient tax collection, town councils had revenue and they became the bastions of the Creoles.

Revolts among different ethnic groups in different regions grew more frequent after 1750: there were only five in the 1740s, eleven in the 1750s, twenty in the 1760s, and twenty more in the 1770s. The Creoles began to realize that only the state protected them from the lower classes. The most violent was the **Tupac Amaru** rebellion in Peru that lasted from 1780 until 1783. He was a descendant of the sixteenth-century Incan emperor who was trying to abolish draft labor of Indians in his province while trying to be recognized by Spain as a noble and heir to the Incas. The Creoles at first sympathized, and this was a rare movement that was not restricted by class or race. Then came his social policy to abolish slavery and a call to wage total war against the Europeans and reconsider property laws. With 40,000 to 60,000 supporters, Tupac Amaru besieged Cuzco in 1781. He was defeated, captured, and torn apart by horses. Nearly 100,000 died in the punishment that followed. Spain reformed the government of Peru as seven intendants replaced a multitude of local governors, but the draft labor system persisted. The tax laws of Spain touched off the **Communero Revolution** of 1781. There were riots in Socorro and other towns of New Grenada (the northern coast of South America) after the government published the tax edicts. An Indian peasant army led by Creole captains marched on Bogotá, was delayed, and then betrayed.

# SPANISH AMERICA DURING THE NAPOLEONIC WARS

## Latin American Precursors

A Mexican and a Brazilian approached Thomas Jefferson while he served as Minister to France. Jefferson refused to commit the United States to helping these rebels. France was more of an inspiration. When Spain controlled French-speaking parts of Louisiana in the 1790s, there were sympathetic writings about the French Revolution. The conspiracies in South America in the 1790s were small and momentary. Police found identical handwritten copies of French speeches in Mexico City and Bahia, 5,000 miles away. The Haitian revolution and the French abolition of slavery caused unrest among blacks and mulattoes. Slave revolts in the United States increased in the 1790s inspired by Haiti. The ruling classes of the Americas looked at Haiti with horror, and this deeply affected the course of Latin American revolutions. There was also fear that the Spanish government was undermining white supremacy. Nonwhites were taking on new kinds of jobs and some were allowed to buy "certificates of whiteness" that would allow them access to previously forbidden jobs and social privileges. The Creoles insisted on their right to a superior position over slaves and free coloreds. Increasing Spanish exports were draining money out of Spanish America, further weakening the elites.

The American Revolution inspired the Venezuelan **Francisco de Miranda**. As a Creole, he could not serve as an officer in the local battalion, so he went to Spain and purchased an officer's commission in the Spanish army. He joined in the Spanish attack on the British fortress at Pensacola, Florida, in 1781. He traveled in the United States and met Washington and Hamilton. He spent time in Russia under the Enlightened Despotism of Catherine the Great, though she would not support his plans to liberate America. He had fought for France at the beginning of its revolutionary wars as a general, but during the Reign of Terror he fled to England, where he became friends with Pitt the Younger. Venezuela was very diverse: whites made up only 20 percent of the population, slaves 10 percent, Indians 18 percent, with the rest being free blacks and people of mixed race. Only 658 families held most of the land. Spain could not reform the whole empire and make it more equitable because Spain itself needed social and economic reforms. In 1795, free coloreds led a slave revolt that reminded many Venezuelans of Haiti. After it was suppressed, Miranda called for Venezuelan independence and a government with an emperor, an appointed chamber, an elected chamber, and two Roman-style censors to check the others.

In New York, Miranda raised a volunteer force and led an invasion of Venezuela in 1806. Despite help from the British navy, Miranda was defeated. The elites rejected the radical revolution that Miranda promoted. He fled to Trinidad and then to Britain. The British were at war with Spain, which was allied to Napoleon.

In 1806, the British fleet that had seized the Cape of Good Hope sailed across the South Atlantic and attacked Buenos Aires. The British had long desired to take the Rio de la Plata away from Spain and settle it themselves. The Viceroy had left the city virtually defenseless and ran away. The city's elite welcomed the British and joined in their celebrations. Merchants and nationalists gathered forces, counterattacked, and made the British occupiers surrender. The victors then deposed the cowardly Viceroy and organized a militia including many of mixed race and African slaves. In 1807, another British force seized Montevideo across the estuary and marched on Buenos Aires. It breached the defenses, but the resistance by the militia and ordinary residents (*porteños*) was so fierce that the British were defeated and abandoned Montevideo.

The situation in Buenos Aires became more tense when the Portuguese royal family transferred to Brazil. Napoleon had invaded Portugal in 1807. The Portuguese court of 15,000, led by the Prince Regent (later King) John

VI, arrived in January 1808. He immediately ended mercantilism and opened legal Brazilian trade with Britain. John was married to Carlota Joaquina, sister of ousted Spanish king Ferdinand VII. She wanted the Rio de la Plata to recognize her as regent over the area while many suspected a Portuguese plot to add the coast to Brazil. This plot divided *porteño* society.

## Resistance of the *Juntas*

When Napoleon took over in Spain, many communities declared themselves free of the Bonapartes and set up *juntas* (boards). These *juntas* then set up a central council, known as the *Junta* **of Seville** from 1808 to 1810. To gain support in America, the *junta* asked the viceroyalties of New Spain (Mexico), Peru, New Granada (Colombia/Ecuador), Buenos Aires, and the captaincies general of Cuba, Puerto Rico, Guatemala, Chile, and Venezuela to send representatives. The French overran Seville, and the *junta* dissolved itself on January 29, 1810. The Creoles rejected Napoleon's takeover in Spain and *juntas* were established in New Granada, Venezuela, Chile and Rio de la Plata (the Buenos Aires/Uruguay/Paraguay region).

Buenos Aires, which had effectively been ruling itself since 1806, declared a revolution in May of 1810 and installed a revolutionary *junta* theoretically loyal to Ferdinand but ruling absolutely. It created a Committee of Public Safety and called for a revolutionary war to liberate the areas up the coast and up the river. However, it refused to free the slaves. It formed the **Army of the North** of more than a thousand men to fight the counterrevolutionaries upriver. Montevideo and the coast had long resented Buenos Aires and resisted attack. The Army of the North drove the conservatives out of Argentina and followed them into Upper Peru, but suffered a severe defeat in June 1811. Uruguay and Paraguay broke off as Creoles formed their own governments.

While almost everyone in Chile opposed independence, there was anger when the corrupt governor backed Carlota's regency plans. Two hundred families dominated Chile and dictated politics. A *junta* overthrew the governor. The situation became more radical, and in 1811, a dictator overthrew the *junta* and stopped just short of declaring independence.

The Creoles in Venezuela also set up a *junta*. Miranda returned to Venezuela, won election to Congress, and established a group modeled on the Jacobin Club he had seen in France. The Congress declared independence on July 5, 1811, but many provinces resisted and a civil war began. Venezuela outlawed the slave trade, but not slavery, so blacks and mixed-race people joined the revolt against the Congress. There was a serious earthquake in March 1812 that the conservative clergy said was God's punishment of Venezuela for rebellion.

# ATTEMPTS AT SPANISH RECONQUEST

Miranda decided to surrender to the royalists. This angered many of his younger associates, including **Simón Bolívar**, and they turned Miranda over to the Spanish authorities. Miranda died four years later in a Spanish dungeon. Bolívar, like many young men of the age, had been deeply impressed by Napoleon's rise to power and had actually attended the Corsican's coronation in 1804. Bolívar returned in 1813 and led a war of bloody slaughter killing all the European-born he could in order to drive a wedge between them and the Creoles. The Spanish aided the army of blacks and coloreds, which beat Bolívar. He escaped to British-held Jamaica and then went to Haiti. Bolívar announced that he was freeing his own slaves and that he would abolish slavery in areas liberated from Spanish rule.

Coup and countercoup by political factions racked La Plata until a stable dictatorship emerged in 1812 supported by newly-arrived revolutionaries from Spain including **José de San Martín** (d.1850). New Granada's provisional government fell into disunity and civil war. In February 1815, Ferdinand sent 11,000 soldiers to regain his lands. The army took Caracas. Fractured New Granada quickly submitted as the Spanish executed five hundred Creole leaders. Many were sick of the battles of the last five years and welcomed the Spanish back. But Ferdinand had disavowed his promise to abide by the Cádiz constitution. This discarded many of the rights gained by the coloreds. Many who had fought Bolívar felt betrayed. He also repudiated the rights of equality granted to the Spanish American lands, which had been represented in the Cádiz Cortes. It suggested that Ferdinand would return to the full absolutism and mercantilism of his grandfather. In August 1815, another veteran army group arrived in Chile, organized 5,000 royalists, and drove out the supporters of home rule.

Then the Spanish suffered setbacks. Disease and an uncomfortable climate took their toll. The Spanish army was increasingly a Spanish American army made up of soldiers who had little to fight for. San Martín and a small Buenos Aires navy forced the royalists out of Montevideo. Argentina declared independence in 1816. San Martín and the exiled Chilean revolutionary **Bernardo O'Higgins** put together a new Army of the Andes in Argentina to take Chile: half of the 3,700 troops were former slaves. The crossing of the Andes was brutal and killed one-third of the army, but San Martín and O'Higgins conquered Chile in 1817. The Chilean revolutionary government then hired the British Admiral Thomas Cochrane to shell Valdivia in 1820 and complete the conquest of Chile. Unfortunately, while San Martín was across the Andes, the Brazilians swept down and seized Montevideo and the coast north of the Plata river.

In New Granada, guerrillas formed among the native and mixed race peoples called *llaneros*. They had fought against Bolívar but saw the King disavow their rights. In 1816, Bolívar invaded the lowlands of Guiana. 7,000 British and Irish veterans of the Napoleonic Wars bolstered Bolívar's forces. How these soldiers were paid is unclear, but one suspects the British government held the purse strings trying to undermine Spanish control. Despite Bolívar's promise of freedom, slaves did not join his army nor did they resume the race war that had driven Bolívar out two years before. Bolívar told the skeptical Creoles that if they kept slavery, they would wind up with a Haitian-style war. Bolívar teamed up with the *llaneros*. However, they were not able to conquer the Venezuelan cities. In imitation of Napoleon and San Martín, Bolívar slogged his 2,000-man army through the flooded Llanos river and then over the Andes at 13,000 feet and took Bogotá by surprise in 1819. With new economic resources and manpower, Bolívar could extend his power in New Granada and Venezuela. Caracas fell in 1821.

# THE REVOLUTIONS OF 1820

The fall of Bogotá shocked and angered the government in Madrid. Ferdinand decided to send a larger army, having lost most of his 1815 expedition. In January 1820, troops in Cádiz mutinied after receiving orders to go to South America. They began a march on Madrid, and other garrisons rebelled. They demanded the restoration of the Constitution of 1812. Ferdinand agreed and was held as a virtual captive to make sure he did not slide back.

The government of Portugal had languished since 1808 under a British protectorate. Even after the French left, Prince Regent John refused to bring the royal family back from Brazil. In 1815, John raised Brazil to an equal status with Portugal so that he could stay in the Americas. Brazil prospered with schools, libraries, and its first printing presses. When his mother, the insane Queen Maria, died in 1816, the Prince Regent became King John VI, but still would not come back. There were many protests and attempted revolutions in both Portugal and Brazil. Inspired by the Spanish revolution, Portuguese insurgents in August 1820 expelled the regency established by Britain during King John's absence in Brazil. The revolution started in the city of Porto, which had suffered greatly since John had ended mercantilism and Britain had seized control of most Portuguese trade with America. They waited until the British commander left the country, then struck and convened an assembly to write a constitution that would be modeled on Spain's Cádiz constitution.

John VI wanted to stay in Brazil. Only when his son Pedro refused to go back to Portugal did John make the voyage across the Atlantic accompanied by his queen Carlota Joaquina and their son Miguel. The new constitution downgraded Brazil and broke it into a group of provinces under Lisbon's control. The Queen and Prince Miguel plotted with army officers and closed down the parliament in 1824. Anarchy resulted. King John died suddenly, and rumors said that Miguel had poisoned him. John left no instructions as to which son should follow as king. Civil war continued until 1834, when Britain's influence created a constitutional monarchy.

Metternich called the Concert of Europe to meet at the **Congress of Troppau** in October 1820 to respond to the turmoil in Spain, Portugal, and the Kingdom of the Two Sicilies. Russia and Prussia supported Metternich's anti-nationalist line, but Britain and France were more cautious. The Concert was showing strains. The conservative three signed the Troppau Protocol which declared that the revolutionary governments were outlaws and vowed to crush them.

When Italian liberals fled to Spain, Metternich identified that nation as the chief haven of revolutionaries. Castlereagh had committed suicide, and his replacement **George Canning** was not willing to support Metternich. At the **Congress of Verona** in October 1822, Metternich demanded action against the Spanish revolutionaries. France was willing to do the job. Canning and the British Cabinet feared that Metternich would next intervene in Latin America. This would threaten a major British market. By 1840, the British cotton industry would be shipping 35 percent of its exports to Latin America. The British withdrew from the Alliance. In April 1823, 200,000 French troops entered Spain. Ferdinand took bloody revenge against the liberals when he regained power.

# South American Freedom

## Bolívar Triumphant

The Spanish revolution compelled a truce with Bolívar. Bolívar was dependent on other generals and was forced to give them vast grants of land to keep peace. Bolívar saw that the revolution had weakened Spain. The Cortes believed it could negotiate a settlement and halted all Spanish offensives against the rebels.

Peru had been the most royalist area and had defeated numerous invasions from Argentina. Its 140,000 whites feared independence because they were outnumbered by a million Indians and mixed-race people. San Martín used a different strategy: attack from Chile and the sea. The British Admiral Cochrane blockaded Peru and forced the governor to flee Lima. San Martín entered the city, called an assembly of the Creole elite, and had it choose him as supreme governor. He expelled the Spanish, declared that children of slaves born after 1821 would be free, and abolished Indian tribute. However, the Spanish continued to hold many mountain fortresses. San Martín met with Bolívar in Guayaquil to discuss the Peruvian situation. The details are unknown, but San Martín resigned all his offices. Perhaps he felt that he did not have the political skill to run these lands or perhaps he wanted to give Bolívar a chance at creating a broad federation. They also had different visions: Bolívar dreamed of a United States of Spanish America from Mexico to Argentina, while San Martín wanted monarchies. When San Martín left for Chile, Peru fell apart. The Creoles appealed to Bolívar to restore order and he entered Lima in September 1823. The **Battle of Ayacucho** in December 1824 in southern Peru decided the issue, and Spain withdrew its remaining troops.

## Brazil

John VI had left his son Prince **Dom Pedro** (ruled 1822–1831) as regent of Brazil. Pedro was originally sympathetic to the liberals in Lisbon, but grew increasingly angry as they downgraded Brazil and demanded that Pedro return to Portugal. Pedro declared himself as the independent Emperor of Brazil in 1822. When Portugal tried to reconquer Brazil in July of 1823, Pedro called on the aid of Admiral Cochrane, who had helped San Martín. Cochrane defeated the Portuguese.

## Reaction in Mexico and Central America

As the Bonapartes took power in Madrid, the government of New Spain (Mexico) called for solidarity between the Creoles and *peninsulares*. This made sense in a viceroyalty where 60 percent of the people were Indian, and 20 percent were of mixed race. A priest named **Miguel Hidalgo y Costilla** called for the independence of Mexico with equal rights for Creoles and Indians in 1810. Some 60,000 ill-equipped volunteers joined him. As the looting and violence grew, Creoles deserted Hidalgo, who was defeated and executed by the Spanish in 1811. The insurgents then rallied behind another priest, **José Maria Morelos**. He declared Mexican independence and appealed to the Creoles. That rebellion also failed and Morelos was shot in 1815.

Mexico then settled into small-scale guerrilla war with perhaps 100,000 dying. Reactionaries in Mexico, fearful that revolutionaries might take control in Madrid during the 1820 Revolution, declared independence. Agustin de Iturbide had led soldiers against each rebellion, but felt he had not been properly rewarded. He suddenly made peace with the last band of rebels and offered his **Plan de Iguala** in 1821. The plan rested on three principles: 1) equality between Creoles and *peninsulares*; 2) the supremacy of the Catholic church; 3) an independent monarchy. Slavery was abolished. In 1822, Iturbide became Emperor Agustin I. Within two years, Mexican leaders began to quarrel over the vast land.

The Central American states were in a league with Mexico at first, then became independent as the Central American federation in 1823. Panama, which was still attached to Colombia, was not part of this.

Once Ferdinand got free and disavowed the Constitution, he wanted to reconquer his American colonies. Britain foiled this by militarily backing the American **Monroe Doctrine** of December 1823. This statement told Europe that the United States would regard any European attack on the Americas as a hostile act. The United States did have not the power to back this up, but Metternich and Ferdinand understood that the British navy would supply the force to keep out their counterrevolutionary armies. Monroe excluded the despised government of Haiti from the umbrella of American protection.

# SOUTH AMERICA AFTER INDEPENDENCE

The legacy of the Latin American revolutions was more violent than the British American Revolution. The Enlightenment was over and had less influence on the revolution and the governments that formed. The army of George Washington had been largely a volunteer force, while the Latin American armies were more of a conscripted force. Finally, the Latin American revolutionaries had brought slaves into the political mix by appealing for their participation in the wars against Spain.

The former British colonies had to stick together because of various threats to their western frontiers. Latin American countries had no uniting concerns. The course of revolutions had created a sharp divide between the conservative Mexican and Central American regimes and the liberated South American area. But even in liberated Spanish America, the Andes mountains and Amazon basin proved formidable barriers. There were few modern roads to knit together the areas. Peru and Upper Peru (Bolivia) divided. Bolívar's Gran Colombia broke apart into Colombia, Venezuela, and Ecuador by the time the Liberator died in 1830. Right before his death, he had said "America is ungovernable. Those who serve the revolution plow the sea."

Paraguay, Uruguay, and Bolivia refused to accept the leadership of Buenos Aires. Uruguayan and Argentine forces beat the Brazilians, and a British-mediated treaty of 1828 created a buffer zone. Indeed the hinterland of Argentina resisted the port's leadership. The early Argentine leader Bernardino Rivadavia led a liberal government in the 1820s. He signed a trade treaty with Britain and confiscated the land of the Church. But Argentina, like many of the nations, fell under the *caudillo*. These strongmen were often rich landowners who could raise private armies and manipulate patron-client relations expertly. Juan Manuel de Rosas came from the provinces, asserted control over Buenos Aires, and ruled as a dictator from 1829 until 1852.

The frequent wars over uncertain boundaries among the nations only strengthened the tradition of militarism and violence that diverted investment money from productive purposes. While Spain would never be able to reimpose mercantilism, South America had a quasi-mercantilist relationship with Britain. Before 1850, Britain sold about £5 million of goods each year to Latin America with about half of that being sold to Brazil. Latin America had no shipbuilding industry and relied primarily on British ships to carry goods. There were no steam engines until the middle of the nineteenth century. The main holders of wealth before the revolution, the *peninsulares* and the Church, did not invest in the local economy. Most of the *peninsulares* returned to Europe, while the Church distrusted or worked against liberal governments.

After independence, Brazil increasingly relied on coffee as a cash crop. Coffee, like sugar, was grown on slave plantations. It accounted for 40 percent of Brazil's exports in 1840 and 60 percent in 1880. Brazil intensified slavery. Half a million slaves came to Brazil from Africa during the 1830s and 1840s illegal slave trade. Brazil only banned the trade in 1851 because the British threatened to blockade Brazil's ports. Brazil did not end slavery until 1888.

## TIMELINE

| | |
|---|---|
| 1780–1783 | Tupac Amaru Revolt |
| 1781 | Communero Revolution |
| 1800 | Gabriel's Rebellion in Virginia |
| 1806–1807 | British attack Buenos Aires |
| 1808 | Portuguese court arrives in Brazil |
| 1810 | Junta of Seville dissolves |
| | Hidalgo rebellion in Mexico |
| 1811 | Venezuela declares independence |
| 1815 | Ferdinand VII sends force to America |
| | Brazil raised to equality with Portugal |
| 1816 | Argentina declares independence |
| 1817 | San Martín and O'Higgins conquer Chile |

| | |
|---|---|
| 1819 | Bolívar takes Bogotá |
| 1820 | Revolution in Spain and Portugal |
| 1821 | Caracas falls to Bolívar |
| | San Martín takes Lima |
| | John VI returns to Portugal |
| | Mexico declares independence |
| 1822 | San Martín and Bolívar meet at Guayaquil |
| | Brazil declares independence |
| 1822–1823 | Congress of Verona authorizes French to crush Spanish revolution |
| 1823 | Monroe Doctrine |
| | United Provinces of Central America |
| 1824 | Battle of Ayacucho |
| 1828 | Independence of Uruguay |
| 1830 | Gran Colombia breaks apart |
| | Death of Bolívar |

# KEY TERMS

Creoles
Tupac Amaru Rebellion
Francisco de Miranda
*Junta* of Seville
Simón Bolívar
José de San Martín
Congress of Verona
Battle of Ayacucho
Plan de Iguala
Monroe Doctrine

# PRIMARY SOURCE DOCUMENTS

**Simón Bolívar**, http://www.fordham.edu/Halsall/mod/1819bolivar.asp

**Monroe Doctrine**, http://avalon.lw.yale.edu/19th_century/monroe.asp

**Slave Life in Rio de Janeiro**, http://faculty.chass.ncsu.edu/slatta/hi216/ documents/slavery/slavelife.htm

**Declaration of Independence of the United Provinces of South America**, http://faculty.chass.ncsu.edu/slatta/hi216/documents/july1816.htm

# Chapter 8

# THE AGRICULTURAL AND INDUSTRIAL REVOLUTIONS

# THE AGRICULTURAL REVOLUTION

As stated before, most people in Europe (and the world) in the eighteenth century were farmers and lived in the countryside. A fundamental change in farming would shake a nation. European farming before the modern period had been extremely varied across the map and dependent on laws, customs, family traditions, soil quality, climate, and many other factors. Generally, we may say that there was a rotation of crops usually involving a grain such as wheat, barley, or rye, and protein-rich crops such as broad beans. Animals and their manure were relatively scarce, which meant both fertilizer and meat were far more limited than today. For most farmers in Western Europe, the only choice was to let part of the soil rest and recover its nutrients. The land would lie **fallow**: farmers would plow and remove any weeds that appeared, but they would not plant crops. They left roughly one-third of the farmland fallow, and this has led historians to create a general model called the **three-field system**. The population grew very slowly, and village life remained much the same from generation to generation. There were a few very fertile, densely-populated areas such as the Netherlands and the Po river valley in Italy that used more intensive techniques. **Thomas Malthus** (1766–1834) had described the early modern situation well: population increased more rapidly than the food supply, thus insuring constant poverty and periodic cycles of famine.

# New Foods and Demographic Revolution

The low point of European population in the early modern period was in 1650. It had just suffered terrible wars, bad weather, and crop failures. After that year, population would grow at an accelerating rate for the next three hundred years. The biggest contributor to the growth from 1650 to 1800 was new food. Explorations had brought the Europeans in contact with many unfamiliar foods, but the most significant were **corn** (which the Europeans call maize) and the **potato**. Corn was developed in central Mexico and had spread through most of the Americas by 1492. Even more important was the potato, one of the hardiest plants in the world. It is native to the Andes Mountains of South America and almost single-handedly supported the complex society of the Incan Empire of Peru. It is an excellent source of carbohydrates, can be prepared in a variety of ways, and has many uses for human and animal consumption. An acre of potatoes could feed up to five times as many people as an acre of wheat. A farmer could harvest a crop of potatoes in three or four months whereas many grains took ten months to ripen. Better food and a decline in the virulence of the plague brought down the death rate and boosted the population. Entire areas of Europe such as Ireland and the southwest German states became dependent on the potato. That proved to be dangerous. From 1650 to 1800 the population increased in England from five million to 9.25 million, France from 21 million to 29 million, the German areas from 17 million to 29 million, and Russia from 17 million to 36 million.

Improvements in agriculture led to a change in many facets of everyday life. Men and women often lived with their parents until they married. For men, the average age at first marriage was about twenty-five to twenty-seven, for women it was around twenty-one. Then they would move out, having saved up enough money to buy or at least rent enough land for themselves. During early adulthood, children often worked for several years away from home. Social pressures had worked to keep the number of children born to unmarried women very low. The spread of the potato allowed farmers to set up a household more easily because they did not need as much land if they planted potatoes. After 1750, the age of marriage began to drop. Earlier marriage meant more children and a larger population.

Other new foods included increased planting of the turnip, which could be eaten by people in an emergency but was mostly for animals. There was also scientific cultivation of the sugar beet with the aim of increasing its sugar content. In the nineteenth century, sugar from beets increasingly took the place of sugar from cane, which could only be grown in the tropics and, as we have seen, was largely the product of slave labor.

# New Tools

The time around 1700 also saw the invention of some simple but ingenious new tools that increased farm productivity. The Englishman **Jethro Tull** (1674–1741) introduced a deeper mold board on the plow. The plow was lighter, and horses could pull it as well as oxen. Plowing would be faster even as it dug more deeply. When one stirs up more soil, it mixes in more oxygen. This means that the microbes that help fertilize soil will increase and work faster making the soil more productive. Tull introduced a new seed-planting method of "seed drilling" in 1701 rather than broadcasting. This meant a family did not have to save as much seed from the previous year's crops and this increased its food supply. It had a modest impact in more advanced Western Europe, but Central and Eastern Europe increased their yield per seed by 24 percent.

Big agricultural machines such as reapers and chemical fertilizer would come only in the nineteenth century. The U.S. wheat yield in 1866 was eleven bushels per acre, about three times medieval Europe's yield. The yield increased to sixteen in 1914, twenty-four in 1960, thirty-six in 1983, and forty in 1998; the growth since 1960 has mainly been because of chemical fertilizer derived from natural gas. The price of wheat in 1919 hit a high of $2.16 per bushel (with inflation, that equals $43.20 in 2007 dollars) as opposed to the current prices of five to eight dollars. What would your life be like if all the prices in the grocery store cost seven to ten times as much? What would you buy and not buy? How much would be left after you paid for food and rent?

# New Means of Cultivation

During the political turmoil in seventeenth-century England, a number of English spent time in the Netherlands and observed the more intensive methods. The scientific revolution inspired some to apply the scientific method to farming. Tull proposed a process of mowing the field while root plants grew. **Charles Townshend** (1674–1738) proposed a scientific model of cultivation based on his experiments on soil fertility. This was known as the **four-crop rotation**: the farmer would plant wheat in the late Fall, it would grow in the winter (thus known as "winter wheat") protected by snow from the cold and then be harvested in early spring. Then the farmer would plant root crops such as potatoes and turnips. The farmer could mow to remove weeds while these grew underground. The farmer would then grow a summer grain such as barley and oats that were mainly for animal consumption; autumn would see him plant so-called artificial grasses such as alfalfa and clover or legumes (peas, beans) to fertilize the soil and replenish nourishment.

Thus two cycles (wheat and root crops) would take nutrition out while the summer grain and the autumn cycle would replenish nutrition and make the soils ready for winter wheat. Scientific farmers found that on many soils, there would no longer be a need to leave a part fallow, so you could plant the entire area year after year.

Farmers also applied science to animal breeding to create larger animals that were carefully bred for meat or milk or (as with the new sport of thoroughbred horse racing) speed. The ability to feed and keep more horses meant that the average English farmer had about 67 percent more horsepower to help him than the French farmer in 1800. **Robert Bakewell** (1725–1795) was a leading breeder. During his lifetime, the average weight of cattle doubled and sheep tripled from twenty-eight to eighty pounds.

# Enclosure Acts

There was strong resistance among farmers to the new techniques. For many they seemed to be physically impossible, and the farmers complained that the scientists must have used special soils in special conditions. They would not risk their family's lives on something so uncertain.

The big landlords, however, were eager to increase their profits and turned nasty. They controlled Parliament. Only 250,000 men (3 percent of the total population) had the right to vote for the House of Commons. But these were not equally distributed, and by one estimate of the time just 5,723 men (.07% of the population) controlled the House of Commons. After 1700, the Parliament passed large numbers of **Enclosure Acts**. On the one hand, they cut off farm lands owned or traditionally rented by peasants from common land and waste land. The commons and the wastes were areas of lesser fertility that would be used by the village communally for less-demanding plants or pastures for animals or foraging areas. The commons and wastes could make the difference between life and death even though the lands were often owned by a local noble or big landlord. Because their productivity was low, peasants had used them by custom. Now they were cut off by fences or hedges with penalties imposed for "poaching." The Enclosure Acts also levied fees for surveying land that many peasants could not afford. The result of enclosure was that many sold or gave up their lands or cooperated with their landlords in converting the land to the new system. From 1761 to 1792, the Parliament enclosed seven times as much land as in the previous thirty years, and the pace accelerated after 1792. By 1800, the nobles or gentry held 80 percent of the land in Britain. Some resisted. In Ireland, the "Whiteboys of Tipperary" destroyed enclosure fences.

## Results of the Agricultural Revolution

From 1700 to 1870, the number of farm workers in England grew by 14 percent, while production of crops grew 181 percent. Labor productivity therefore grew 146 percent (2.81 divided by 1.14). Measured another way, the land productivity of wheat, oats, and legumes doubled. Farmers not only eliminated most fallow land but reclaimed swampy and hilly and infertile land so the total amount of land planted grew 72 percent. Production of potatoes went from 1.31 million bushels to 50.14 million bushels. The general population of England and Wales rose from 5.75 million to 25 million (335 percent) in this time. England had been a food exporter from 1660 to 1770; now it had to import food. Sixty percent of the English workers had been mainly food producers in 1700; that fell to 22 percent by 1850. The increase in population would tend to lead to a rise in food prices, but this was offset by the increase in productivity, which brought prices down. Sara Horrell found that 48 percent of the budget went to food in the 1787 to 1796 period in Britain, but only 40 percent on average went to food in the 1830 to 1954 period. By another estimate, in 1688 58.5 percent of the British G.D.P. was spent on food, drink, and textiles; that would fall to 16 percent by the 1990s.

The agricultural revolution spread to northern France by 1770. A hundred years later the process was largely complete in that country. From 1780 to 1810, the amount of French land planted with potatoes increased by more than one hundred times. From there it spread across the rest of western and central Europe. The process was faster than Britain's and also the enclosure process was not used except for a few cases. The new methods resulted because with each new generation, farm land was split among more and more farmers until they were left with "microplots": farms too small to support a family. At that point, families would plant potatoes or introduce the four-crop rotation.

# INDUSTRIAL REVOLUTION

## Basic Shifts

The Industrial Revolution involved three basic shifts. Firstly, machines replaced, amplified, and transmitted human labor. Secondly, wood burning gave way to coal burning as world coal production grew from 10 million tons in 1800 to 1 billion tons in 1900, a hundredfold increase. Thirdly, animal or water or wind power gave way to the steam engine. Instead of many separate activities carried out by families across the countryside, unified factories would carry out production with many different machines and either would be centered in cities or new cities would grow up around the factories.

# Why England?

England had several advantages for industrialization: 1) **Financial**: the Bank of England provided a strong anchor for a credit system to provide financing for projects. Interest rates were lower than most other European nations. The first English country bank was founded in 1716. The number of banks outside the capital of London grew from twelve in 1750 to 400 in 1793 and 900 in 1815. 2) **Geographic**: England, a long and narrow island surrounded by seas, had many navigable waterways, making transportation cheaper. 3) **Economic**: the Agricultural Revolution, pioneered in England, made for lower food prices and thus more disposable income for manufactured goods. Landowners used their agricultural profits to develop many of the coal fields. 4) **Natural resources:** coal and iron were abundant. Because the gentry ran the country, there were few regulations on agriculture or industry and landless workers could move where they pleased.

These four factors were necessary to start an industrial revolution. Nearby Ireland had similar geographic advantages and also went through the agricultural revolution. However, Ireland did not industrialize. It did not have a lot of coal and iron. Also, its banking and credit system was underdeveloped. Ireland suffered as a British colony. Cromwell had brutally completed the colonization process in the 1650s by taking land away from most Catholics. Although 90 percent of the Irish were Roman Catholics, Protestants owned 86 percent of the land and were often absentee landlords. What wealth Ireland produced was frequently transferred to Britain. Those renting the land had no incentive to improve their land because that would only raise the rent. Ireland's textile industries suffered from British competition, and Ireland actually deindustrialized during the late 1700s: 48 percent of the Irish had been employed in farming in 1775; it was 75 percent in 1845. The Agricultural Revolution brought rapid population growth in Ireland as it did in Britain, but it also brought a dangerous overreliance on the potato. Not only was this the main food for many, but raising potatoes was the main job of many. If anything should happen to the potato crop, the Irish would have nothing to eat and no job to provide money to buy other food. 1,750,000 Irish left for England and America even before the Great Hunger of the 1840s.

# New Textile Inventions and Innovations

After agriculture, textile production was the second biggest occupation. Most clothes were made of wool, which comes from sheep. Silk and cotton were very expensive and had to be imported, often from China and India. In the putting-out system, merchants gave wool to peasants to spin into thread, then weave into cloth, and then sew together as clothes. In 1717, Thomas Lombe set up the first true factory, where these functions would be carried out in one central place. In 1733, **John Kay** invented the **flying shuttle**, which sped up the weaving process. This created pressure to speed up the spinning of the thread to meet the weavers' demand. It took ten spinners to meet the need for thread of a single weaver working with the flying shuttle. The problem of thread was solved when the **spinning jenny** was invented by **James Hargreaves** in 1765. Coarser yarn could be turned out faster by the **water frame** of **Richard Arkwright** after 1775. Finally, **Samuel Crompton's "Mule"** (1779) combined the speed of the water frame with the fine thread of the jenny. The Mule could spin two to three hundred times faster than a hand spinner. However, the Mule required water power, so businessmen built factories near water and cottage spinning declined. The number of hand-weavers kept growing to weave the enormous amounts of spun thread, which grew tenfold from 1770 to 1790. In the 1820s, **Edmund Cartwright's Power Loom** (invented 1785) became dominant in weaving. These inventions all occurred in England. It was not because Englishmen were smarter than men of other nations. These inventors had incentive because credit was cheap, and many of these inventors became very wealthy men. They could borrow money at low interest rates to set up a new business or expand existing business. Often they borrowed from friends, relatives or members of their church. Life was harder for businessmen in France and Spain because interest rates were much higher and it was harder to make a profit. They found it easier to put money into land.

The next key problem was the supply of cotton. The North American colonies and India were the main sources of cotton. Cotton production was very slow because cotton seeds had to be picked out by hand, and raw cotton is difficult to work with. A worker could process only six pounds a day. Nevertheless, Britain had tripled its cotton cloth production from the 1740s to the 1770s. In 1793 the American **Eli Whitney** invented the **cotton gin** to pick out seeds automatically. This caused an upsurge in the cotton industry as the gin increased production fiftyfold. Britain imported 2.5 million pounds of cotton in 1760, 22 million in 1787, 50 million in 1800, and 366 million in 1837. By 1830, cotton cloth comprised 50 percent of the value of British exports. It also caused the expansion of cotton plantations across the southern

United States and with it slavery. Before the cotton gin, only the long-staple cotton grown on the American coast had been profitable. Now, short-staple cotton from slightly cooler climates could also turn a profit, greatly expanding the cotton range.

# The Transportation Revolution

As textile production grew after 1760, it became more important to ensure cheap and reliable transportation. Roads were mostly unsuited to wheeled vehicles: a rainstorm turned them into quagmires. Only a few special coaches on the British roads of the 1760s could travel sixty miles a day. Water transport was cheaper and more efficient. One horse could pull 100,000 pounds loaded onto a water barge, but only 250 pounds on land. After 1760, Britain and France launched many projects to build canals to link rivers and to deepen many waterways. In 1815, engineers led by **John McAdam** built new roads made with crushed stones held together by tar over a solid foundation to accommodate wagons.

The "rail road" had long existed in the mines. The rails were usually made of wood that was joined together. Miners would push carts on grooved wheels loaded with tons of rock. The heavy weights were constantly breaking and splintering the wooden rails, which needed frequent replacement. Innovations in iron and steel made better rails possible; mines installed the first iron rail track in 1767. In 1801, the first general railroad was established, pulled by horses to link up canals. The barge would be unloaded onto special carts that sat on iron rails.

Transport improvements caused the price of commodities to fall as goods became cheaper. The first steam-powered railroad line was built in 1830. The railroad expanded horizons of travel and movement, made cheap overland transport possible, and shrank distance for the first time in European history.

# Growth in Iron and Steel

The European iron industry had grown steadily from the fifteenth century, when the water-powered blast furnace operated in Italy to increase the production speed of cast iron. Blast furnaces are used to extract the metal from the raw ore. Heating was done with **charcoal**, the result of wood burned in the absence of air to make a smokeless fuel. Britons had cut down many of the forests to make charcoal or to build ships or warm people in their homes. From 1540 to 1640, coal and iron production in Britain increased

800 percent, but limits on mining from water flooding and the nature of coal prevented further expansion.

With the price of wood climbing, especially in Britain, people began to turn to coal for heating. Although very efficient, coal was very smoky and could not be used in houses that did not have chimneys. Iron makers could not mix coal with iron because coal had many impurities that made the iron brittle. Another problem was that coal would turn soft and clog the furnaces. **Abraham Darby** borrowed the process of charring coal to remove impurities in coal from brewing industry. This created **coke**. He used it to smelt iron in 1708. British coal production quintupled in the eighteenth century, while iron production rose eightfold from 1740 to 1796.

# The Application of Steam Power

The problem of pumping water from mines still limited coal use. Before 1700, the only sources for the continuous driving of machinery were wind, water, and living muscle. Scientific experiments of the late 1600s in the areas of vacuum and atmospheric pressure had shown the power of steam, pistons, and vacuum power. Thomas Savery (c.1650–1715) built an early steam engine in 1698, but it was **Thomas Newcomen** (1663–1729) who built the first continuous engine in 1712, which pumped 120 gallons of water a minute from the mine. He used steam to create a vacuum which worked a pump at a cycle of twelve strokes a minute. The Newcomen engine produced five horsepower, about the same as an average water mill. By the time of his death, a hundred of his engines were in use, mostly in the coal belt of the British Midlands.

In 1763, a small working model of the Newcomen engine was brought to a professor at Glasgow University for repair. **James Watt** recognized the great waste of energy in the engine and worked to improve its efficiency. A problem arose with the Watt engine that the main cylinder had to be snugly contained or steam would escape. Ironmaster **John Wilkinson** had devised in 1774 a new way of boring holes into cannon and the same thing could be done to cylinders and other automatically guided precision tools to within a thousandth of an inch. The first Watt engine set to work pumping water in 1776. In 1797, Richard Trevithick developed the **high-pressure steam engine**, which was more efficient than Watt's engine and could produce twenty horsepower, four times the power of the Newcomen engine. Trevithick invented a locomotive that could haul ten tons at five miles an hour.

Steam power sped up production in industrial areas. Blast furnaces pumped air to speed iron manufacturing. Henry Cort simplified the entire iron production process in the 1780s and produced high-quality iron. Later, steam powered the entire textile process. Factories could be located away from water sources. Canals linked coal fields to the centers of industry. Britain began to export iron in 1797. British iron production was 260,000 tons in 1806. It reached three million in 1844. By 1852, Britain accounted for half of the world's iron production and was exporting more than a million tons a year. In 1777 Abraham Darby III built the Iron Bridge, the first large work of civil engineering in iron. In 1829, **George Stephenson**'s locomotive *The Rocket* operated from Liverpool to Manchester at twenty-eight miles per hour.

France, Belgium, and the German states quickly followed Britain's railroad lead. By 1840, Britain (excluding Ireland) had built 2,390 kilometers of rail, France 410, the German states 469, and Belgium 334. By 1860, Britain had 14,603 kilometers, France 9,167, and the German states 11,089. By 1862, Britain had built more than half of the rails it would ever build. Belgium reached that mark in 1867, Germany in 1876, France in 1877, the United States around 1884, Italy in 1886, and Russia in 1898. Other countries reached this mark after 1900 including Japan around 1920 and China around 1960.

# ADAM SMITH: ECONOMIC THEORY FOR THE REVOLUTIONARY AGE

With the tremendous growth in farm and manufactured goods, the emergence of a national work force and more cohesive national states united by railroads, an international market was emerging more clearly. The old principles of mercantilism were clearly outdated as were regulations dating from the Middle Ages. **Adam Smith** (1723–1790) of Great Britain published the *Wealth of Nations* in 1776. Smith had met with Voltaire and applied Scottish Enlightenment theories to economics: by serving their own self-interests and applying reason, people will actually serve the greater good by bringing into effect the "invisible hand" as long as they are properly informed (as with Rousseau). The wealth of a country comes not from its hoard of gold and silver, as the mercantilists would have it. Wealth depends on a nation's productivity. An important step is the division of labor: each person doing one small repetitive task can increase productivity. Production lines were already common in Enlightened Europe. The larger the market, the larger the division of labor could be, and thus all restraints on trade should be lifted. Smith was the founder of the classical liberal economic school.

Many heads of big corporations who cite Smith with approval want to "get the government off their backs," but Smith also attacked big corporations venomously, especially those that had separated boards of directors from management and from the stockholders. This leads to managers cheating the true owners of the company. Also if companies get too big, they invariably manipulate and distort the free market so the invisible hand cannot operate properly. Smith advocated government interference of a sort that only Communist governments have ever implemented.

With attacks against restraints on trade, Smith set up an economic liberal philosophy that would combine with political liberalism to create one of the most powerful political movements of the nineteenth century.

# THE SPREAD OF INDUSTRIALISM

Even in Britain, the impact of industrialism was gradual. Between 1811 and 1821, the plurality of economic product (and probably employment) shifted to industry. As late as 1870, half of the total steampower in manufacturing was still in textiles. The great majority of industrial workers in 1851 were still craftsmen in small shops. Britain did not massively apply steam in industry until the thirty years after 1870. British exports grew 50 percent from 1775 to 1800 despite the loss of the thirteen colonies. They grew another 142 percent from 1814 to 1845.

# TIMELINE

| | |
|---|---|
| 1698 | First Engine (Savery) |
| 1708 | Use of Coke in Smelting Iron (Darby) |
| 1712 | First Continuous Engine (Newcomen) |
| 1730s | Townshend promotes four-crop rotation |
| 1733 | Flying Shuttle (Kay) |
| 1733 | Jethro Tull, *The Horse Hoeing Husbandry* |
| 1765 | Spinning Jenny (Hargreaves) |
| 1765 | Improved Steam Engine (Watt) |
| 1775 | Water Frame (Arkwright) |
| 1776 | Adam Smith, *Wealth of Nations* |
| 1779 | Crompton's "Mule" |
| 1781 | Rotary-action steam engine (Watt) |
| 1783 | Steamship (d'Abbans) |
| 1785 | Power Loom (Cartwright) |
| 1793 | Cotton Gin (Whitney) |

| 1797 | High-Pressure Steam Engine (Trevithick) |
| 1803–1804 | Steam Engine Locomotive (Trevithick) |
| 1807 | The *Clermont* (Fulton) |
| 1815 | Macadamized road (McAdam) |
| 1829 | The Rocket (Stephenson) |

# KEY TERMS

Three-Field System
Thomas Malthus
Jethro Tull
Four-Crop Rotation
Enclosure Acts
Flying Shuttle
Spinning Jenny
Water Frame
Crompton's "Mule"
Power Loom
Cotton Gin
McAdam
Abraham Darby
Thomas Newcomen
*The Rocket*
Adam Smith

# PRIMARY SOURCE DOCUMENTS

**Accounts of the "Potato Revolution,"** http://www.fordham.edu/halsall/mod/1695potato.html

**Letter from the Leeds Cloth Merchant**, http://www.fordham.edu/halsall/mod/1791machines

**Adam Smith**, http://www.wsu.edu:8080/~dee/ENLIGHT/WEALTH1.HTM

**Adam Smith**, http://odur.let.rug.nl/~usa/D/1776-1800/adamsmith/wealth02.htm

**Edwin Chadwick**, Report on Sanitary Conditions, http://www.victorianweb.org/history/chadwick2.html

# Chapter 9

## THE EGYPTIAN CHALLENGES

Napoleon's brief time in Egypt had proved the weakness of the Turkish Empire and challenged the Muslim world. The response caused a bitter dispute between modernizers such as Muhammad Ali of Egypt and Muslim fundamentalists such as the Saudis and Wahhabists in Arabia.

## THE OTTOMAN EMPIRE IN DECLINE

The Turkish Empire had been declining for more than a hundred years, and Austria and Russia had steadily forced it back. The original Ottoman system had depended on constant growth and being able to reward military leaders with land grants. The child levy for Janissaries ended around 1650, and Janissary status became hereditary. The Janissaries and officials who came out of that corps had understood Christian Europe and sometimes aided their families. When that ended in the eighteenth century, the Christian part became resentful of Istanbul. After its 1683 failure at Vienna, the Ottoman system turned inward: if lords wanted a reward, they had to get it from someone else, and that involved bribing the Sultan. The administration was corrupt, and the economy was inefficient. It lost control over Yemen and much of Arabia. Southern Arabia's loss of the coffee monopoly in the eighteenth century was a major blow. The Turks kept power over the port of Jidda and controlled Mecca and Medina during the times of pilgrimage. In 1814, an estimated 70,000 pilgrims had traveled to Mecca. This provided vital revenues through the governors of Syria and Egypt who assembled the pilgrims and provided protection for them.

The Sultans in the early days of the empire had governed regions, but after 1600, they grew up in the palace with little education or practical experience. Large landowners and Muslim religious leaders foiled attempts by the Sultans to reform the government. Jews, Armenians, and others had used the printing press, but there was no press authorized to print in Turkish until 1727. Even so, the press was forbidden anything on religion or law, and produced about a book a year until it was shut down in 1742. The Turkish printing press was not revived until 1784. "Doctors of the law" (*'ulema*) had the right to interpret Islam. Their view of Islam was very rigid, and they were opposed to all western ideas and reforms. Their interests coincided with the Janissaries, who opposed all military reforms and modernization. By 1800, 400,000 claimed Janissary status, but only 20,000 were available to fight. The French ambassador in 1807 said: "To make an alliance with Turkey is the same as putting your arms around a corpse to make it stand up!"

Farmers rented land from landlords who were almost always absent. Local lords pressed the farmers for more than legally required, and Istanbul lacked the power to protect its loyal subjects. There was increasing religious intolerance, and significant numbers of Jews left for Western Europe. The European part suffered constant violence from the Empire's wars with Austria, Russia, and Venice. The Janissaries were supposed to protect the people, but often teamed up with local merchants to fleece the local population. The only choice was to look to strong local leaders. The people would back local strongmen who took the title of **bey** rather than the Istanbul-appointed governor (pasha). By 1600, the Janissaries seized power in Tripoli and elected their own *dey* who shared power with the pasha. By 1700, a hereditary family of beys held much of the power in Tunis. Around that time, the *dey* in Algiers won the title of pasha and ruled that area in league with the merchants and the rulers of the grain-producing hinterland. In 1747, a group of Mamluks from Georgia took over Baghdad.

Under the peace treaties of 1699, the Ottomans gave up the right to tax trade, which meant they had to find other revenue or go without. The wealthiest men were non-Muslims and so were cut off from influencing policy or pressing reform. It was impossible that they could force a calling of a Turkish Estates-General. Christians and Jews were not bound by the Muslim ban on usury (the lending of money at interest rates) and so assumed the leading financial role in the Empire. In the late eighteenth century, the Ottoman economic position became even more dire. Goods produced in Europe or from its colonies in Asia and the New World competed with Middle Eastern goods such as sugar and coffee in Europe and then in the Middle

East itself. The French were selling high-quality textiles to rich and common people alike.

**Selim III** (ruled 1789–1807) attempted long overdue reforms. He levied new taxes to pay for a new corps of soldiers who would not be linked to the Janissaries. He sent soldiers into southeastern Europe to roust out the Janissaries. He attempted to collect fees from the vast majority of Janissaries who were not performing any military duties. He introduced technical training for officers and the first programs for administrative education.

# THE RISE OF MUHAMMAD ALI

## Egypt under the Georgian Mamluks

In the Arab world, there was growing discontent with its Turkish overlords. The Turks saw their Arab provinces as underpopulated backwaters, safe against invaders, and tended to ignore them. They had increasing difficulty controlling Egypt. The Turks had conquered the previous ruling military class of Mamluks, but the governors began to lose authority. The government in Istanbul feared that a long-serving governor in Cairo could establish it as a power base against the Sultan and so made sure to change governors frequently. The result was that no governor got control over the Mamluk elite.

Not only was Egypt a source of revenue from the Meccan pilgrims, but it was also the granary of the Ottoman Empire, as it had been for empires going back thousands of years. The Mamluks grew in power and swelled their ranks with new recruits from the Caucasus mountains and Russia. Boys would be enslaved in these areas, sold to Egypt as soldiers, converted to Islam, and then freed as adults. In 1768, Ali Bey proclaimed himself as governor and refused to pay tribute to Istanbul. He briefly conquered Syria, but was betrayed by a subordinate and died in 1772. Power soon fell to two other Mamluks from Georgia, **Murad and Ibrahim**. The Mamluks gained control of the Ottoman regiments. Murad and Ibrahim periodically fought with one another and sometimes refused to pay taxes to Istanbul or provide the necessary grain supply to the holy cities of Mecca and Medina. In 1785, Murad gave the French the right to ship goods across Suez so as to shorten their route to Pondicherry in India. This caused the Sultan to dispatch a force to Egypt. The Turks chased the beys out of Cairo, which degenerated into civil war. Ibrahim and Murad found new support to the south and east. The

Turks could not finish subduing the beys because a new war loomed with Russia and Austria. The beys were back in Cairo by 1791.

Napoleon drove them out again. He slaughtered many of the Mamluk and bedouin forces as well as regular Turkish units stationed in Egypt. He had promoted clerical government, emphasized the centrality of Cairo to the Islamic tradition, and even called himself a "muslim" of sorts. Napoleon's invasion was a shock to Selim III who had considered the French to be allies. It caused a shift to conservative advisers and Selim's era of reform ended.

## Ali Seizes Power

Muhammad Ali was born to a prominent Albanian merchant family in the same year as Napoleon. As a young man, he was a successful tax collector. The French tried to interest Russia in a joint war against the Ottomans. In 1801, the French force finally surrendered to the Turkish authorities, and the Sultan asked for military units to take over Egypt. The British tried to prop up Mamluk rule, but left within two years. Muhammad Ali arrived as a second commander in his cousin's Albanian force, but soon began a rise to power by marrying Ali Bey's widow and gaining some of the former ruler's political base. When the Albanian leader was killed in a riot, Muhammad Ali assumed command. Murad Bey had died of plague, but Ibrahim was still maneuvering for power and allied with Muhammad Ali. Muhammad Ali's Albanian mercenaries made him valuable to all sides of the conflict. By 1804, the Albanians had installed Osman Bey al-Bardisi as strongman in Cairo, but he pressed the people too hard to raise taxes to pay the Albanian soldiers. Meanwhile, Ali assured the people that he would preserve order.

The Albanians drove Ibrahim Bey and Osman Bey from Cairo and invited the Janissary Mayor of Alexandria to become governor. But soon this governor (Ahmed Khorsid) brought in troops from Syria and tried to destroy the Albanians. Ali had made a key alliance with Omar Makram, a cleric who had organized resistance against Napoleon in Cairo and then fled with Ibrahim Bey. Makram came out of the French occupation with great prestige as a religious and military leader and persuaded the *'ulema* of Cairo to back Muhammad Ali over Khorsid. In May 1805, Sultan Selim appointed him as Pasha of Cairo and he became pasha of all Egypt in October 1806.

Some Mamluk beys resisted Muhammad Ali's appointment, and while he was fighting them in Upper Egypt, a British naval force arrived in Alexandria. Makram organized resistance to them, and Ali negotiated a peace that made Egypt a major naval supply post for the British navy. Ali nationalized all the land in Egypt and reserved a monopoly on trade for the state. Large amounts of revenue now flowed into his coffers. Ali used the money to enlarge the army beyond his Albanian mercenaries. The *'ulema* backed him as he claimed growing rights over the Mamluks' hereditary lands. In 1809, Ali pressed the religious foundations for money. Makram broke with Ali and led protests, but Ali arrested him and forced him into exile.

In 1807, the Janissaries rose up and deposed Selim. They got the head of the *'ulema* in Istanbul to declare his reforms as contrary to Islamic law. A reformist force marched on Istanbul, but the conservatives murdered Selim before it arrived. The reformers then installed Selim's brother **Mahmud II** (ruled 1808–1839) to continue the modernization.

# Wahhabism

Beyond the Ottoman frontiers in Arabia were regions with small merchant towns in oases of central and eastern Arabia or ports on the western side of the Persian Gulf. In central Arabia, a religious reformer named **Muhammad Ibn 'Abd Al-Wahhab** (1703–1792) called for a return to Islam as understood by the Prophet and his companions. He rejected all later interpretations of Islamic law and illegitimate innovations such as saint worship and lavish mosques. He considered tobacco and hashish to be intoxicants as forbidden as alcohol.

Wahhab stirred up controversy by forbidding grave worship and destroyed the grave of one of the Prophet's companions. He also insisted on the stoning of all adulterers. He fled to the market city of Dir'iyya in the northeast Nejd and in 1744 made an alliance with the Saud tribe ruled by **Muhammad ibn Sa'ud** (d.1765) to form a state that claimed to live in strict accord with the *shari'a*. Wahhab convinced Sa'ud that it was his duty to wage a jihad on all other forms of Islam and in 1763, he began the conquest of his neighbors. They rejected the claim of the Ottomans to be the true protectors (caliphs) of authentic Islam.

Muhammad ibn Sa'ud was succeeded by his son Abdul Aziz (ruled 1765–1803), who had married Wahhab's daughter. Abdul Aziz extended Sa'ud power along the eastern coast of Arabia and up into Mesopotamia (Iraq). In 1802, his troops outraged the Shi'ite Muslim world by sacking the holy city of Karbala and destroying its graves and monuments. In this campaign, the Saudis got to within sixty miles of Baghdad. But the Saudis went too far. Wahhabi pirates began to attack British trading ships in the Arabian Sea. The Saudis also captured the holy cities of Mecca and Medina and the Hijaz coast of the Red Sea. They damaged the graves in Mecca, threatened the grave of Muhammad himself, and challenged the authority of the Ottomans.

The Sultan now ordered Muhammad Ali to destroy this threat. In 1811, the Egyptian pasha appointed his seventeen-year-old son Tusun to command the force against the Saudis. He summoned the Mamluks to the Cairo citadel to celebrate and join forces, but treacherously slaughtered them and issued orders for Mamluks to be killed across the country. A few, including Ibrahim Bey, escaped to Sudan.

Tusun and his troops came down the Red Sea by ship. They forced the Saudis out of the holy cities. Tusun's brother Ibrahim took over the campaign in 1816. He led the Egyptian force through the desert, destroyed the Saud fortresses, and wiped Dir'iyya from the face of the earth. The Saud ruler and the Wahhabist religious leaders were brought to Istanbul and executed on the Sultan's orders. The Egyptians had broken the Saudi threat. The Sultan rewarded Ibrahim with the governorship of the Red Sea coast.

# THE GREEK WAR OF INDEPENDENCE (1821–1829)

## The Serbian Phase

Resentment had grown in Serbia over the Turks favoring Greeks in religious and trade matters. Many Serbs moved into the Habsburg lands after the Austrian conquests of the late seventeenth century. This gave the Serbs a base of operation and some military experience. The Habsburgs warred with Turkey from 1787 to 1791 and took Belgrade but gave it back, disappointing many Serbs. After the war, unemployed Janissaries allied with Bulgarian bandits to loot Serbia. Selim III gave local Serbs the right to form militias to defend themselves and provided troops to fight the Janissaries and their allies. Napoleon's attack on Egypt in 1798, however, led to a diversion of troops and left the Serbs helpless. At the beginning of 1804, the Janissaries killed close to a hundred Serb notables. The Serbs raised an army of 30,000 under **Karageorge Petrovic**, a poor farmer who had been trained in the Habsburg army, then had joined the Serb militia.

Fighting dragged on for ten years as demands escalated from autonomy to independence. The Turks finally granted authority in 1815 to a rival Serb leader, **Milos Obrenovich**, who murdered Karageorge, stuffed his head, and sent it to the Turkish governor.

## The Greeks Rebel

While the Serbian revolt had been led by peasants, the Greeks were led by outsiders, then notables and upper clergy, and lastly peasants. Greeks and Romanians in Russia formed a secret society hoping for a general Balkans uprising to spread from Serbia. The Russians helped intermittently, depending on their relations with France and Turkey. The hope for a general Balkans revolt ended with Karageorge's murder, and a Romanian uprising was a debacle. Greek intellectuals inspired by French nationalism joined the revolt in 1821. Greek exiles returned to aid the cause. The Turks responded savagely, people all over the world helped the Greeks, and the British government provided a big loan. The British Romantic poet Lord Byron named his yacht *Bolívar* after the Latin American liberator and sailed to Greece. Byron did little fighting, then died of a fever. Austria opposed this national revolution. When the Greek leader Alexander Ypsilanti crossed the border, the Austrians imprisoned him in the grim fortress of Theresienstadt.

# Muhammad Ali Intervenes

During the Greek revolt, Muhammad Ali's new navy commanded by Ibrahim had taken the island of Crete. In 1825, Sultan Mahmud III promised Crete to Muhammad Ali and the governorship of southern Greece for Ibrahim if they would help against the Greeks. A Turkish-Egyptian army of 10,000 rolled across Greece and had nearly overrun it by 1826. Feeling himself in a strong position, the Sultan in June 1826 issued a decree that the core of the Ottoman army would be a mainly Turkish force organized on the European model. This led the Janissaries to rebel. The Sultan bombarded the Janissary barracks, and the new army and the mob of Istanbul slaughtered thousands of Janissaries. The word went out across the Empire, and the Janissaries were wiped out as an organized force. The massacre got rid of a troublesome element, but it left Muhammad Ali as the supreme military power in the Empire.

The Greek cause seemed lost, but France, Britain, and Russia agreed to work for Greek autonomy. The Greeks hired Admiral Cochrane, who had played a key role in the Latin American revolutions, to command their small fleet.

# Independence

Britain, France, and Russia insisted that the Turks cease operations. When Ibrahim pointed out that the Greeks were still fighting, the European powers destroyed his navy at the **Battle of Navarino** (1827). The Russians declared war on Turkey in 1828 and began to march down the Black Sea coast. Muhammad Ali reached agreement with the British and French to bring Ibrahim's army back to Egypt.

The **Treaty of Adrianople** (September 1829) created an independent Greece with a Bavarian prince on its throne, but many Greeks remained in the Ottoman Empire. Turkish control of Romania became only nominal, Serbia gained autonomy: it would have the right to collect taxes in the name of the Sultan and the Turkish garrisons in Serbia would be restricted. Russia gained a little territory and payment from Turkey.

# THE EGYPTIAN CRISES

## The First Crisis

Muhammad Ali had continued to build Egyptian power. As the Industrial Revolution grew in Britain, he dedicated large tracts of land to raising cotton. In 1826, he imported the first steam-run power looms from Britain. In 1836, Egypt produced more than a million bolts of cotton cloth. He built dams and improved irrigation to get more productivity out of the land. He oversaw new canals and hired European engineers to build steam-driven pumps for irrigation of the fields. This allowed two crops of cotton each year. He ordered the planting of high-quality cotton cash crops as well as a summer grain in a modified form of the four-crop rotation. He made a sustained attempt to train officers, doctors, engineers, and officials in new schools, and sent them on missions to Europe to learn trades. He initiated a massive program to translate vital European technical works into Arabic. During Muhammad Ali's time in power, the Egyptian population nearly doubled, acreage grew by one-third, revenue grew 300 percent while trade volume increased 900 percent. He increased the size of the army, brought in French officers to train it, built an arms factory in Cairo and a shipyard to Alexandria. In 1820, he had dispatched 5,000 troops under his third son, Ismail, and conquered Sudan to the south. All of this was done without resorting to foreign loans or assistance from the Ottoman government.

By 1831, Muhammad Ali had rebuilt his forces and wanted Syria from Turkey for his help in the Greek War. When Turkey did not satisfy him, Ali's son Ibrahim marched up the Mediterranean coast. In 1832, the Egyptians beat a big Turkish army and threatened Asia Minor. Ibrahim sought to depose the Sultan and pressed to within 150 miles of Istanbul. Russian ships moved to the Straits to "protect" Turkey and forced the Ottomans to agree to a treaty in 1833. Ali gained all of Syria and Crete, and Russia gained the right to intervene in Turkey when it wanted. The British feared that the Russians might be trying to gain control of the Straits and threaten commerce. This remained a cornerstone of their foreign policy through the century.

# The Second Crisis

Ali declared independence in 1838, and the Sultan was determined to punish him. The Egyptians whipped the Turks again while the Turkish navy defected to the Egyptian side. Ali's forces pushed into Arabia as far as the Persian Gulf. France supported Ali, but the other four powers lined up behind Turkey. Ibrahim wanted to take the Sultan's throne, but Ali knew the great powers would never stand for that. The British demanded that Syria be put between the Turks and Egyptians and grabbed the strategic port of Aden. Tensions mounted, British and Turkish troops landed in Beirut, and Ibrahim's army fell back. In a treaty of 1841, the Sultan and the five great powers recognized Muhammad Ali and his heirs as hereditary rulers (*khedives*) of Egypt and Sudan, but theoretically still under the Sultan. He would have to pay a sum to the Ottomans, reduce the size of his army, and give up Crete, Syria, Mecca, and Medina. Ali also had to remove his import barriers and end his monopolies. This would allow the British to flood the Egyptian market with their cheaper goods. The Straits would be closed to all warships when the Ottomans were at peace. The Concert had again held and prevented war among the great powers, but the Turkish decay still threatened the stability.

# Aftermath

After the second crisis, age rapidly overtook Muhammad Ali. Ibrahim finally had to appeal to the Sultan to make him the ruler in place of his father, but he died almost immediately, followed by Muhammad Ali. Tusun's son Abbas took over as *khedive* but proved unpopular and was assassinated in 1854.

# TIMELINE

| | |
|---|---|
| 1744 | Wahhab-Sa'ud Pact |
| 1768 | Ali Bey of Egypt refuses to pay tribute to Turks |
| 1789–1807 | Selim III sultan |
| 1798–1799 | Napoleon in Egypt |
| 1801 | Muhammad Ali arrives in Egypt from Albania |
| 1802 | Sauds attack Iraq |
| 1803 | Sauds occupy Mecca and Medina |
| 1804 | Serb revolt begins |
| 1807–1808 | Janissary uprising kills Sultan Selim |

| | |
|---|---|
| 1808–1839 | Mahmud II sultan |
| 1811 | Muhammad Ali launches attack on Sauds |
| 1818 | Egyptians destroy First Saudi State |
| 1820 | Egyptians conquer Sudan |
| 1821–1829 | Greek War of Independence |
| 1824 | Muhammad Ali takes Crete |
| 1825 | Muhammad Ali intervenes in Greece |
| 1826 | Sultan wipes out Janissaries |
| 1827 | Battle of Navarino: Russian/British/French fleet destroys Egyptian fleet |
| 1829 | Treaty of Adrianople grants Greek independence |
| 1831–1832 | First Egyptian Crisis |
| 1838–1841 | Second Egyptian Crisis |
| 1848 | Death of Muhammad Ali |
| 1854 | Egyptian khedive Abbas assassinated |

# KEY TERMS

Selim III
Muhammad Ali
Mahmud II
Mamluks
Janissaries
Muhammad Ibn 'Abd Al-Wahhab
Muhammad ibn Sa'ud
Battle of Navarino
Treaty of Adrianople

# PRIMARY SOURCE DOCUMENTS

**Napoleon**, http://napoleonsegypt.blogspot.com/2007/08/bonaparte-puts-sunni-clerics-in-control.html

**Al-Jabarti**, Muhammad Ali's Tax Inspectors, http://historicaltextarchive.com/sections.php?action=read&artid=14

**William Eton**, http://www.fordham.edu/halsall/mod/1799Ottomans.asp

**Lord Byron on Greece**, http://www.fordham.edu/halsall/mod/byron-greece.html

**Al-Wahhab**, http://islamicweb.com/beliefs/creed/Clarification_Doubts.html

## Chapter 10

# FERMENT AND TURMOIL IN THE MUSLIM WORLD

The Wahhabists and other Islamic fundamentalists were reacting against reformist movements of the eighteenth century. Even as modernizers and fundamentalists vied for power, Islam spread in West Africa and a revived Arab-run slave trade disrupted East Africa.

## BRITISH DIRECT RULE IN INDIA

From 1660 to 1763, the British East India Company had been a power unto itself: it could coin money, hold jurisdiction over English subjects, and make war or peace with non-Christian powers. From 1660 to 1700, it made an average annual profit of 25 percent. Robert Clive used his victories to buy up effective control of company stock. Parliament under King George and the King's Friends tried to unify the British empire by restricting the Company's dividends and imposing a tax. In 1767, the Company failed to pay its annual tax of £400,000 to Britain. Famine and smallpox swept Bengal as about one-third of all residents died, and the Company's finances plunged. Clive was recalled, tried by a Parliamentary committee, and, though acquitted, committed suicide.

The Company named **Warren Hastings** (governed 1772–1785) as the new governor of Bengal. The **Regulating Act** (1773) established a governing council in Calcutta to rule Bengal, Madras, and Bombay, with Hastings as Governor-General, but the council would have three directors named by Parliament and just two named by the Company. To help with finances, the Company would be able to reclaim all taxes paid on tea if it would re-export tea from Britain to America. This had led to the retention of the Tea Tax and the subsequent Boston Tea Party in America.

Hastings became more engaged in Indian politics, supporting various rulers. The most vigorous challenge to the British came from Mysore, the state centered around Bangalore that dominated most of southern India. A Muslim mercenary named **Haidar Ali Khan** (Sultan 1762–1782), an ally of the French in their British wars, had conquered Mysore in 1762. Khan tried to build a Muslim-Hindu alliance against the British. When the British attacked French outposts as part of the American Revolutionary War, Haidar raised an army of 83,000 and inflicted a stinging defeat on the British in 1780. He died in the middle of the war and was succeeded by his son **Tipu**, who forced a peace treaty that discredited the Company's control. Parliament recalled Hastings and accused him of naked aggression. Like Clive, he was acquitted, but he was the last "Company governor."

The **India Act of 1784** put Company directors under Parliamentary supervision. **Lord Charles Cornwallis** (Governor-General 1786–1793), the losing general in America, was named to succeed Hastings. The **Cornwallis Code** (1793) was the foundation of British rule in India until independence in 1947. It made a major shift in Bengal landowning policy and effectively gave tax farmers full power over land; this soon created a ruling class loyal to British interests based in the banking centers of Calcutta. It created incentive to bring more land under the plow; this in turn led to rapid population growth in nineteenth-century Bengal. The Code established courts with British judges, set the foundations for a civil service, abolished internal tariffs, and placed the salt and opium trades under government control. It established a new landlord system where tenant farmers paid rents.

The British were determined to get revenge on Tipu Sultan for their humiliation. Tipu attempted to build an Islamic alliance against the British including the Ottoman Empire, the Persian Kingdom, and the Sultanate of Oman. However, none was able to render army or naval assistance. Much later, the French grasped the importance of Tipu, and Napoleon intended for his Egyptian force to reach Mysore and challenge the British in India. Napoleon's defeat left Tipu in a precarious position. In 1799, the British led 50,000 soldiers in storming Tipu's capital. The "Tiger of Mysore" was killed in battle, and the British took the Malabar coast of southwestern India around Calicut.

# SUFISM

Sufism dates from the early days of Islam. It incorporated elements of both Christian monasticism and Indian mysticism. Sufist orders were established starting in the twelfth century where one was initiated into the order and began a progress toward the divine. Obeying Islamic law (*shari'a*) was not as important as having a direct experience of God. An initiate was called a **Fakir**, a term often misapplied to various itinerant magicians. Many came to know the Persian equivalent Dervish for dancing ecstatically in an attempt to dissolve in the Divine. Disciples were bound to a teacher and would submit to fasting, seclusion, and sleep deprivation to aid in their passage. Sufists were willing to combine Islam with other traditions and this helped Islam spread through south and southeast Asia and trans-Saharan Africa. Sufist orders worshiped saints, visited their tombs, and incorporated some practices not traditional in Islam. Saints, both men and women, both living and dead, were "friends of God" who could intercede on the behalf of others. Visiting the tombs of dead saints could invoke their supernatural power. Saints could generate worldly power, and "god-guided ones" (*Mahdis*) could gather political movements in opposition to unjust rulers. Areas that had been holy in older traditions were converted by Sufists into Muslim holy places. This was regarded as heresy by more conservative Muslims, who periodically killed Sufists. The Wahhabists destroyed shrines in Mecca and Medina that they connected to the Sufists. A Sufi mystic named Shaykh Salim Chisti had great influence on the Mughal emperor Akbar. Akbar built a capital city and placed the mystic's tomb in a mosque so as to identify Mughal authority with a Muslim saint. Aurangzeb's half-brother Dara Shikuh tried to find a blend of Hinduism and Sufism, but the Emperor put him to death for heresy in 1659.

By the eighteenth century, there were many Sufi "paths" for individuals who did not want to escape the world. They emphasized the need for people to live according to the rules and regulations established by Muhammad in the original Islamic community. Sufi organizations spread through the Middle East, often taking the form of informal clubs where merchants, for example, would study the pronouncements of Muhammad on trade. In Cairo by 1800, almost every male belonged to a "path."

In northern India in the eighteenth century, attempts were made to modernize Islam in response to the challenges of the age of revolution. **Awadh** (or **Oudh**) had been a part of the Mughal Empire. Emperor Aurangzeb presented his adviser Mullah Asad bin Qutub Shahood with the **Farangi Mahalli** (French Palace) in Lucknow. Mullah Asad established a family-run school. Aurangzeb appointed the Shi'ite Persian adventurer **Sa'adat Khan** as governor of the Awadh district in 1722. Khan was killed while commanding

Mughal forces during the 1739 war. His nephew became the main power in the Empire and made Awadh virtually independent. The Farangi Mahalli school therefore taught in a Sufi Muslim tradition in a district ruled by a Shi'ite Nawab when Lucknow itself was mostly Hindu. The school taught Sunni and Shi'ites alike and cooperated closely with the Oudh court. Students came from Arabia to China and all points in between. It combined scholarly and mystic learning. A further influence came in 1764 when the forces of the British East India Company defeated the Nawab of Oudh at the Battle of Buxar. The Farangi Mahalli became a center of logic and jurisprudence. The Lucknow school remained family run and promoted a model syllabus teaching rationalist Islam.

**Shah Waliullah** (d.1762) of Delhi also urged flexibility in applying the *shari'a*. The goal of the Prophet, he said, was to create a just community. As conditions change, so too must the application of the laws. The mystical and intellectual traditions of medieval Islam were not heresies.

But both Waliullah and Abd' al-Raazaq of the Farangi Mahalli promoted their ideas, modernizing as they might be, as restorations of the true vision of Muhammad. The would not or could not embrace a revolutionary Islam that was moving forward in accordance with Allah's plan. British influence began to grow in Oudh after 1774 when Hastings provided English mercenaries to fight an Afghan raid. In 1801, the British forced the Nawab to disband his army and Oudh became effectively a British puppet. A backlash set in typified by the Wahhabist-influenced **Sayyid Ahmad** (d.1831) who promoted a fundamentalist "way of Muhammad."

# ISLAM IN EASTERN AFRICA

## Rise of the Slave Trade

In the seventeenth century, the sultan of Oman had ousted the Portuguese from many of their trading posts and fortresses along the Arabian and east African coasts. Oman then took control of part of the African coast. In the middle of the eighteenth century, the French developed their islands in the Indian Ocean and imported slaves from East Africa, an area that had not been part of the Atlantic slave trade. Pierre Poivre planted spices on Mauritius in 1747. Coffee grew as a cash crop on Reunion and the Dutch colony of Java. Slaves also flowed throughout the Muslim world. Zanzibar, under Oman's control, became the major slave trading center. The French were buying about

5,500 slaves a year, but even more were going to Muscat and India. Zanzibar also became a major exporter of ivory and rhinoceros horn.

# Impact of the *Mfecane*

The interior area of eastern Africa between the Nile sources and the Zambezi river had long been quiet and isolated. This changed with the arrival of the Ngoni-speakers in 1835. As they fled the *Mfecane*, they crossed the Zambezi and began to disrupt things with their violent military tactics and novel political institutions. After 1848, the strong Ngoni state broke into six smaller states.

# Oman at its Peak

The Muscat prince **Sayyid Said** (ruled 1806–1856) had projected Arab power in the Indian Ocean as the British and French dueled for power. When the British defeated Napoleon, they asserted their power along the Indian and Arabian coasts and forced Said to focus on East Africa. In the 1830s, he conquered Mombasa and moved his center to Zanzibar. There he encouraged Indian bankers to immigrate, practice their religion freely and run finance and trade in the capital. He also promoted the growing of cloves as a cash crop. Swahili and Arab traders moved into the interior from trading cities in order to revive slave trade. Said developed Arab trading centers along Lake Tanganyika and elsewhere. They traded guns for ivory and slaves. After the 1850s, traders turned tribes against each other as they introduced guns in large numbers, and major slave trading began. Strong tribes in the area of modern Kenya, Rwanda, and Uganda kept the Arab traders out. To the south in the lake region and Congo river watershed, Swahili, Arab, and African adventurers formed their own armies and looted and enslaved freely. In 1860, 100,000 slaves lived on Zanzibar with 4,000 owned by the sultan himself.

# The Egyptian Takeover of Sudan

Further to the north, Muhammad Ali of Egypt pressed up the Nile, using his firepower and better-trained troops to gain lands. After 1825, the Sudanese reached accommodation with the Egyptians. Islam had been growing in Sudan since the fifteenth century when Muslim traders had brought it from the north. Sufism was very attractive to many in Sudan as they sought to draw upon the saint's power and get him to intercede with Allah, who was a remote figure to many people.

# THE *JIHADS* IN WESTERN AFRICA

In the Middle Ages, powerful Muslim kingdoms had ruled the savanna region around the bend of the Niger river. The collapse of Songhai in 1591 and the turmoil of the slave trade had weakened Islam. Even the most devout Muslim states tolerated pagan practices in western Africa. Arabs migrating from the western Sahara brought Sufism to the area. Merchants also produced and distributed magical charms and amulets, which often contained Koranic scriptures. For many African pagans, these charms introduced them to the world of Islam. Devout Islam persisted in only a few urban areas. Muslims, semipagans, and pagans had lived together in relative peace. A group of **Fulani** clerics was influenced by the Arab **Qadiriyya Brotherhood**, which promoted fundamentalist Islam.

Along the Senegal river in the 1700s, radical Fulanis staged *jihads* (holy wars) and established theocratic states where the clerics ruled. Futa Toro near the mouth of the Senegal river established a theocracy in 1775, and Futa Jalon in the Niger/Senegal watershed followed in 1776.

In Hausaland southeast of the Niger bend, there was a complex religious and social pattern. The Hausa rulers were pagans. The Fulani were divided among rural pagans, nominal Muslims in the cities and fanatical **Torodbe** clerics in the cities. The Fulani were vital to Hausaland's success but were second-class citizens and resentful. The Fulani clerics would use Sufism not as an emotional appeal as in the east, but as a rallying call for purification.

**Usuman dan Fodio** began to preach in 1774 in Gobir along the Sokoto Rima branch of the Niger river. He instructed the '*ulema* and finally the pagan Sultan of Gobir. Relations began to break down after the Sultan's death and Usuman became more radical in his demands and urged his followers to arm themselves. In 1804, the Sultan killed one of Usuman's followers, and the cleric urged his followers to flee Gobir in imitation of the prophet Muhammad's *hijra* and then engage in *jihad*. He called for an end to misgovernment and rule by Islamic law. From 1804 to 1808, Usuman's brother and son **Muhammad Bello** (ruled 1817–1837) conquered the Hausa states and established a Fulani empire called **Sokoto**. He caused disruptions as far as the Lake Chad kingdom of Bornu. After Bello's death, Sokoto helped stabilize the region after the chronic warfare of the previous two hundred years and trade grew. Sokoto exported local brass, pewter, and cloth, while importing spices, beads, and perfume from Tripoli. Slavery and the slave trade remained very common with some people owning up to a thousand slaves. The conquered Hausa felt they had to stick together to preserve their culture and so the *jihad* increased their solidarity. The Sokoto Muslim state ended up not being very rigorous because it needed to recruit Fulani pagans and promoted Fulani unity as much as religious fervor.

Another Muslim *jihad* swept **Macina** just southwest of Timbuktu. **Ahmadu Bari** (d.1844), a believer in the Qadiriyya brotherhood, drew inspiration from the Sokoto *jihad* that he witnessed and launched a holy war against the semipagan and animist groups dominating Macina in 1818. He took over the Niger River from Jenne to Timbuktu. Ahmadu banned the use of alcohol and tobacco as well as dancing.

**Umar** (d.1864), the son of a Torodbe cleric at Futa Toro, had made the pilgrimage to Mecca where he came in contact with Wahhabists. There he joined the Tijaniyya brotherhood, which was more puritanical than the Qadiriyya. He also spent time in Egypt to observe the modernizing government of Muhammad Ali. He married into the Bornu ruling family near Lake Chad, then lived for a while at Muhammad Bello's palace and married one of his daughters. Umar began his *jihad* in 1852 at the sources of the Niger and Senegal rivers using firearms brought from the coast. He defeated the pagan Bambara in 1854, then tried to attack the coastal French fort of Saint Louis in 1857 but was defeated. The freed slaves and mixed-race residents of Saint Louis and Gorée were strongly devoted to France and had no use for Muslim *jihad*. Umar moved up the Niger River and took Segu in 1861. Macina, ruled by Ahmadu's grandson, had grown worried about Umar's empire-building and backed the Bambara. Umar used this as a reason to conquer Macina and kill its king. Umar captured Macina but the resulting riots led by the Qadiriyya brotherhood killed him.

Muslim *jihads* were able to penetrate down the Niger river part of the way and damage the forest and coastal kingdoms. Yoruba kingdoms were racked by war and a slave trade reorienting to the north. **Dahomey** under **Gezo** (ruled 1818–1858) west of Lagos gained in power. **Ashanti** also controlled the area north of Accra, but the Fante area along the coast remained independent when British helped them against the Ashanti in 1831.

# The West African Coast

The abolition of slavery in Britain in 1772 and American slaves freed by British soldiers during the American Revolution created a substantial African population in Britain. In 1787, British philanthropists paid for a settlement for former slaves at Freetown on the coast of Sierra Leone. Former slaves from Nova Scotia and Jamaica reinforced the town. An elite emerged of Christian, English-speaking Africans. By 1850, Freetown had 40,000 inhabitants. Freed American slaves founded Liberia in 1822, and it became an independent nation in 1847. Other cities grew on the coast including Cape Coast, Accra, and Lagos that had an African population with a European orientation. The settlements remained on the coast because African diseases of the interior still ravaged Europeans and western-born Africans alike who had no resistance to these diseases. **Samuel Ajayi Crowther** (d.1891) was a Yoruba who came to Freetown in 1822 as a boy rescued from a slave ship. He became a missionary and then Episcopal bishop for all West Africa. Crowther and others believed that Western culture was vital for African development.

The dream of independent, prosperous west African states faded as quarrels and shocks from the *jihads* to the north and east proved disruptive. The Europeans were constantly drawn in: they explored up the Niger river to persuade chiefs to abandon the slave trade for legitimate commerce.

# TIMELINE

| | |
|---|---|
| 1722 | Sa'adat Khan becomes governor of Awadh |
| 1762 | Haidar Ali Khan conquers Mysore |
| 1773 | British Parliament passes Regulating Act for India |
| 1774 | Usuman dan Fodio begins to preach |
| 1775 | Futa Toro becomes Muslim theocracy |
| 1784 | India Act |
| 1787 | Freetown established |
| 1793 | Cornwallis Code |
| 1799 | British defeat Tipu of Mysore |
| 1801 | Oudh becomes British puppet |
| 1806–1856 | Sayyid Said rules Muscat, Oman, and Zanzibar |
| 1808 | Sokoto established |
| 1817–1837 | Muhammad Bello rules Sokoto |
| 1818 | Ahmadu Bari launches jihad in Macina |
| 1822 | Liberia founded |
| 1847 | Liberia independent |
| 1852 | Umar begins jihad |
| 1864 | Umar killed |

# KEY TERMS

Warren Hastings
India Act of 1784
Cornwallis Code
Sayyid Said
Usuman dan Fodio

# PRIMARY SOURCE DOCUMENTS

**Regulating Act for India**, http://www.fordham.edu/halsall/mod/1773indiaact.asp

**dan Fodio**, http://www.lasalle.edu/~mcinneshin/344/wk06/jihaddocs.htm

**Journals of Samuel Crowther**, http://books.google.com, pp. 347–51.

# Chapter 11

# SHAKA, "THE NAPOLEON OF AFRICA"

## THE BOERS AND THE CAPE COLONY

The British seizure of the Cape of Good Hope during the wars against Napoleon would indirectly touch off huge conflicts and transformations throughout southern Africa. The Dutch had established the outpost at the Cape in 1652. There had been a small-scale migration of Dutch, Germans, and French Protestants. Slaves were brought from Java and Madagascar. Frontier farmers (*trekboers*) spread out from the Cape to establish enormous ranches and grow grains in the favorable climate. On the eve of the British takeover, there were about 75,000 people in the Cape Colony with its frontier about a hundred miles south of the Orange River. Of these, there were 25,000 free whites. The rest were slaves, people of the Khoikhoi groups that lived to the northwest of the Cape, and those of mixed race. A racial system even more inflexible than the Americas emerged on the Cape. The Boers ran into a new people, the **Xhosa** who spoke a Bantu language, between the Sunday and Great Fish rivers. War began in 1780 when a Boer farmer killed a Xhosa. The ranchers felt they were not getting enough support from the Cape, which was five hundred miles from the border, and tried in 1795 to declare their own republics. The British put down this Boer revolt. The first three wars between the Boers and the Xhosa saw the Boers pushed back to the Sunday river. The British took over in 1806 and gained permanent right over the colony in 1814. Their import of 5,000 settlers from Britain along with promoting racial justice and limits on slavery caused a backlash among the Boers and more pushed to the frontier.

# ORIGINS AND PREDECESSORS

## The Crisis of the late 18th Century

Migration and expansion had always alleviated pressures within the Bantu-speaking groups and tribes. This could work as long as they could take new land from hunter-gatherers who had fewer numbers and less-advanced weapons. **Nguni** groups had reached the very fertile, disease-free coast of southeastern Africa, and their numbers exploded in the late eighteenth century with no place to go. Portuguese traders established an outpost at Mozambique and brought American corn (maize) to the area. Corn provided more nutrition for the land planted but required more water. By 1778, Bantu and Boer settlements were close to each other.

The crisis became acute when the price of ivory dropped after 1800 because of new discoveries in eastern Africa. From 1803 to 1806, bad drought gripped the region. Adding to the instability was a shift in the slave trade. The British had outlawed the slave trade in 1807, and their ships would enforce this in the Atlantic. The slave trade now shifted to the east coast of Africa and southeastern ports began to export slaves. Confederations of tribes rose in the north Drakensberg corridor: the **Ngwane** in southern Mozambique under the Swazi royal house and their king Ngwane II (c.1750), the **Ndwandwe** under Zwinde (d.1820), and the **Mthethwa** (or Mtetwa) led by **Dingiswayo** (c.1780–1818).

Dingiswayo had plotted against his father and gone into exile. This brought him into closer contact with the Portuguese and other European ideas. He took over about 1807, made an alliance with the Tsonga people to the north, and united around thirty tribes. He altered Mthethwa society radically: the custom of puberty rites for young men involving circumcision was eliminated. Young men would prove their manhood on the field of battle. He organized a larger army not by tribal groups, but by age grades in order to erode tribal and clan differences. This would be a more efficient army and also one that would enhance the powers of the chief. Other men and women were organized in hunting for elephants or slaves, or agricultural work, and to serve the orders of the elite for a given number of years. Mostly through diplomacy, Dingiswayo convinced clans to join his confederation. Around

1811, the Mthethwa defeated the Buthelezi clan and persuaded a lesser clan, the **Zulu**, to join it.

## Shaka's Early Life

### Shaka's Boyhood

The chief of the Zulu clan was Senzangokona. He had many wives, but Shaka was born in the 1780s to **Nandi**, who was not the chief's wife. Others taunted Shaka through his boyhood about his parentage. Shaka had to find another avenue to prove himself and military prowess was the way to do it, just as Napoleon had. He joined the Mthethwa before the rest of the Zulu did, and attracted the support of Dingiswayo, who helped Shaka become Zulu leader when Senzangokona died in 1816. When Shaka became chief, the Zulu army numbered 400 at most; by the time of his death a dozen years later, it numbered more than 40,000.

### New Military Tactics

Shaka completely revolutionized military tactics. In the place of the long throwing spear, he introduced the *assegai*, a short stabbing spear. He trained the Zulu warriors to fight in formations, not as individuals. They adopted the "buffalo horn" tactic. Troops would advance holding heavy cowhide shields in front of them to ward off thrown weapons. They would then close the distance and warriors from the middle would run to the flanks to envelop the enemy. Foes in a loose formation often turned and ran; those who remained would be slaughtered or captured. Shaka put the army on a constant war footing, and there was nonstop drilling. By 1818, Shaka had already absorbed a few neighboring clans and built his army to 2,000.

# SHAKA'S RISE AND FALL

The drought south of Maputo Bay had a catastrophic effect because there had been a shift to water-intensive corn-growing. This perhaps drove the confederations into war. The Ndwandwe under Zwide routed the Ngwane. That group retreated northward and became the Swazi nation. The Ndwandwe then turned on the Mthethwa. In a great battle of 1818 in which Shaka and the Zulu were not present (we do not know whether that was planned or not), the Ndwandwe utterly broke the Mthethwa and killed Dingiswayo. The Zulus were left with no overlord.

# The *Mfecane*

### Shaka Gains Supremacy

*Mfecane* means "the crushing." Shaka gathered the remnants of the Mthethwa, integrated them into the Zulu, and then met the Ndwandwe at **Gqokoli Hill** in 1819. Despite being heavily outnumbered, the Zulus won, pursued and smashed the Ndwandwe, leaving most of those remnants to move north of the Limpopo river or join the Zulu. Shaka now ruled supreme in the land between the Tugela river and Maputo Bay. The area between the Tugela and Natal Rivers was devastated, and Shaka threatened the southern Drakensberg area.

### Zulu Society

The Zulus now grew enormously as they incorporated other Nguni tribes into their pre-existing structure. Many did not want to fight the Zulus after seeing the results. Shaka controlled the territory and authority of territorial subchiefs; he could appoint and remove them at will. The leaders of his regiments were common-born and owed all authority to Shaka, since they could never hope to be tribal leaders. Shaka's most important innovation was the introduction of permanent military barracks on the king's land, which bound together young men from all different backgrounds. All were trained in personal loyalty to Shaka. Similar to the power of French nationalism that had swept Europe during the Revolution, Zulu nationalism was a force that bound people with a strength more powerful than the cohesion of their neighbors.

## The European Response

The British gradually became aware of the carnage going on to the north and east. The Governor of the Cape Colony, Lord Charles Somerset, sent Lieutenant Francis Farewell to Zululand to investigate, and much of what we know about Shaka comes from that mission.

At Farewell's first meeting in 1825:

> *The King told his visitors about the glories of his realm. His vast wealth in cattle of which they would get an idea on the morrow and the following days. His regiments which were the terror of all his enemies. The magnificence of his capital, Bulawayo. Then he very pointedly asked Farewell and his companions if they had ever seen a more orderly governed state than his Zululand, or subjects who were more moral and law-abiding.*

*Thereafter he made many inquiries about King George, the size of his army, the nature of his government and country, and the number of his cattle and wives. He applauded the wisdom of his brother king in having only one wife. 'That accounts for his advanced age; but he would have been wiser still to have none at all like myself.'*

A doctor accompanying Farewell treated Shaka after an assassination attempt and in gratitude the Zulu king granted Farewell trading rights and land at Port Natal (today Durban).

## The Spillover Effect in Eastern Africa

For self-protection, other groups ran away and/or banded together into larger entities. The 1820s and 1830s saw other large states set up: Swaziland, Lesotho, and the Ndebele of southwestern Zimbabwe. **Mzilikazi** of the Ndebele had been one of Shaka's commanders but had a dispute and fled the Zulu king's wrath. He led the Ndebele some 500 miles into the Transvaal and devastated the Tswana and Sotho towns with a ferocity worthy of Shaka. One remnant of the Nwandwe confederation conquered the Tsonga and the Portuguese trading posts around Maputo Bay and formed the Gaza empire in southern Mozambique.

Another group fleeing the *mfecane* was the **Ngoni** people. This small tribe fled north and was further defeated by other refugee tribes. By the 1830s, it reached an area north of the Limpopo river where Shaka's tactics and organization had never been seen before. The Ngoni were able to defeat and absorb the inhabitants. They crossed the Zambezi river, looting and pillaging all the way and eventually stopped north of Lake Malawi, where they founded the city of Mapupo, some 1,500 miles north of Zululand. After 1848, their leader Zwangendaba died, and the Ngoni split up. They moved in different directions and caused even more havoc.

The Kololo moved to the northwest and set up a kingdom on the Zambezi river floodplain above Victoria Falls.

## Shaka's Death

A growing number of Zulu leaders were appalled by Shaka's bloodthirstiness and never-ending desire for war. After his mother Nandi died in October 1827, Shaka seemed to lose all reason. He ordered a prolonged period of mourning including the sacrifice of many cattle and no planting for the spring of 1828. He also ordered groups of young men and women to dance naked together. If a man showed any sign of an erection, it would be taken as a sign of disrespect for the period of mourning and he would be killed. Shaka drew up plans for a major invasion of the south, including the Natal and the Cape Colony. Shaka was murdered on September 22, 1828, and there was general relief.

## Shaka's Legacy

It is estimated that all told between one and two million died in the *mfecane*. Losses were greater on the interior plateau where the wars among groups fleeing Shaka nearly depopulated the region.

**Dingane** became Zulu king and resumed expansionist policies, but began to have problems to the south. Port Natal became a gathering area for Zulu dissidents as well as British merchants and missionaries. Gun-carrying Boer cattlemen defeated Dingane's forces in 1838 and pushed for Natal. The Zulus were forced to evacuate the land south of the Natal River. Dingane's prestige fell, and he was replaced by another son of Senzangokona, **Mpande**, who had worked with the Boers and advocated a conciliatory policy with them. The British defeated his successor **Cetewayo** in 1879, ending the independence of the Zulu nation.

# THE GREAT TREK

The British tightened their hold on the Cape Colony. They introduced a new system of land registration and taxation that was greatly resented. In 1828, Britain imposed freedom-to-work laws and banned discrimination based on color. It abolished the old courts and made English the official language. Finally, Britain ended slavery in 1834 in all of its colonies.

Wars resumed between the whites and the Xhosa. Regular British soldiers now led the fight and pushed the Xhosa beyond the Keiskama river. To the dismay of the Boers, the British brought in some 5,000 colonists. While the colonists did not become farmers as the government intended, it was the first injection of a large British population into South Africa. When London denied the Boers the land beyond the Great Fish river, many Boers decided to set out on their own. Some 10,000 Boers left in their ox-drawn carts for the north beyond the Orange and Vaal rivers. In 1836, the Boers came into conflict with Mzilikazi's Ndebeles. The next year, the Boers drove the Ndebele out of the Transvaal and across the Limpopo river. Mzilikazi sent forces across the Zambezi but this more tropical area harbored the tsetse fly and sleeping sickness that destroyed any of the Ndebele herds that ventured north. The land between the Limpopo and Zambezi rivers became Matabeleland.

Another group of Boers headed east toward Natal and clashed with Dingane and the Zulus. After some setbacks, the Boers inflicted a decisive defeat on the Zulus at the **Battle of Blood River** (1838).

The Boers, however, found government difficult, having rebelled against authority. The British took over the Natal area in the 1840s. The other Boer settlements gradually coalesced into two states: Transvaal and the Orange Free State.

The widespread violence left what was potentially the richest part of Africa impoverished. Its white and black residents remained backward with few roads, no railroads or modern harbors, and little industry. The pre-Enlightenment religious fanaticism of the Boers allowed no place for modern science or education, only military technology. It became the land that time forgot until gold and diamonds were discovered at the end of the century.

# TIMELINE

| | |
|---|---|
| 1652 | Dutch settle at Cape of Good Hope |
| 1780 | Boer-Xhosa War begins |
| 1805–1807 | Ndwandwe and Mthethwa confederations form |
| 1806 | British take over Cape Colony |
| 1816 | Shaka becomes Zulu leader |
| 1818 | Dingiswayo killed by Ndwandwe |
| 1819 | Zulus rout Ndwandwe at Battle of Gqokoli Hill |
| 1825 | Francis Farewell meets Shaka |
| 1827 | Nandi dies |
| 1828 | Shaka dies |
| 1834 | Slavery abolished in Cape Colony |
| 1836 | Boers fight with Ndebele |
| 1837 | Matabeleland established |
| 1838 | Boers defeat Zulus at Battle of Blood River |
| | Mpande replaces Dingane as Zulu leader |
| 1848 | Ngoni disperse from Mapupo after king's death |
| 1852–1854 | British recognize Boer republics of Transvaal and Orange Free State |

# KEY TERMS

*trekboers*
Dingiswayo
Zwinde
Battle of Gqokoli Hill
*mfecane*
The Great Trek
Battle of Blood River

# PRIMARY SOURCE DOCUMENTS

**Shaka Documents**, http://www.lasalle.edu/~mcinneshin/344/wk07/Zulu Docs.htm

# Chapter 12

# NATIONALISM AND LIBERALISM

## Nationalism

Metternich and his allies dreamed of turning the clock back to 1789, but the French Revolution had unleashed powerful forces. The most powerful was nationalism. A nation is a group of people with common language, traditions, culture, history, and sometimes religion. Nationalists insist that such a group needs its own government. Nineteenth-century governments tried hard to create these nations by imposing a language in education to replace local dialects. Some languages were practically invented in the nineteenth century to give people an identity. Many individuals had fluid nationalities and might pass back and forth between two or even three national identities. The governments imposed the dialect of a small area (Paris, London, Piedmont) upon France, England, and Italy. Fluid identities could lead to "checkerboards" of nationalities, as often happened in east-central Europe. To create a nation in these areas would automatically deprive another group of its nationhood. This led to instability, revolt, and war.

## France after Napoleon

Louis XVIII had gradually moderated during his twenty years of exile in Vienna. He knew that he had to govern with some kind of constitution, so in 1814 he provided a Charter as a "gift." The King kept considerable authority but had to share power with a Parliament, which consisted of a Chamber of Peers appointed for life by the King and a Chamber of Deputies elected for five years; a Deputy had to be at least 40 years old and pay 1,000 francs in taxes. The voters were all men, thirty years or older, and had to pay at least 300 francs in taxes. Only 0.3% of the French population could vote, sharply down from the most democratic days of the 1792 Convention. All French were called equal under the law, which continued to be the Napoleonic Code. They were eligible for all civil and military positions and free from arbitrary arrest and imprisonment without due process. Although King Louis had become a moderate, the rich supported the reactionary political group called **the Ultras** that wanted to abolish the Charter and return to absolutism. The Ultras grew stronger in 1824 when Louis XVIII died and was succeeded by his youngest brother **Charles X** (ruled 1824–1830), who was reactionary and not very bright. He decreed that he would not pay some of the interest on the government bonds held largely by the middle class and used the money to pay nobles compensation for lands lost during the revolution.

# Britain

Tension gripped Britain as reformers grew frustrated, and the social impact of the agricultural and industrial revolutions took full hold. A very conservative government headed by **Lord Liverpool** (Prime Minister 1812–1827) and Foreign Secretary Castlereagh governed for the rich. The **Corn Law of 1815** kept out foreign (mostly Russian) wheat by imposing high tariffs. Workers would have to pay more for their bread even as a sharp reduction in the armed forces put pressure on the job market. Violence flared as **Luddites** smashed industrial machines that threatened jobs, and British troops fired on protesters who demanded reform and their rights.

# The German Confederation

After Napoleon, Germany had thirty-nine states including the Austrian Empire, and the five kingdoms of Prussia, Hanover, Bavaria, Württemberg and Saxony. The Confederation joined them together loosely and met in Frankfurt. Austria was its leader, and Metternich used the Confederation to carry out his will. Article XIII of the Federal Constitution called for states to grant constitutions. In the aftermath of Napoleon, five states put out constitutions that were all royal grants like the French charter. Prussia and Austria, the two biggest German nations, did not put out constitutions. Many young men had fought Napoleon and died for "German liberation." Student unions (*Burschenschaften*) were formed in a number of universities by returning soldiers. Their stated mission was to "improve student morality, break down local patriotism, and stir up youth with nationalist ideals." The student union of the University of Jena held a big meeting at **Wartburg** Castle in 1817 to celebrate the anniversary of the Battle of Leipzig. Speakers complained about those princes who had not granted constitutions. Metternich convened the Confederation and put out the repressive **Karlsbad Decrees** (1819) that dissolved the student unions, instituted proceedings against subversive individuals and organizations, and imposed strict censorship over the press and universities. The Confederation's **Final Act of Vienna** (1820) upheld monarchs and denounced parliaments as "un-German."

The Prussian King Frederick William III had promised a constitution but after Napoleon went down, his fellow monarchs and the *Junkers* (nobles living in eastern Prussia) convinced him to turn toward reaction. He pulled back on his earlier reforms.

# THE REVOLUTIONARY RIPPLE OF 1820

We have already seen how the revolutions in Spain and Portugal in 1820 interacted with revolution in Latin America. In January 1820, the troops in Cádiz mutinied after receiving orders to go to South America. They marched on Madrid, and other garrisons rebelled. They demanded the restoration of the Constitution of 1812. Ferdinand agreed, but the rebels held him as a virtual captive to make sure he did not slide back. In August 1820, inspired by Spain, the Portuguese liberals expelled the regency established by Britain during King John's absence in Brazil. French troops authorized by the Congress of Verona crushed the Spanish revolution in 1823.

Many Italian soldiers had served under Napoleon and dreamed of a more liberal government. Southern Italy was ruled by a king who was the uncle of King Ferdinand of Spain. As a member of that royal family, he had promised in 1812 to uphold the Spanish constitution. Italians in Naples demanded that he grant similar rights to them. In 1820, there had been a military revolt, and the King agreed to call a parliament. This alarmed Metternich, who feared that constitutions and Italian nationalism might take away Austria's Italian lands. He summoned the great powers to the **Congress of Laibach** in January 1821. It authorized Austria to crush the revolt in the Kingdom of the Two Sicilies. The Austrian army would remain in Naples until 1827. A smaller liberal mutiny in Piedmont-Sardinia had called for the installation of the Spanish Constitution of 1812, and the Austrians crushed that as well.

Austria's wars in Italy were expensive and Vienna called the Hungarian Diet in 1825 to raise taxes. The Diet's demands for more Hungarian rights led to some reforms, but radicals sought greater autonomy.

## The Decembrist Revolt

The Russian Emperor Alexander died in 1825 and was succeeded by his more autocratic brother **Nicholas I** (ruled 1825–1855). Younger officers, influenced by ideas of the West and some of whom had been in Paris after the defeat of Napoleon, backed Alexander's other brother Constantine, who they saw as more moderate. They rebelled in December after refusing to swear allegiance to Nicholas. The conspirators told the Moscow soldiers that Constantine was the real Emperor and started a cry of "Long live Constantine, long live the Constitution!" The soldiers thought that "Constitution" was Constantine's wife. Its pitiful failure met with very harsh punishments. This was the last of the revolts of the early 1820s. In Europe, only the Greek revolt succeeded.

Nicholas set up a network of secret police and informers. Fearing Russian nationalism, he employed many Germans (mostly landowners from the Baltic Sea coast) to run the country. This brought about a gradual reaction from **Slavophiles** who praised Russian and Slavic history and culture. Nicholas' censorship was severe: he banned anything from or about the United States Many young intellectuals went into exile including Alexander Herzen (d.1870) and Mikhail Bakunin (d.1876), the father of modern anarchism. Nicholas did reform the law codes and freed 20 million peasants from serfdom who were living on the crown's own lands.

# THE REVOLUTIONS OF 1830

## France

King Charles X faced ever more opposition from the liberals. In 1830, the liberals for the first time in France used a no-confidence vote against the King's chosen ministers. When the liberals won a parliamentary election, Charles X issued **Four Ordinances** (July 26, 1830) that suspended press liberty, dissolved the Chamber, took away the right to vote from the upper middle class, and set the date for a new election. Charles then left town. Liberal journalists led by the editor **Adolphe Thiers** (1797–1877) signed a letter of protest. The next day, the police demolished the presses. Liberal leaders, including the banker Jacques Lafitte, the famous Marquis de Lafayette, and the historian François Guizot all returned to Paris. Barricades went up as the mob of Paris pillaged gun shops and cut down trees to barricade the streets. Eight thousand armed men clashed with the Swiss Guards, who were the only reliable troops in the area for the King. On July 28, the barricades spread and the violence grew.

About eight hundred civilians died and about four thousand were wounded while about two hundred troops died. The revolutionaries gained control of Paris. Parliament offered to mediate, but the King refused. Thiers and his friends put up posters urging that the crown be offered to the King's cousin Louis Philippe, son of Philippe Égalité, the Duke of Orléans and a Jacobin during the Terror. Lafayette and Louis Philippe appeared together wrapped in the revolutionary tricolor flag. Charles left Paris again, fled to Britain, and on August 2 abdicated in favor of his grandson. Republicans called for Lafayette to accept the presidency, but the elderly liberal preferred that Louis Philippe take the throne. On August 3, the Chamber revised the Charter. On August 7, it declared the throne vacant and two days later elected Louis Philippe king. He agreed to uphold the Charter and embraced the tricolor flag. Voting rights were expanded slightly so about 0.5% of the people now had the right to vote. The government ended censorship and restored Napoleon's religious toleration.

# Belgium

The Congress of Vienna's merger of Belgium with the Netherlands to the north had never worked well. There were different traditions, religions, and languages. As the news came from France of the overthrow of Charles X, unrest broke out leading to a full revolution on August 25. Delegates wrote a very liberal constitution with a sweeping bill of rights. Belgium would have a king, but he would share power with a two-chambered parliament elected by 1 percent of Belgian men. Britain and France presided over the **London Protocol of 1830** that declared Belgian independence. Another German prince became king.

# The German Confederation and Switzerland

The ouster of the French king provoked responses, and constitutions were given in Brunswick (where the Duke was deposed), Hanover, Saxony and Hesse-Kassel. When the German nationalists gathered in Hambach in 1832, Metternich again summoned the German Confederation to crack down on the liberal movement. Its **Six Acts** assured rulers of their right to override assemblies and denied assemblies the right to deny a prince income or pass legislation prejudicial to Confederation as approved by Austria and Prussia.

In 1837, Queen Victoria took the throne of Britain. German laws stated that no woman could rule as a prince, so after more than 120 years, Hanover separated from Britain and Victoria's widely-hated uncle Ernst August became king. One London newspaper said that Ernst August had committed every crime in his life except suicide. He started his rule in Hanover by abolishing the constitution. When seven professors at the University of Göttingen (including the famous brothers Grimm) protested, Ernst August fired them. When Prussia hired some of the professors, liberals hoped that Prussia could unite Germany. The liberals advanced the idea of free trade led by Prussia. In 1834, a number of smaller states plus Bavaria and Württemberg joined Prussia in a **Customs Union** that brought down the trade barriers. By the 1850s, most German states (except for Austria) belonged to the Customs Union.

In Switzerland to the south, some cantons began to allow representative government and press freedom in 1828. After a short war in 1847, all the cantons allowed every man to vote.

Metternich did seek some reforms in the Austrian Empire. He promoted the idea of provincial diets sending representatives to a national Reichsrat but other officials were even more conservative than the Chancellor. In 1835, Emperor Francis I died and was succeeded by his mentally-deficient son **Ferdinand** (1835–1848). Metternich and Kolowrat joined Ferdinand's uncle Ludwig as the real rulers of the Empire. Metternich tried to counter Prussia's Customs Union with freer trade within Austria, but Ludwig and Kolowrat shot the idea down. After a Polish uprising inside Austria in 1846, Metternich got the great powers to let Austria take the independent republic of Cracow.

# Italy

There were rebellions in Modena, Parma, and other areas. The Austrian army again crushed all revolts and occupied parts of Italy until 1838. Italian nationalists had varying reactions. **Giuseppe Mazzini** (1805–1872) formed a group called Young Italy and, from his exile in France, tried to organize a movement for a united Italy rather than focus on the divided states. This excited a young man from Piedmont named **Giuseppe Garibaldi** (1809–1882), who joined the Piedmontese navy in order to organize a revolt. He was discovered in 1834 and condemned to death, but escaped and lived for a time in New York and in South America. Another who died in the Italian uprisings of 1830–31 was a veteran of Napoleon's Grand Army, Andrea Orsini, whose son Felice will enter the story later in Chapter 15.

# Poland

Polish nationalists had been unhappy about the Vienna settlement. Autonomous "Congress" Poland had a constitution, bicameral legislature, religious toleration, and civil liberties. Polish was the official language, and the kingdom retained the Napoleonic Code. Alexander's brother Constantine, seen as a reformer by the Decembrists, was regarded as a tyrant in Poland. Polish students wanted to imitate the German *Burschenschaften* and promoted nationalism. When Emperor Nicholas proposed attacking France and Belgium to crush the new governments, Polish officers saw their chance and drove out the Russian garrison in January 1831. Aristocrats and nobles led the revolt but the masses were not involved. Nicholas reacted with a massive force of 180,000 soldiers and defeated the Poles by September 1831. A wave of Polish nationalists fled west.

# LIBERALISM AND REFORM IN BRITAIN

## Liberalism

The term "liberal" began with Spain's leftist opposition to Napoleon and Joseph Bonaparte, but by the 1830s, it applied to a broad movement across western civilization. It was intellectually rooted in the Enlightenment with its faith in progress, the perfectibility of humanity, and the social contract between the people and the ruler, aimed at realizing individual freedom.

The program of the liberals included:

1.  Freedom of the individual, based on human or constitutional rights, including freedom of speech, conscience, and thought. Liberals supported equality before the law, but this did not mean equality of education or property.
2.  A constitutional state with a separation of powers. The constitution was the supreme law in a state of laws designed to protect the citizens. No one was above the law, not even a king. Nor would anyone be below the law, that is selected for legal prosecution when other people were not.
3.  Political participation by a larger number of men to elect representatives to a parliament. Generally, the liberals did not call for universal manhood suffrage or for Rousseau-style direct democracy. They believed in votes only for the educated middle- and upper-class men who would elect representatives. There was a lingering fear of the radicalism that had happened in the French Revolution, when all men got to vote for a constitutional convention. In practice, the liberals supported opening the vote to more and more people until by 1920, most men and women had the right to vote in Western Europe and the United States.
4.  A free economy with freedom of occupation, trade, entrepreneurial activity, coalition, competition and movement. They were influenced

not only by the ideas of Adam Smith, but also the French economist Vincent de Gornay who had coined the phrase *laissez-faire, laissez-aller* ("let it be, let it go") which effectively meant allowing businesses to do as they pleased. Smith had warned that this practice allowed businesses to grow too large and distort the market. Another influential liberal economic thinker was **David Ricardo** (1772–1823). Ricardo agreed with Malthus that population would always be near its maximum. He devised an "iron law of wages" that pay would always be low because there would always be more workers than jobs, therefore pay would not rise above the lowest level necessary for survival.

Liberals in the Italian and German lands had a priority: national unification. Liberals in areas such as Poland or Hungary saw their first goal as gaining independence from the dominant country that ruled them (Russia and Austria in these cases). Many countries continued to be absolutist or at least have some absolutist tendencies, such as a dominance by noble families and an established church. Thus the liberals often took on the nobles and the church as enemies, pushing for an end to tax money going to the church, religious toleration, and an end to any remaining noble privileges.

# Liberal Reform in Britain

In Britain, the liberals gained some victories in the late 1820s. They reformed criminal law in the spirit of Beccaria's Enlightenment teachings and removed the death penalty from more than a hundred trivial crimes such as petty larceny. They allowed non-Anglican Protestants to hold public office and reduced the Corn Law tariffs somewhat. A major fight occurred over rights for Roman Catholics. Ireland had a strong majority of Catholics but none of them could serve in Parliament. The Irish Catholic **Daniel O'Connell** (1775–1847) established a Catholic Association and illegally ran for a seat, forcing the Parliament to consider the issue. Not wanting another John Wilkes-style debacle, the Parliament gave in and allowed **Catholic Emancipation** in March 1829. This was the first time a political association had compelled the Parliament to pass a law and gave the reformers new hope. Attempts at a similar Jewish Emancipation failed until 1858.

# The First Reform Bill

The British political system was wildly uneven. The population shifts from the Agricultural and Industrial Revolutions had created even more rotten boroughs and pocket boroughs. The rottenest borough was Old Sarum, a deserted hilltop whose eleven voters all lived elsewhere but sent two members to the House of Commons. Meanwhile, the industrial cities of Birmingham, Manchester, Sheffield, and Leeds sent no members at all. There were no real elections for two-thirds of the seats in the House.

Catholic Emancipation, the overthrow of Charles X, and an economic recession built pressure for political reform. **Willliam Cobbett** (d.1835), the son of a farm laborer, had traveled to the United States and returned in 1819 with the bones of Tom Paine. He called for political reform and improvement in the condition of the rural worker. Reformers used riots, tax strikes, and a run on the banks to increase this pressure. The Parliament passed the **First Reform Bill** in 1832. It gave the vote to 20 percent of the men in England and Wales, 12.5 percent in Scotland, and 5 percent in Ireland. Together, about 3 percent of all people in Great Britain could vote as opposed to 0.5 percent in France. It eliminated fifty-six rotten boroughs and moved more than one-quarter (143) of the seats from the rural south to the industrial north of England. Cobbett won election to the House of Commons. The government wanted to show that it was not intimidated by violence and sent another 481 political prisoners to Australia.

A more liberal government took power after the elections. It abolished slavery in the British colonies while compensating the slaveowners with £20 million. The Factory Act of 1833 limited work hours for children under age thirteen to nine hours a day and those under eighteen to sixty-nine hours a week. The **Poor Act of 1834** forced all relief recipients to enter workhouses and separated them from their families. It put the able-bodied together with the old, sick, insane, and children. The liberals reformed town and city governments in 1835 so that all homeowning men would have the right to elect town and city councils. In 1840, the government reformed the postal system to allow all letters weighing less than half an ounce to go anywhere in the U.K. for a mere penny. This transformed communication as much as the telegraph that was being developed at the same time.

# Challenges in Ireland, Canada, and Jamaica

Colonial problems brought down Lord Melbourne's liberal government. Violence had continued in Ireland because the Catholics were still being forced to pay taxes to support an official church that they did not attend. The Poor Law could not cover the massive poverty of Ireland. The Melbourne government was able to put in municipal reform for Ireland that placed power into the hands of the wealthier rather than a self-appointed Protestant elite.

Seventy thousand loyalists had left the United States after the Revolution, more than the total of émigrés who left France permanently in the 1790s. Half were granted land in Nova Scotia, and about ten to twelve thousand settled in Québec. The Constitutional Act (1791) granted a House of Assembly to be elected in Upper and Lower Canada every four years; it was supposed to govern its own taxation so there would be no complaint of "no taxation without representation." Britain neglected Canada after the War of 1812. With the American threat receding, Canadians felt more confident in asserting their rights. British-appointed governors and "legislative councils" of elites ran the provinces. The Houses of Assembly had limited power. The government also discriminated against the French speakers of Québec. In 1837, riots swept Montreal, while rebels led by **William Lyon Mackenzie** attacked Toronto. The rebels were driven off but alarming evidence showed that they were supported by the United States, and there were a few Americans who took it upon themselves to "invade" Canada in solidarity. Britain transported 153 Canadian patriots to Australia as punishment. The Melbourne government sent **Lord Durham** as governor-in-chief of all the provinces. He recommended in 1839 that Canada be granted more rights as one nation with Britain keeping only foreign policy, trade, and land distribution rights. The 1840 **Act of Union** forced the two Canadas together but did not reform the system. The Governor would name the executive council and legislative council and ignore the elected Assembly.

Violence also erupted in Jamaica. The end of slavery hurt the planters even as sugar from beets was substituting for sugar from cane. The planters had exploited the former slaves terribly and treated them at least as brutally as they had in the days of slavery. By a narrow margin, Melbourne got Parliament to suspend the constitution of Jamaica and restore order.

# The Trade Union Movement

Workers found it easier to organize after 1825, and union membership grew. In 1833, the Grand National Consolidated Trades Union was founded. **Robert Owen**, a factory owner and socialist, was one of the leading forces in the union. Owen ran a model establishment with good pay and facilities for workers, and full-time education for children. Unions had no legal protection until 1855. Many officers took off with union money. The unions took up the cause of factory reform to improve conditions, but the act of 1833 was only a half-measure. The G.N.C.T.U. fell apart when Owen argued with others. Only the skilled unions, whose workers were hard to replace, survived. The G.N.C.T.U.'s failure showed that nothing could be done without the vote, and workers now turned to Chartism.

# Chartism

In 1836, William Lovett formed the London Working Men's Association to seek the vote for workingmen. It introduced the **People's Charter** that called for 1) universal male suffrage; 2) annual elections; 3) equal electoral districts; 4) removal of property qualifications for Members of Parliament; 5) the secret ballot; 6) payment of Members of Parliament. Some of these ideas dated back 200 years to the Levellers. Chartism was strongest among old-time artisans threatened by industry. When Parliament rejected the Charter in July 1839, riots in Newport killed ten people. Chartism revived with economic hard times in 1841, but Parliament rejected it again in May 1842. The government broke the back of the Chartists by transporting more than a hundred of their leaders to Australia. The elites portrayed Chartism as an anti-industrial measure, and that alienated possible middle-class supporters.

# The Ministry of Sir Robert Peel

Peel rebuilt the Tories on more moderate lines and accepted reform. The 1841 elections gave the Tories a majority of seventy-six, their first win since 1830. Peel's government came to focus on a move toward free trade. Liberal manufacturers founded the Anti-Corn Law League in 1839. "Corn" is the British term for all grain, mostly wheat. What Americans call corn, Europeans call "maize." The League was an expression of liberal economic ideas and promoted the policy that workers should pay less for their bread. The Chartists attacked the League as just employers who wished to lower wages under Ricardo's Iron Law. Peel faced strong resistance from his own party until the potato blight hit Ireland. Peel persuaded the Parliament that reducing the tariffs would allow the Irish to buy food. The majority of the Tories, led by Benjamin Disraeli, denounced Peel and brought down his government. John Russell took over a coalition of Whigs and Peel supporters and completed a move toward freer trade by 1850. The process showed that violence was not necessary to carry out big changes.

A series of reports in the Peel years detailed the miserable conditions of poor and industrial workers in cities and in mines. The worker of 1850 could buy far less food than the worker of 1500. Cholera from south Asia devastated cities such as London and Paris because it bred in impure water, and the filthy conditions encouraged its spread as people drank water contaminated by waste sewers. Parliamentary acts reformed conditions in the factories (1844) and coal mines. Then Russell pushed through a Public Health Act in 1848. However, no government would challenge the entrenched religious interests that controlled education. Even as other countries enacted public education, Britain fell further behind.

# GREAT AWAKENINGS

Religious fervency grew across the Western world in the 1820s and 1830s, and this interacted with liberal and revolutionary movements in complex ways. Organized religion was hurt by its conservative and absolutist ties. Industrialism in England and the growth of cities weakened community ties in general and religious activity was a casualty of that. Many turned to non-official religion. In Britain, this meant new converts to non-Anglican Protestantism. Union leaders often received their first training in governing and speaking at Methodist chapels. Evangelicals promoted the abolition of slavery, missionary expeditions to Asia and Africa, temperance, and poor relief. After the municipal government reforms, many Dissenters took power in towns. However, many people's spirituality was left cold by the plain approaches of Calvinism and Methodism that clashed with the Romantic feelings for beauty, awesomeness, and mystery. Some wanted to lower barriers between Anglicanism and Catholicism, and a few became Catholics.

In the United States, there was a growing backlash against austere Calvinism, with its insistence that most people are destined to hell from their birth. Many preachers felt that this hard-line attitude had encouraged the Deism of the American Revolutionary period and promoted a less harsh Christianity. In 1818 and 1833, Connecticut and Massachusetts, respectively, disestablished their Congregationalist churches. Evangelical fervor was especially strong in western New York and in New England. New religious communities were born including the Mormon Church. Many social movements, including the abolition of slavery, religious missions abroad, women's rights, and temperance movements were led by those who started in the evangelical movement.

# NORTHERN EUROPE

While northern Europe was more quiet, it was also affected by nationalism and liberalism. Napoleon's Continental System hurt Denmark and Norway. Things got so desperate in Norway that people ate bread mixed with tree bark. Icelandic rebels tried to declare their independence from Denmark so it could trade freely with Britain. In the last war against Napoleon, Sweden aided the Quadruple Alliance while Denmark stuck with Napoleon. When Napoleon lost the Battle of Leipzig, the victors took Norway from Denmark's control. Norway briefly tried to gain independence, but Britain wished to reward Sweden. The Swedes did have to accept the Norwegian Constitution of 1814 in return for peaceful rule. The Norwegian Parliament had more rights than the Swedish Estates and was elected by all property-owning men, which made it the most democratic constitution in Europe at the time. The Parliament ordered the sale of the remaining Church lands in 1821. Sweden and Norway united as a trade zone in 1827. Peasants in Norway also began to gain some political experience when elected local councils were introduced in 1837. Within a generation, the peasants would have the political knowledge to challenge the ruling classes. The 1843 Swedish town reform gave the local vote to all taxpaying men.

Denmark tried to follow Metternich's lead by handing out lengthy prison terms and censoring liberal publications. Denmark's province of Holstein, as part of the German Confederation, was supposed to have a constitution, but like other northern German rulers, King Frederick VII ignored this. When revolution broke out in 1830, demonstrators demanded constitutional reform. The Danish King established four provincial diets. Only the wealthier property owners could vote or serve.

# THE JACKSONIAN BREAKTHROUGH IN THE UNITED STATES

## An Era of Bad Feelings

One-party rule had effectively lasted since 1802 but began to break down in 1822. A succession system had been established where the Secretary of State succeeded the President after two terms. The next in line was **John Quincy Adams**, son of the former president. Many doubted his commitment to states' rights and disliked him personally. This spurred the ambitions of others: William Crawford, the Treasury Secretary from Georgia, **John C. Calhoun**, the War Secretary from South Carolina, **Henry Clay**, the House Speaker from Kentucky, and **Andrew Jackson**, a general and former Senator from Tennessee. The New York Senator Martin Van Buren, supporting Crawford, denounced President Monroe (and by extension Adams) for abandoning Jeffersonian principles. Van Buren, a protege of Aaron Burr, was trying to reforge the alliance between the great landowners of upstate New York and the southern planters.

### The Presidential Election of 1824

The Congressional Caucus nominated Crawford, but he suffered a stroke and was paralyzed. Partisans of the other candidates denounced the caucus nomination as undemocratic. Calhoun pulled out to run for vice-president for both Adams and Jackson. The state legislature of Tennessee nominated Jackson. In a sense the election went as the Framers had intended: it was thrown to the House. But Jackson won a strong plurality of both popular and electoral votes, and there was skullduggery: the Adams electors cast votes for the disabled Crawford to keep Clay out of the top three. This meant that members of the House could not vote for him. Nonetheless, Clay made a "Corrupt Bargain" with Adams: Clay would throw his support in the House to Adams, and Adams would appoint Clay to the "succession" job of Secretary of State.

### The Democratic Party

The Jacksonians were outraged and began organizing the machinery of a party that would return to the true traditions of Jefferson: the Democratic Party. Jackson, another early ally of Burr, joined with Van Buren. Despite his influence, Burr was a political outcast because he had shot and killed Alexander Hamilton during a duel in 1804. The Jackson/Van Buren alliance swamped the Clay/Adams group in the midterm elections of 1826 and trounced Adams himself in the presidential election of 1828. Voting participation rose markedly and the Democrats introduced the **political convention** to reach grass-roots partisans. While voting records are incomplete, it seems that participation as a percentage of population roughly tripled from 1824 to 1828 and would reach 10 percent by 1832 with a peak of 14 percent in 1840. Only a few parts of France had reached this level of participation in the vote for the constitutional convention of 1792. Clay had to follow suit by building a rival political party: the Whigs.

# Jackson as President

Jackson opened the "era of the common man," to the dismay of many elites. Many of Jackson's followers were rough westerners. Cheap newspapers became available based on steam presses in the 1830s. Candidates ran for the House as representatives of their local areas. Jackson saw himself as the direct representative of all the people and the embodiment of the nation. Jackson was at odds with Vice President Calhoun over states' rights, and he got into a bitter dispute with Clay. He vetoed the bill reauthorizing the national **Second Bank of the United States**, both because it was run by a supporter of Clay and he thought it was an unreasonable enterprise by the nation. This shocked the Whigs because it was a rare policy veto. He ruined the bank by withdrawing the government deposits. The Clay-controlled Congress censured Jackson in 1834.

The Jackson period transformed the United States government as surely as the revolutions of 1820 and 1830 had in Europe. The Presidency emerged as the supreme branch of government. Popular vote for presidential electors, political parties, and the abandonment of the last vestiges of "virtual representation" in House elections created more democracy and closer ties between the voters and their government. This did not mean necessarily better or fairer government, as the tragedy of the Cherokees showed.

### Relations with Indians

Jacksonian nationalism and intense democracy victimized the Indians. Popular demand wanted the Indians removed in some fashion so that their land could be taken. Dislocation and forced transportation led to disease, distress, and death. When the Cherokee Indians sued the state of Georgia, the Supreme Court ruled that the state could not nullify Cherokee laws. Jackson refused to recognize the court ruling and retorted: let John Marshall enforce it. More than 5,000 Cherokees died on their forced march from Georgia to Oklahoma.

# SOCIALISTS AND REVOLUTIONARIES IN EUROPE

## The Origins of Socialism

Liberalism mainly appealed to the middle classes. There was very little in the liberal political program for the lower classes. In the 1830s, another political movement called socialism began to take shape. **Socialism** believes in a fair distribution of property, a fair social order, equal rights, and well-being for the lower classes (usually this means industrial workers and the peasantry). Socialist ideas had been growing for a while. The Diggers during the English Civil War in the 1640s had called for income redistribution. Rousseau had blamed private property for many of the ills of the world, and Jefferson had famously stricken Locke's enshrinement of property as a basic right in favor of the "pursuit of happiness" in the American Declaration of Independence.

# The Hungry Forties

With the Industrial Revolution in Britain, many noticed that although national wealth was increasing, many people's conditions became increasingly wretched. Nobles held most positions of leadership and much of the land, which was still the main form of wealth outside Britain. The "Hungry Forties" saw peasant revolts break out in Ireland, Wales, Russia, Galicia, and Silesia. While meat had been a main part of the diet in the sixteenth century, the typical peasant meal was now a lot of potatoes with a little milk or cheese and maybe some pork in the autumn months. An Irish working man of the time typically ate twelve pounds of potatoes a day. In Lille, France, 66 percent of workers were on the relief roll in 1828. Fewer than half could expect to eat meat more than once or twice a year; 30 to 50 percent of their budgets went to buy bread. In the French city of Mulhouse, more than half of the children of workers died before their fourth birthday.

The winters were cold and hungry and hard liquor production skyrocketed as people tried to keep warm. It was common in London for employers to pay workers and craftsmen on Saturday night at the end of the work week from a table in a pub, where many workers would then waste their wages. The pub owner naturally gave a cut to the paymaster. In Antwerp, a survey of the whole population (including children) in 1820 found an average consumption of two bottles of beer a day, one bottle of wine and one bottle of gin every month. Ten percent of all calories came from alcoholic drinks. A later survey of people over the age of fourteen in wine-loving France showed that the average person drank six bottles of wine, two bottles of beer and three shots of hard liquor every week. By the 1820s, Americans on average were drinking five gallons of hard liquor (mostly whiskey) each year. That is about two shots a day. In reaction to the spread of alcoholism, temperance societies sprang up, starting with Ireland in 1818. Because alcoholism often led to violence against women, they took the lead in the movement to restrict or ban alcoholic beverages. Never before or after were things so tough for the common person as in the 1840s.

# Socialist Ideas

### Socialist thinkers begin to carve out an ideology:

The **Count de Saint-Simon** (1760–1825) had been at the Battle of Yorktown with Washington and Lafayette and later fought in the French Revolution. He called on scientific and industrial leaders to reorganize the state based on the brotherhood of man. He considered economic progress to be the driving force of history. Science and technology would solve social problems. Social classes would collaborate guided by an elite of engineers and entrepreneurs. Saint-Simon is often known as the father of modern socialism. His followers called for the abolition of inheritance rights, public control of the means of production, and gradually giving women equal rights as men, including the right to vote.

**Louis Blanc** (1811–1882), another French socialist, wrote *The Organization of Work* in 1840. This book attacked the competitive system. It is ruinous to common people and to the upper classes since it produces continual crises. Blanc believed that there should be a nationally-planned economy. In a democratic republic, the state would create national workshops in the most important industries; it would regulate production and allocate functions to prevent sudden booms and busts that hurt the workers. Because workers would get fair pay from the state, they would know that they were not being exploited by the owner and would have greater productivity and thus make the nation as a whole richer. Blanc tried to raise seed money in the 1840s to start a few experimental national workshops to prove his ideas, but not surprisingly, few banks or wealthy people were interested.

The Englishman **Robert Owen** (1771–1858) came at socialism from another direction. He was a rich factory owner and tried to build model industrial villages in which he provided education, housing, and insurance facilities for workers. Owen believed that this would make his workers more productive and loyal than workers at other factories. Owen encouraged the formation of the first big labor union in Britain to help gain workers' rights. Many other factory owners regarded Owen as a fool and refused to cut into their profits.

There were also writers and leaders who might vaguely endorse socialism, but their main aim was to have a violent Jacobin-style revolution that would overturn the political and economic order. Auguste Blanqui (1805–1881) wrote of a "duel to the death between dividends and wages." "Mechanized man" must wage war against a bourgeoisie with whom he shared no common interests. Blanqui supported the most hopeless of conspiracies and spent most of his adult life in jail. His political leaning was probably more **anarchist** (no government at all should exist) than socialist. Another French writer **Pierre-Joseph Proudhon** (1809–1865) published *What is Property?* in 1840. He answered his own question: Property is theft! Profit is actually money owed to workers because their labor has increased the value of the materials used in the manufacturing process. He promoted the idea that small businesses paying workers fairly could build a network and compete successfully.

# THE REVOLUTIONS OF 1848

## The Revolution in France

In August 1845, a fungus destroyed half of the potato crop in Ireland. This was catastrophic because most Irish lived on the potato and made their money growing the potato. Now they had no food to eat and no money to buy other kinds of food. The colonial power of Britain was slow to help. Ireland shipped out wheat and meat even as people starved. At least a million Irish died, and millions fled the country after 1845 as the blight destroyed the entire crop of 1846 and 1847. Across Europe, the loss of the potatoes caused food prices to skyrocket. In Paris, the price of rye for bread and potatoes doubled. Soup kitchens opened up. In the Prussian capital of Berlin, people fought over scarce potatoes when they appeared. The crisis put a strain on the poor transportation and distribution system. Outside of England there were few railroads in 1848.

In the summer of 1847 the French opposition held great feasts to feed the hungry and talk politics since it could not hold meetings. Daniel O'Connell had used this tactic in rallying support for Catholic Emancipation in Britain. The government of Louis Philippe and his Prime Minister François Guizot put in no reforms, took no action, but did ban meetings. The opposition planned a "monster banquet" in Paris for Washington's birthday, February 22, 1848. The government tried to ban it, then set up conditions. Students and workingmen assembled in the streets. Louis Philippe turned on Guizot and dismissed him on February 22 in an attempt to save his crown. This did not clear the air; it only encouraged the revolutionaries. The crowd headed for Guizot's home on February 23. They were met by soldiers, and forty died in the confusion. News of this "massacre" caused the protesters to build 1,500 barricades. The National Guard proved unreliable. Louis Philippe feared a repeat of the Terror and quit as king.

With the King, the Chamber, and the Charter discredited, power fell to the liberal newspapers. Their editors picked a temporary government of liberals and socialists headed by the poet **Alfonse de Lamartine**. The temporary government immediately proclaimed a republic, announced elections where all men would have the right to vote, recalled the troops from abroad, and made service in the National Guard compulsory for all males. It set up a mobile guard of 15,000 in Paris to keep the peace. Later, the government abolished slavery in all French territories.

Radicals wanted the state to intervene in the economy and clean out the bureaucracy. Louis Blanc, who was part of the temporary government, called for nationalization and decentralization of industry. But Lamartine was a liberal defender of property. The government set up "National Workshops" that were the result of a compromise between the two. An opponent of Blanc's with every incentive to cripple the National Workshops was put in charge. Unemployed workers could sign up on a sheet to get work in or around Paris. Those who got a job through the government were paid two francs a day for working. But what if you signed up for work and the government did not have a job that day? Should you get nothing and risk the starvation of your family? The government would pay one-and-a-half francs (later one) franc a day for not working. People poured into Paris. Many ended up being paid for doing nothing. The National Workshops had been designed for 12,000; by the end, 120,000 were enrolled and 80,000 more were trying to join. Government needed a 45-centime tax to keep the budget in order. This caused anger in the countryside against Paris and the Lamartine government.

# The Revolution in Austria

Excitement greeted the news from Paris. The nationalist **Louis Kossuth** called for Hungary to have its own constitution. Fighting broke out in Vienna, and Metternich was forced out on March 13. Two days later, the Hungarian Diet put out a constitution giving Hungary autonomy. Without Metternich, Austria did not have strong leadership, and the Austrian emperor had a severe mental disability. Austria gave in to the Hungarians on March 31. Then the Czechs demanded and gained their rights on April 8. A Constituent Assembly convened in Austria seeking a Belgian-model constitution. The Assembly ordered peasants freed from serfdom, and the Emperor signed the decree on September 7. This was the main demand of the peasants, and they had no interest in further revolution.

# Revolution in Italy

Most of the Austrian troops were tied down in Italy as the provinces of Lombardy and Venetia rose and sought independence. The revolt had begun in the Lombard capital of Milan when news from Vienna reached it on March 17. Venice rose on March 22, and the Austrian troops withdrew to strategic positions in forts. King **Charles Albert** of Piedmont-Sardinia (ruled 1831–1849) invaded Lombardy and reached Milan on March 26. Lombardy, Parma, Modena, and Venice voted to join with Piedmont-Sardinia. The unification of northern Italy, at least, seemed likely.

# Revolution in Prussia and the German States

Frederick William III had died in 1840 and was succeeded by his son **Frederick William IV** (1840–1861), who was rather unstable and romantic. In 1847, the King desperately needed money for the budget and to fund a railroad. He called a United Diet in 1847 but when he would not grant it permanent status, the Diet turned down all loans.

The Prussian cities had already seen hunger riots and riots by artisans whose work was being threatened by cheap British industrial goods. When Metternich fell, Frederick William IV promised to convene a Prussian parliament, grant a constitution, and sponsor reforms. On March 18, fighting broke out in Berlin after crowds clashed with troops. More than 250 died. The commanding general felt that he could only retake Berlin by pulling out and laying siege, which would destroy much of the city. The King ordered the troops out of Berlin and was essentially a hostage of the revolution. The mob poured into the palace courtyard with the corpses, and the royal couple had to salute them. The King abolished lord-run local courts that were the last vestiges of serfdom, satisfying the Prussian peasants. The King appointed a liberal Rhenish merchant named Ludulf Camphausen to form a government. The United Diet set a fairly liberal suffrage for elections to a Prussian Parliament. Camphausen ordered credit expansion to help banks and merchants, but did little for city workers.

Especially in the overcrowded states of southwestern Germany, crowds with liberal petitions marched even as workers' riots in the cities smashed industrial machines. In the countryside, peasants destroyed landlords' records. Governments offered little resistance. In Bavaria, demands for reform combined with calls for the king and his mistress to leave town. Once liberal ministers were in power, they began to use the old tools to keep order. They feared that the peasants would try to seize property, and the liberals strongly protected property rights. The revolution offered little to the peasants.

The revolutionaries were also German nationalists in many cases and saw their chance. All the states in the German Confederation agreed to choose representatives to meet in Frankfurt and draw up a liberal constitution for a united Germany. They repealed all of the Metternich-era antiliberal measures. The **Frankfurt Parliament** started on May 18. Election laws differed according to state. Many had indirect elections and only allowed a few rich men to vote. In those states that did extend the vote to the lower class, many declined to show up for the elections in March and April. There was a Jacobin-like uprising in southwestern Germany in April that tried to establish a republic, but the authorities crushed that attempt.

Of 800 members in the Frankfurt Parliament, only about 500 showed up at any time. Most were lawyers, although Professor Dahlmann, a member of the "Göttingen Seven," was a representative. Austria sent representatives, but Bohemia and Moravia refused to participate. Political groups ranged from conservatives to ultra-radicals. Some say that the Parliament should have declared its authority and acted dictatorially or at least employ revolutionary methods. It did enact agricultural reforms, including the abolition of all feudal dues. The artisans in the cities turned against the revolution because they were opposed to change and liberalization.

The Parliament drafted the Fundamental Rights of German People. This provided for equality under the law, abolished all class privileges, allowed freedom of association, the press, assembly, teaching, and said no one could be put in prison without a charge. Under the constitution, all men would vote for members of a People's House for three-year terms by secret ballot. The members of the House of States would be picked by state governments and by state parliaments. The Parliament voted to exclude Austria from united Germany and offered the crown to Frederick William IV of Prussia by a vote of 290 to 248. Twenty-nine of the remaining thirty-eight states approved the Constitution; that was more than the three-fourths that put the U.S. Constitution into effect. The Germans had to wait for Frederick William's decision.

# Impact on Britain and the British Colonies

Chartism's last gasp came in April 1848 when news of the revolutions reached London, but strong police action caused the activists to disperse. In 1848, as revolution swept Europe, the Canadian governor allowed reformers to form a cabinet that had a majority of the popularly-elected Assembly supporting it. In 1849 Britain abolished the mercantilist Navigation Laws that had restricted Canadian trade.

# Women's Rights Movement

Liberals and nationalists focused on constitutions and rights and creating nations. Humanitarians tended to look at extending rights and votes to men or freeing slaves or ending the slave trade. Very few radicals were willing to consider full rights for women. Most girls received a limited education. The spread of the Industrial Revolution, urbanization, and the fall of living standards, along with the rhetoric of the time, began to inspire women. Many favored abolition of slavery and other reforms but ran up against prejudice that women should not speak publicly. Some had grown up as the daughters of politicians and preachers where speech was vital to the cause. For some, moral reform, however defined, was vital to protecting their families. As part of the religious surge, some evangelical preachers allowed women to offer public prayers. The alcoholism and violence against women that hit their high point in the 1840s also motivated women to seek equal legal rights, the vote, and limits on the sale of alcohol. A number of American states recognized women's rights to property, to wages, and to child custody.

Women attending the world anti-slavery convention in London in 1840 were not allowed to speak. On the ship back to the United States, female abolitionists **Elizabeth Cady Stanton** (1815–1902) and **Lucretia Mott** (1793–1880) discussed forming a society to promote women's rights. The 1848 revolutions seemed to open a new chapter. In May 1848, Mott addressed the American Anti-Slavery Society on the events in France and how French leaders were now calling former slaves brothers. She reflected on what a change it had been from ten years before when rioters in Philadelphia had stormed a meeting of the women's anti-slavery society and destroyed the hall. Mott and Stanton convened the **Seneca Falls Convention** in 1848 where they drafted a Declaration of Sentiments modeled on the Declaration of Independence. The revolutions emboldened Mott to include a demand for the vote. About three hundred delegates attended, and one hundred signed the Declaration. Seneca Falls marked the beginning of the organized women's rights movement in the United States.

# THE FAILURE OF THE REVOLUTIONS

## France

The April 23 elections for the Constituent Assembly reflected a great reaction in the countryside. Almost 85 percent of the eligible voters participated. Many peasants voted for the first time under Church influence and were disgusted at free-spending Paris. The moderate republicans controlled the assembly and forced Lamartine to drop Blanc. On May 24, it ordered the dissolution of the National Workshops. The younger unemployed could join the army, those from rural areas were paid to go home, others could undertake public works outside Paris. Attempts to delay this action failed.

On June 23 when the army enlistments were supposed to begin, the workers met at the square where the Bastille had once stood and set up barricades. The Minister of War **Eugene Cavaignac** put down the revolt in four bloody days. The government killed 1,460 people, tracked down and executed three thousand, and arrested twelve thousand. These "**June Days**" represented a conflict of the middle class against the workers as well as a conflict between Paris and the French countryside. A dictatorship replaced the government's executive committee and got rid of social reform. Lamartine was completely discredited.

In October 1848, the Constituent Assembly agreed on a constitution modeled upon that of the United States. There would be a strong president, but the constitution limited him to a single four-year term. The president would share power with a National Assembly elected every three years. All men would have the right to vote, about 25 percent of the total population.

Lamartine and Cavaignac both ran for the presidency and received little support. The overwhelming winner was **Louis Napoleon Bonaparte**, nephew of the former emperor. Napoleon I's only son had died in Vienna in 1832, and Louis Napoleon had proclaimed himself the leader of the Bonapartes. He had been active in the Italian revolutions of 1831. He had tried to overthrow Louis Philippe without success and had been exiled to the United States. After six months in New York and Philadelphia, he had returned to Europe and resumed plotting. The Revolution of 1848 brought him back to France. In 1839, the book *Napoleonic Ideas*, with Louis Napoleon's name on it, appeared. It was a hodgepodge of liberal and socialist ideas designed to appeal to the lower classes. Louis Napoleon called himself a socialist, and his book seemed somewhat inspired by Saint-Simon.

# Northern Europe

The revolutions of 1848 saw some movements in Norway for political reform similar to English Chartism: widen the voting franchise, pay members, have a secret ballot, and hold more frequent elections. The newspaper editor Marcus Thrane, who had traveled in England, led the reformers. Norwegian reformers called for the removal of tariffs, the improvement of working conditions, and the formation of a large democratic party based on the middle and lower classes. Thrane was a Saint-Simonian-style socialist. The reformers sent a petition with 30,000 signatures to King Oscar. The government responded by sending 117 to prison for revolutionary activity. Thrane served seven years, then urged emigration to America as a way of escaping the conditions and left in 1862. King Oscar had seemed to be moving toward a representative system in Sweden, but riots in Stockholm in March 1848 left thirty dead and alienated Oscar from further political reforms.

A Danish liberal editor, Orla Lehmann, promoted Danish nationalism and called for the abolition of noble privileges. He organized demonstrations in 1848. Liberal nationalists demanded a full written constitution that would incorporate Schleswig, which was mostly German speaking. The October 1848 elections for a Constituent Assembly allowed the vote to male householders who were over the age of thirty but not on poor relief. Only one-third bothered voting. Lehmann and a liberal cleric wrote most of the constitution of 1849. Denmark became a limited monarchy: the King would share power with a bicameral national assembly. All men over thirty living independently had voting rights for the lower house. Older and richer men only could vote for the upper house. Ministers of government were not responsible to the Parliament and could issue provisional laws between sessions. The King could not levy taxes without the Parliament's consent. The constitution guaranteed civil liberties: freedom of religion, of the press, of public assembly. The constitution applied only to Denmark proper, not Schleswig-Holstein.

## Bohemia

The Czechs called a pan-Slav Congress to transform the Austrian empire into a federation where Germans, Magyars, and Slavic peoples would have equal power. On June 13, a full rebellion broke out in the Bohemian capital of Prague. The Austrian military commander **Alfred von Windischgrätz** bombarded Prague, and it gave up on June 17.

## Italy

In July 1848, the Austrian forces rolled back in, under the command of **Joseph Radetzky**. At the **Battle of Custoza** (July 23–27, 1848) Radetzky defeated Charles Albert. The Austrian regained Milan on August 6. For six months things stayed quiet, but in February 1849 there was a new revolution in Rome that drove out the conservative Pope and proclaimed a republic. Mazzini was one of the leaders, and Garibaldi headed the defense squad. The United States was the only nation to recognize the Roman Republic. Charles Albert again attacked Lombardy and was defeated. Louis Napoleon ordered French troops to retake Rome for the Pope in order to please conservative Catholic voters. The city of Venice held out for months against Austrian bombardment until August of 1849. The Revolution had failed in Italy and it remained divided.

## Events in Vienna

Vienna had begun its own version of the national workshops, and similar problems developed as in France. The Constituent Assembly sought a Belgian-style Constitutional Monarchy. One-quarter of the representatives were peasants. It abolished the last laws that required peasants to donate labor to the landlord. On October 6, 1848, revolt broke out in Vienna centered on a soldiers' mutiny when they were ordered to attack Hungary. Students and workers backed the mutineers. General Windischgrätz brutally suppressed the rebellion by October 30 killing and wounding about four thousand people. The general installed his cynical brother-in-law **Felix zu Schwarzenberg** as chief minister. Schwarzenberg engineered a change in emperor. The mentally-disabled Ferdinand resigned in favor of his eighteen-year-old nephew **Francis Joseph** (ruled 1848–1916). The Austrian Constituent Assembly was about to approve its constitution but Francis Joseph and Schwarzenberg dissolved it in March 1849 and put out their own very conservative constitution. The regime arrested many protesters.

# Hungary

The Austrians had been stirring up trouble in Hungary by encouraging the non-Hungarian groups such as the Croats, Serbs, and Romanians to try for their own independence. When Austria tried to send troops to Hungary, Kossuth's power grew. In December 1848, the Hungarian Parliament refused to recognize Francis Joseph as the new Emperor, effectively declaring independence. The Hungarians defeated Windischgrätz in April 1849. Kossuth took over as president of a Hungarian republic. The Austrians appealed to Russian Emperor Nicholas, who sent 140,000 troops in 1849 and crushed the revolt. There was massive retaliation by the Austrians starting with the execution of thirteen leading Hungarian generals. Kossuth escaped to the United States.

# Prussia

In May 1848 the Prussian National Assembly split between the liberals and democratic radicals. It did not get control over the army and police and had to use its own civic guard against unrest in Berlin, angering the lower classes. When the Assembly debated abolishing manorial rights, the *Junkers* set up their own political party and newspaper and looked for popular support. They could pressure their own peasants, people of rural towns, and Protestant churches. Some disenchanted artisans also backed the *Junkers*. The Assembly decided to abolish all noble titles and decorations and dropped the phrase "King by the grace of God." In November 1848 Frederick William IV, inspired by the crushing of the Vienna revolt, suspended the Assembly and called in the army.

The King put out the **Prussian Constitution of 1850**. This established a bicameral legislature with an upper House of Lords and a lower house elected by a three-class franchise. This meant that 17 percent of the male taxpayers elected two-thirds of the seats in the lower house. This would be a strong barrier to democratic and social reform legislation in Germany down to the end of World War I in 1918. Not surprisingly, few from the lower class bothered voting. The Parliament had to approve the budget, but another article allowed the government to collect existing taxes and duties.

# Germany

Frederick William IV also dealt with the Frankfurt Parliament. He wanted to be the first German Emperor, but did not like being bound by a constitution or sharing power with an elected assembly or weakening the state of Prussia by breaking it into eight provinces. The King refused to "take the crown out of the gutter." One-quarter of the members of the Parliament tried to continue governing. In the southwest and Saxony, radical revolts broke out. The Saxon revolt saw rebels as different as Richard Wagner, the court composer, and Mikhail Bakunin, the Russian anarchist, on the barricades. Frederick Engels, the Communist writer, was part of a doomed rebellion in the Rhineland. Prussian troops crushed these small revolts. The last holdout was the fortress of Rastatt, which was taken July 23. Among those who fled was Carl Schurz, who would become a prominent reformer in New York. The German revolution was over.

Frederick William IV then tried to unite Germany on his own terms while Austria was still weak by forcing the smaller German states into an **Erfurt Union** (1849–50). Austria, backed by Russia, forced Prussia to back down. Under the **Punctation of Olmütz** in November 1850, Prussia agreed to the reestablishment of the German Confederation with Austria as leader.

# General Causes of Failure of Revolutions of 1848

We may sum up the reasons for the failure of the revolutions as follows:

1. The middle class feared the revolutionary radicalism of workers.
2. The revolutionaries lacked political experience.
3. The army and bureaucracy remained loyal to established authority.
4. In some cases, foreign intervention made the difference (Russia in Hungary, France and Austria in Italy). Without this, Hungary would have gained its independence and northern Italy down to Rome would have united in 1849.
5. The peasants were satisfied with a few reforms and thereafter sat on the sidelines or backed the conservatives. This is very important

because most soldiers were of peasant background. Not only were most people peasants, but boys growing up in the cities of the Hungry Forties were often scrawny and rejected for military service. As long as the army supported the revolution or at least the king doubted its support, the revolution could advance.

# Results of the Revolutions of 1848

1. The national desire for the unification of Germany remained, but the politically disappointed middle class turned more to economic endeavors. Many would go into business in the 1850s.
2. Many emigrated from Germany, especially democrats from the overcrowded southwest; this weakened the democratic movement and helped ensure that when unity came, Germany would be united as an autocratic Prussian empire.
3. Reality proved stronger than ideas, and a more realistic intellectual era would begin. Romanticism faded after the failure of the Revolutions of 1848. The new mood would be realism as represented by Otto von Bismarck: The great matters of time are not decided by debates and majority votes but by blood and iron!

# TIMELINE

| 1815 | Congress of Vienna |
| 1820 | Revolutions in Spain, Portugal, southern Italy |
| 1821–1829 | Greek War of Independence |
| 1822 | Congress of Verona; Britain refuses to back intervention in Spain |
| 1825 | Decembrist Revolt in Russia |
| 1829 | Andrew Jackson becomes U.S. President |
| 1830 | Revolutions in France, Belgium, Italy |
| 1831 | Revolution in Poland |
| 1832 | First Reform Bill in Britain |
| 1845–1848 | Potato famine in Ireland |
| 1848 | Revolutions across Europe |

# KEY TERMS

The First Reform Bill
Decembrist Revolt
Andrew Jackson
The Hungry Forties
Louis Blanc
Louis Kossuth
Frankfurt Parliament
Seneca Falls Convention
"June Days"
Battle of Custoza

# PRIMARY SOURCE DOCUMENTS

**Klemens von Metternich,** http://www.fordham.edu/halsall/mod/1820metternich.html

**Louis Kossuth,** http://www.h-net.org/~habsweb/sourcetexts/kosswash.html

**John Stuart Mill,** http://www.wsu.edu:8080/~wldciv/world_civ_reader/world_civ_reader_2/mill.html

**David Ricardo,** http://www.fordham.edu/halsall/mod/ricardo-wages.html

**Seneca Falls Conference,** http://www.fordham.edu/halsall/mod/Senecafalls.html

**Louis Blanc,** http://www.fordham.edu/halsall/mod/1840blanc.html

**Carl Schurz,** http://www.fordham.edu/halsall/mod/1848schurz.html

## Chapter 13

# WESTERN EXPANSION IN ASIA AND AUSTRALIA

# THE TRADE BALANCE REVERSES

## General Considerations

One of the main features of the global economy of the eighteenth century, as in previous eras, had been a long-term trade imbalance between Europe and Asia, particularly India and China. The Europeans gradually found substitutes. Trade laws limited the import of Indian luxury cloth. Cheap cloth, increasingly made by the British factories, replaced it. German, French, and British makers of ceramics figured out the secret of making fine porcelain that had been a Chinese monopoly for centuries. By the late 1700s, tea was the main import from Asia. The Dutch were buying ten times more tea by value in 1790 than they had been sixty years before.

After 1800, Europe completed substitution for imports and was advancing its exports. This had a catastrophic effect on Asia: it had steadily matched that trade surplus by population increase, so wealth did not grow on average. Shifts in trade and the continual expansion of western ideas would open a revolutionary situation in Asia. Globalization took hold: after 1800, factors outside of England began to affect English land prices.

# China's Problems

China was huge in size and population, and the government was unable to take careful measurements. We are not even sure of the population because some provinces falsified their numbers. Somewhere between 300 million and 350 million lived in eighteenth-century China, four-fifths in the countryside. China has much less fertile land than India or Europe, so most of those people were squeezed along the coast or into the major river valleys. Centuries before, most of the forests had been felled for farmland, depriving China of large-scale wood resources. The land was carefully managed with improvements and water control. About seven million acres were added in the eighteenth century. Human labor provided the overwhelming percentage of motor power. There were few draft animals, tools, or storage facilities. An eighteenth-century attempt to install a mechanical pump at a well failed when workers refused the water unless it was drawn by hand. Productivity was low and education was concentrated in a bureaucratic class that seldom dealt with agriculture or commerce.

There were many innovations on the farm, but unlike Britain, they did not increase productivity because the population grew so quickly. It is an imperfect comparison, but in some ways China was like a giant-sized Ireland. Champa rice, introduced from southeast Asia, could yield three crops a year on superior soil. On sandier soil, the new food of sweet potato served as the poor man's food of southern China. Other new crops included corn (maize), tobacco, and peanuts.

Tea and silk, the major export products, were also the result of large-scale rural labor. There was little credit, and limited currency in copper coin and silver bullion. Paper money was still avoided in memory of the disastrous Ming Dynasty experience. China regarded itself as relatively self-sufficient. It did not encourage trade. The empire confined most foreign merchants to live in Gwangzhou (Canton) from 1760 to 1834. The small-scale trade with Portugal went through the isolated port of Macao. Foreigners had to trade with licensed Chinese monopolists (Cohung), who were under the superintendent of Chinese customs at Canton (called by Europeans "the Hoppo"). Chinese merchant firms (hangs) were licensed to trade between China and East Indies in junks that could carry up to 1,000 tons. The government levied an equal amount of tariffs on exports as on imports and so was neither mercantilist nor free trading in policy. The government provided no legal safeguards of trade. There were neither investment markets nor joint-stock companies. Unlike European countries, nationalist competition did not press China: Japan was isolated, Korea and Vietnam were small and weak.

China had no institutionalized science and invention as had developed in seventeenth-century Europe and constituted a Scientific Revolution. The government regulated all printing and there were no convenient printing centers over the Chinese borders that could defy the emperor's strict censorship. In the latter part of the century, 150,000 books were burned because they were deemed anti-Manchu in part or in entirety. A census of all works was conducted and a little over half of all the books were recopied by hand and a little under half were destroyed. The government heavily taxed new businesses, which rarely could attract any venture capital. If a new endeavor succeeded, the government could confiscate it for a monopoly. Merchants therefore put their profits into land and/or education for their sons. The severe inequality of income meant there was no real domestic market to speak of. According to Kenneth Pomeranz, the Chinese grain trade was 2.4 million tons, which equals about fifteen to twenty pounds a person per year, depending on what the population was. On a per capita basis, that is less than ancient Athens, which annually imported at least 220 pounds of grain per person around 400 BC. Regulation of grain prices made it very difficult for a peasant to make any profit and this discouraged productivity except for the need to feed extra mouths at subsistence level.

From 1775 to 1799, the chief minister **Heshen** plundered the empire for his own benefit and installed relatives and cronies across the land. Some have suggested that he was the emperor's lover. He strengthened his position when his son married the emperor's favorite daughter in 1790. He deliberately extended military campaigns so as to extort more money. Officials falsified tax receipts and production reports, so it is very difficult for us to get a true sense of Chinese economic and government activity in these years. Heshen's corruption squeezed the peasants, who also suffered under a regressive tax system. Because officials stole the money needed to maintain the dams and canals of the Yellow River, that river flooded catastrophically. In 1799 the Emperor died, the government swiftly charged Heshen with various crimes and allowed him to commit suicide. At his death, stupendous amounts of wealth and many pawnbrokers were found to be under his control. His total assets were estimated at fifteen years of government revenue: the 2013 U.S. equivalent would be $50 trillion! Heshen may be the biggest thief in history. Tellingly, the only imported goods in this fortune were 460 European clocks.

# Qing Expansion

The Qing worked to emphasize Chinese culture to minorities such as the Hakka ("guest people") of the south, who were related to the hill tribes of southeastern Asia. The Manchus expanded their territory into less civilized areas: Mongolia, Tibet, and Xinjiang (Chinese Turkestan) in the 1750s. From 1720 to 1750, interventions led to China putting Tibet under the Dalai Lama, who would be protected by China. These conquests plus the Manchu homelands virtually doubled the size of China. In the 1720s, the Qing government replaced native chieftain rule in distant areas with direct bureaucracy. From 1765 to 1769, China invaded Burma with 70,000 troops. While the Chinese soldiers had some successes, they were weakened by the tropical climate and diseases of Burma. The Burmese forces attacked the Chinese lines of communication while avoiding the main force and forced the Chinese out.

In the days of Heshen, Chinese military power waned. In 1769, Thailand had warred with the lords of Vietnam over Cambodia. The Thai victory and heavy burdens on the Vietnamese people led to the **Tay So'n rebellion**. This defeated the Trinh and Nyugen lords, killed many ethnic Chinese residents, and drove the Emperor of Vietnam, a Chinese client, out. In 1788, China invaded Vietnam. This turned into a fiasco when the Vietnamese staged a surprise attack during the New Year feasts. There were other "police actions" against the Gurkhas of Nepal, two rebellions in Szechuan, and a rebellion in Taiwan (1788–89). The second Szechuan campaign cost the equivalent of two years of government revenue with an unknown amount going into Heshen's pocket.

## The White Lotus Rebellion, 1796–1804

This uprising showed how weak and corrupt the military had become under Heshen. It began in an inaccessible area of the Han and Yangtze rivers. It was essentially an ordinary peasant rebellion, but the army led by Heshen's brother could not put it down. The government finally had to pen up villagers and supplies to keep food and recruits from rebels, then armed the villagers as a militia. The rebellion shattered the myth of Manchu invincibility.

# BRITISH SUPREMACY IN INDIA

**Richard Wellesley** arrived in India in 1798 as the governor-general along with his younger brother Arthur, the future Duke of Wellington. He only lasted until 1805 but set the foundations for British rule and left proteges. Wellesley extended British control in the south by linking diverse ports. The British destroyed the Mysore state that had been negotiating with the French. They attacked Ceylon (Sri Lanka) in 1803 and completed its conquest in 1818.

The Mughal Empire had reached a sorry state. **Shah Alam II** (ruled 1759–1806) had effective control only over Delhi. Even this city was not safe, as Sikhs from Punjab attacked it repeatedly. In one raid, the Mughal Emperor was blinded. Wellesley moved up the Ganges river from Bengal. As we have seen, Oudh became a virtual puppet state. Wellesley was concerned that the Maratha state, which held most of the Mughals' land, had a French-trained and equipped army. The French could use this power over Shah Alam to force the Mughal Emperor to issue anti-British decrees. In 1803, the British drove the Marathas from Delhi and put Shah Alam under their "protection." By 1805, the British had smashed the Maratha army and driven French adventurers out of India. These British victories were costly. Wellesley had started with about 9,000 regular soldiers, but lost 2,000 in his campaign against the Marathas. The British turned increasingly to training native Indian troops, who they called "Sepoys." By 1824, there would be an army of 200,000 of which 90 percent consisted of natives of south Asia. London felt that Wellesley had been a little too aggressive and recalled him from India in 1805.

When bandits based in Maratha territory began raiding the south, the British launched a campaign from December 1817 to January 1818 and brought central India under their control. But another challenge arose. **Ranjit Singh** (d.1839) had united the Sikhs by 1803 with his capital at Lahore and launched a series of campaigns conquering the Punjab from Afghan and local princes. French and Italian veterans of the Napoleonic Wars helped him equip and train his army. By 1820, the Sikhs controlled Punjab and Kashmir. Singh built a secular empire and employed Sikhs, Muslims, Hindus, and Christians in his army and government. There was no religious discrimination, but Singh was suspicious of Muslim mullahs who tried to spread their religion.

The British were surprised that the population did not rebel. People were happy that once they paid taxes to the British or their allies, they were left in peace for the year, not beleaguered by bandits, wars, or additional requests. In the heyday of the Mughal empire before 1739, the government had taxed perhaps 50 percent of all income. The British taxes were the same or slightly lower. In 1813, the British Parliament extended Britain's sovereignty to all Company possessions and allowed missionaries to go to India. This led to schools to train an Indian elite. The natives trained here would help the British run India, but eventually they would lead the move for independence. Wellesley established an administrative school at Fort William to train British civil servants.

Calcutta, with a population of 250,000, became the center of a "Bengal Renaissance." This movement combined new appreciation and research into past Indian history and literature with an understanding of western values and scientific method. Scholars revived the ancient Uphanishads of south Asia in order to show that Hindu superstitions had crept into traditions over the years. A return to the true path of Indian religion would purge Hinduism of *sati* (a tradition where a widow throws herself on the funeral pyre), polygamy, child marriage, and other superstitions. **Ram Mohan Roy** (1772–1833) was a towering figure of the Bengal Renaissance. He worked for twelve years for the British East India Company while translating ancient Vedic scriptures into English. Roy founded the Calcutta Unitarian Society and then the Brahmo Sabha in 1828. The Brahmos started as Christian-influenced Hindus who believed in one supreme God. It became a religious and social reform movement that pushed for property inheritance rights for women and an end to Hindu superstition. It eventually split from Hinduism entirely. In 1817, Roy set up the Hindu College in Calcutta backed by British philanthropists such as David Hare. In 1822, Roy established Vedanta College which focused on English, science, medicine, and technology. While promoting the necessity of western learning to the people of Bengal, Roy also protested British actions such as the imposition of censorship in 1823. In 1830, he sailed to Britain as the Mughal Emperor's Ambassador to Britain, and he died in Britain in 1833.

# THE OPIUM WARS

## Background

Smoking opium came to China after the introduction of tobacco-smoking from America via Manila in the seventeenth century. During the late eighteenth century, China imported an average of sixty-seven tons of opium per year. From 1800 to 1821, this jumped to an average of 300 tons a year. Prices fell 30 to 50 percent after 1821. By the 1830s, China was importing up to 2,660 tons and 1 percent of the entire population was considered addicted to opium. Population pressure, lower living standards, the increase of corruption, and general demoralization spurred drug addiction. It was not that people had suddenly developed disposable income. Instead they were foregoing necessary food, shelter, and clothing to get opium. The Chinese empire had banned opium smoking and selling in 1729, and banned imports in 1796, but corrupt officials kept bringing it in.

British India was dependent on opium for 5 to 10 percent of its revenue. At first, there was competition between British East India Company opium and non-Company opium grown in western India. In the 1830s, the Company got control of ports such as Bombay and was able to tax it.

## The Canton System

The British East India Company's monopoly in China decayed as other British traders stayed as nominal representatives of other European governments. In 1834, Britain replaced the monopoly and sent a superintendent of trade. In 1839, China moved strongly against the opium trade. It had upset the exchange ratio between silver bullion and the copper cash used in everyday transactions. Tensions rose when China detained 350 British merchants and stripped them of their opium, which was then destroyed. The British sent steamships with cannon and 4,000 regulars and Sepoys from India against the antiquated junks of China with their primitive cannon. The Chinese military was set up to deal with bandits or rebels; it had no large land or sea units trained together with sufficient striking power. Its naval vessels were much smaller than Chinese trading junks. The British moved up the Pearl river and captured Gwangzhou. Then the squadron moved to the Yangtze and took Shanghai. Seventy ships sailed up the Yangtze to its intersection with the Grand Canal. That was enough.

The **Treaty of Nanjing** (1842) brought an end to the war. China ceded Hong Kong to Britain. The Chinese government was fined to reimburse the cost of the opium. Other ports, including Shanghai, were opened to British trade. The British gained the right of **extraterritoriality**, which meant that any Briton accused of a crime in China would be tried by a British court, not a Chinese court. By the 1850s, the opium trade was up to 4,000 tons a year, and the Chinese economy was crumbling.

# THE GREAT MUTINY

## Burmese, Afghan, and Sikh Wars

Rebels had used British-controlled lands in India as bases for operations against Burma. The Company ignored the complaints, and in 1823, Burma moved into Company land to crush the rebel movement. The British counterattacked with 5,000 troops, took Assam and Rangoon, but then suffered the same problems of climate and disease that had laid the Chinese soldiers low. Burma gave up some lands in 1826.

The Company worried that the Persians and Russians were moving into

Afghanistan, which was more divided after suffering defeats at the hands of the Sikhs. An attempt to take Afghanistan began in 1839 with 21,000 British and Indian troops taking Kandahar and Kabul. But in 1841, a rebellion surrounded the British garrison of 4,500. It surrendered, headed back for India with 12,000 refugees, but then was massacred by the Afghans. This caused a wave of unrest through northern India as the British appeared vulnerable. The Baluch rulers in Sind at the mouth of the Indus river tried to defy British orders and lost their lands in 1843. The only remaining independent group was the Sikh Empire. In a four-year conflict, the British defeated the Sikhs and their Afghan allies and took the Punjab.

The British began reshaping Indian economy and society in the 1830s. They abolished certain Hindu practices including *sati*. The 1833 Charter took away the British East India Company's privileges except for its monopolies on opium and salt. From 1813 to 1833, cotton manufacture in Bengal collapsed, throwing millions of Indian men and women out of work. The British had previously imported Indian cottons; after 1833, India would be inundated by cheaper British cottons. Imports of cotton goods increased by a hundred times from 1814 to 1829, and then sixfold to 1890. The first railroad in India opened in 1853. A Bengal railroad would open the growing cotton fields and help reduce British dependence on American cotton. The telegraph followed in 1854. In 1855, a 1,600-mile-long railroad linked Calcutta and Bombay. The British extended their idea of a unified postal service to India in 1854, which allowed anybody to send a message anywhere in India for a penny. This not only exerted a unifying force but stimulated literacy as well.

In 1856, British broke a treaty directly and annexed Oudh. This was followed by laws forcing Sepoys to serve abroad if necessary and laws allowing widows to remarry. A fear grew that the Christians were undermining Hinduism through the Brahmos movement and direct conversions to Christianity.

This all exploded in mutiny. In 1857, the British introduced Enfield rifles with new greased cartridges. The grease was feared to be made of pig (unclean to Muslims) and cow (sacred to Hindus). It was actually vegetable oil. When the Sepoys refused to bite open the cartridges, they were dismissed. The revolt started in May of 1857 in Meerut, about twenty-five miles from Delhi. The mutineers marched to Delhi to "restore" the Mughal emperor. The force stopped here, but other regiments rose. Oudh had a national uprising. The revolt was mostly confined to the upper Ganges valley, and the capitals of British India (Bombay, Madras, and Calcutta) were not affected. The war got uglier on both sides. After a Sepoy massacre of four hundred men, women, and children at Cawnpore, British soldiers tied rebels to cannons and blew them apart.

By 1858, the British had suppressed the mutiny and forced the last figurehead Mughal emperor to quit. The government dissolved the British East India Company, and Britain took full control in India. It completely reorganized the army and civil service. The total cost was £36 million, a full year's revenue from India.

# THE AUSTRALIAN SETTLEMENT

## Prison Islands

After it lost the thirteen North American colonies in 1783, the British decided that southeastern Australia would be a good place to deport criminals who were overcrowding British prisons. No European ship had been to Australia since Cook in 1770. The first convicts, 548 men and 188 women, arrived in Botany Bay in January 1788 along with about two hundred nonconvicts. The fleet had traveled 12,000 miles over 252 days, and forty-eight people had died. They quickly found Botany Bay too barren and moved north to what would become Sydney harbor. The fleet had bought animals at Cape Town, but had no draft animals for labor or plows to turn the soil. The convicts would have to dig in the ground with the own labor. One precious bull and one cow survived for breeding stock, and no plow would come to Australia until 1803. The worst felons went to remote Norfolk Island, about 1,000 miles from the eastern Australian coast.

When their terms expired, the government gave the convicts thirty to fifty acres of land. While they could return to Britain, few chose to leave Australia. Discharged soldiers received eighty to a hundred acres. The first free British settlers arrived in 1793. When the British suppressed rebellion in Ireland in 1798, they sent many of the rebels to Australia. In 1804, the authorities put down an Irish convict rebellion brutally. From 1788 to 1840, the British transported perhaps 160,000 convicts. Of the early convicts, 80 percent were thieves and city dwellers sent to a wilderness where they lacked skill or experience. Before 1800, there were only twenty free settlers. Soldiers made up the balance and lorded their power over the convicts. The officers got the best land and the most skilled convicts to work that land. In 1808, they overthrew the British governor, the luckless William Bligh, and ruled as a *junta* for two years.

After 1815, the nature of the colony began to change. Britain allowed free immigration. By 1810, there were three thousand free settlers, who objected to any attempt to give convicts social equality. Australia also developed a frontier.

Passes had been found from the harbor across the rugged Blue Mountains to the vast grassy plains suitable for sheep-raising to feed the hungry wool mills of Britain. The merino sheep of Europe was crossbred with the hardier Bengal and Afrikaner sheep. The whites freely attacked natives and took their hunting grounds, and when the natives became aggressive, extermination began. Lawlessness marked the frontier populated with escaped convicts. Settlers began to plow the farmlands of the interior. The trappings of government and regular society started to appear with civil courts in 1814 and a bank in 1817. The Governor was the absolute power and always a military man until 1823, when a legislative council was set up. The most brutality occurred in Tasmania where the authorities systematically exterminated the natives. The aboriginal population fell from 650,000 in 1800 to 90,000 in 1900.

# Free Colony

In 1829, Britain established a precarious settlement on the west coast at Perth. This was 2,400 miles from the eastern settlements, separated by a vast desert. In the 1830s, the authorities sold land at a price of five shillings, then twelve, then twenty shillings per acre. They set aside half of the proceeds to go to public works and used the other half to encourage immigration. In 1849, the last convicts were brought to New South Wales. By that time, fewer than 25,000 were under sentences. The free population of Australia already greatly outnumbered convicts and emancipists. There were about 140,000 persons with an economy based on raising sheep for the British factories. Britain sent convicts sporadically to Western Australia because it desperately needed labor. Britain abolished convict colonies in Tasmania in 1853 and on Norfolk Island in 1855.

# The Australian Gold Rush

Edward Hammond Hargreaves had sailed from Sydney to join the 1849 gold rush in California but failed to get rich. When he returned to Australia in 1851, he saw the unmistakable signs of gold. On February 12, 1851, he discovered gold in the state of Victoria leading to a gold rush. Australian colonies had just received the rights to make their own legislatures, fix tariffs, determine who voted, and alter the constitution, all subject to ratification in Britain. This paralleled similar developments in Canada. In 1855, the first railroad in Australia linked Sydney to Goulburn. The first steamship arrived at Sydney in 1852. The colonies of Western Australia, New South Wales, South Australia, Victoria, and Tasmania adopted constitutions. Most included two legislative houses that were elected on a limited franchise. In the

1850s, the authorities established universities in Melbourne, Sydney, Perth, and Adelaide. The final convicts came to Perth in 1868, and the Tasmanian convict system was dismantled in 1886. In 1871, there were about one-and-a-half million people of European descent living in Australia.

Gold was discovered in New Zealand in 1861. At the time, the British were in the middle of a brutal conflict with the native **Maoris**. As was often the case, the initial contact with Europeans had been lethal for the natives as the Maori population fell from about 130,000 in 1740 to 85,000 in 1840. The British had separated the colony from New South Wales in 1841 and given the white settlers self-government in 1852. After defeating the Maoris, the British guaranteed them some seats in the New Zealand parliament.

# TIMELINE

| | |
|---|---|
| 1765–1769 | China-Burma war |
| 1769 | Thailand defeats Vietnamese |
| 1770 | Tay S'on revolt begins in Vietnam |
| 1775–1799 | Heshen chief minister of China |
| 1788 | China invades Vietnam |
| | Settlement in Botany Bay |
| 1796–1804 | White Lotus rebellion |
| 1798–1805 | Richard Wellesley governor of British India |
| 1799 | Chinese Emperor dies, Heshen falls from power |
| 1803 | Ranjit Singh unites the Sikhs |
| 1823–1826 | British-Burmese War |
| 1829 | Settlement at Perth |
| 1839–1842 | Opium War |
| 1839–1841 | British-Afghan War |
| 1842 | Treaty of Nanking |
| 1851 | Gold discovered in Australia |
| 1857 | Great Mutiny in India |
| 1861 | Gold discovered in New Zealand |

# KEY TERMS

Heshen
Tay S'on revolt
Richard Wellesley
Ranjit Singh
Ram Mohan Roy
Opium War
Treaty of Nanking
The Great Mutiny

# PRIMARY SOURCE DOCUMENTS

**Reception of First English Ambassador to China**, http://www.fordham.edu/halsall/mod/1792macartney.asp

**Lin Cixu to Queen Victoria**, http://academic.brooklyn.edu/core9/phalsall/texts/com-lin.html

**Ram Mohan Roy**, http://chnm.gmu.edu/wwh/p/101.html

**Elisa Greathed**, http://www.fordham.edu/halsall/mod/1857greathed.asp

# Chapter 14

# THE WORLD OF NAPOLEON III

By the middle of the nineteenth century, the revolutions of the western world had repeatedly buffeted and battered the rest of the world in many ways. The West had come to dominate the world, and no figure personified that more than Louis Napoleon Bonaparte, the dominant figure in Europe in the 1850s and 1860s. Louis Napoleon had expansive interests and vaulting ambitions that involved him in nearly every corner of the world, even more than his famous uncle.

## "Neo-Romanticism" And Neo-Bonapartism After 1820

By 1824, a majority of the population in France had been born after 1789 and did not remember the French Revolution first hand. Mazzini's Young Italy movement spawned a liberal Young Germany movement. Lord Byron fought for Greek independence. French romantics opposed royalists as Bonapartism revived. People forgot how many Frenchmen had died in Napoleon's wars. Neo-Bonapartism grew in France after the revolutions of 1830. Victor Hugo wrote an admiring poem. Adolphe Thiers, a writer and Prime Minister under Louis Philippe, not only wrote a positive twenty-volume history of Napoleon's Consulate and Empire, but completed the Arc de Triomphe in Paris, and named streets and bridges after Napoleon's victories. In 1840, he arranged to bring Napoleon's bones back from St. Helena.

# YOUNG LOUIS NAPOLEON

## The Family

Louis Napoleon was born in Paris in 1808, the son of Napoleon's brother Louis Bonaparte (then the King of Holland) and stepdaughter Hortense Beauharnais. His parents' marriage was stormy: at one point Hortense took a bastard son of Talleyrand's as a lover and bore Charles Demorny (after 1862 known as the Duke de Morny), who was important in French business and political circles by the 1840s. Napoleon stripped Louis of his title in 1810 because he put the interests of the people of Holland ahead of his brother's and defied the Continental System. So it was not that far a fall when the Quadruple Alliance defeated Napoleon at Leipzig in 1813.

Napoleon died on St. Helena in 1821, but none of his relatives took up the cause. His son lived under lavish house arrest in Vienna as the Duke of Reichstadt until he died in 1832. Napoleon's brothers lived on: Lucien until 1840, Joseph to 1844, Louis until 1846, and the youngest, Jerome, until 1860. None of them tried to keep a Bonaparte movement together or advance and protect the legacy of Napoleon. At the time that Louis Napoleon began to advance his claims, his father, grandmother, three uncles, and an aunt were all alive with closer ties to Napoleon than he. The only relative with real ambition was his cousin Prince Napoleon (known dismissively as "Plon-Plon"), a radical with a reputation for immorality who spent his life in his older cousin's shadow, while working with radical leftists and casting doubts on Louis Napoleon's family ties.

Louis Napoleon was frail and not very tall. He was moody and an introvert, reminding many of his dreamy, indecisive father. Many mistook his detachment for stupidity. He was quiet, slow-moving and deliberate, with little of the fire of his uncle. The Bonapartes gave Louis Napoleon little support in his plots. At one point, he was engaged to marry Plon-Plon's sister Mathilde, but she broke off the engagement because it seemed Louis Napoleon would not amount to much. Nevertheless she served as official hostess until he married.

## The Intriguer and Revolutionary

Louis Napoleon grew up outside of France, particularly in the cities of Augsburg and Arenenburg, and for the rest of his life spoke French with a slight German accent. He and his older brother became involved in the uprisings in Italy. In 1831 the Bonapartes briefly took control of the town of

Civita-Castellana in the northern state of Romagna, one of the Papal States. Austrian troops intervened and the Bonapartes fled. Louis Napoleon's older brother died in a measles epidemic that swept the region.

In October 1836, Louis Napoleon appeared before Napoleon's old regiment, the Fourth Artillery, which was stationed at Strasbourg. He called for a march on Paris and the overthrow of Louis Philippe. The commander arrested him. Louis Napoleon wanted to avoid bloodshed; his model was his uncle's return from Elba in 1815. He believed that he could gather support in a march on Paris. The government did not want to give Louis Napoleon publicity, so it gave him some money and put him on a ship to the United States. He spent six months there, mostly in New York and Philadelphia, then returned to London and Switzerland, where he became friendly with the journalist Victor Fialin (later the Duke de Persigny).

In 1840, Louis Napoleon secured the support of the northern army commander and sailed from England to Boulogne. Both soldiers and townspeople met him with indifference. The conspirators retreated to the boats, but the boats capsized in the turmoil, and the authorities fished out Bonaparte.

The Crown now arranged a formal trial. Louis Philippe was alarmed by neo-Bonapartism sweeping high and low culture. The image of Napoleon was appearing on mugs, almanacs, playing cards, calendars, and practically everything else. The trial backfired. Louis Napoleon denied that the regime had any authority to try him and announced: "I stand before you as the representative of a principle, a cause, a defeat. The principle is the sovereignty of the people, the cause is that of the Empire, the defeat is Waterloo." He was sentenced to life imprisonment in the fortress of Ham.

In Ham, he wrote another pamphlet, "The Extinction of Poverty" (1844). He called for the government to move the unemployed out of the cities and put them in special barracks where governors of twenty-year agricultural colonies would be elected. The famous socialist Louis Blanc visited him in prison. In Spring 1846, he escaped from prison and fled to England. His father's death had left him a small inheritance. In the April 1848 elections for the Constituent Assembly, three Bonapartes were elected: Pierre, the son of Lucien; Plon-Plon; and Lucien Murat, the son of Caroline Bonaparte. Louis Napoleon was elected in a June by-election, but did not take the seat because many were appalled that an escaped criminal had been elected. After the June Days, he was elected in another by-election and took his seat this time. His German accent upset many who had forgotten that his famous uncle had a Corsican accent. Nevertheless, he began to gather more followers, and his support grew. Some felt they could manipulate him. Adolphe Thiers, eager to regain power, signed on as a supporter.

# LOUIS NAPOLEON AS EMPEROR

## The Second Republic

The French constitution of 1848 had created a system where the president had to share power with an assembly. Louis Napoleon's popularity grew even more after his intervention crushed the Roman Republic and restored the Pope's power in 1849. The Constituent Assembly condemned Bonaparte because the constitution had stated that France "should never turn her arms against the liberty of any nation." The assembly elections of May 1849 sharply rebuked the moderate republicans who had unleashed the June Days. Of 750 deputies, only about a third could be described as republicans. The monarchist right won about four hundred seats, but it split between the Legitimists (those who wanted Charles X's grandson to be king) and Orleanists (those who wanted Louis Philippe's grandson to become king). The radical left won about two hundred seats. There were perhaps only fifty moderate republicans left in the assembly.

Louis Napoleon assembled a group of advisers. Along with Morny and Persigny, he added two leading generals: Emile Fleury and Leroy de Saint-Arnaud. They ensured that Bonapartist officers were placed in key military positions.

## The Republic and Its Discontents

The election of the monarchists touched off a new round of riots, known as the June Days of 1849. The Assembly took advantage and ordered the arrest of thirty-three republican deputies, closed political clubs, imposed a tougher press law, and introduced property and residence requirements that took the vote from one-third of the electorate. Louis Napoleon signed the bill reluctantly because he needed funds from the Assembly to pay off his debts, and he hoped the Assembly would change the constitution to enable him to run for a second term as president. Although seventy-nine of the eighty-six departments in France petitioned for a revision, the Assembly refused to let Louis Napoleon run.

Louis Napoleon dismissed the ministers of Assembly's choosing who had tried to limit his power and declared he would choose his own ministers. In January 1851 he appointed a supporter to control Paris and its military garrison. The President attended all the bridge openings, railroad dedications, and harvest festivals he could. He showed interest in local problems and talked to businessmen and peasants alike. In short, he ran a political campaign.

## Napoleon III's Takeover

On the night of December 1/2, 1851, the authorities arrested most of the Assembly leaders and opposition to the President, including Cavaignac and Thiers, who had dropped his support for Bonaparte. Posters announced that the President had dissolved the Assembly and restored universal male suffrage. People voted on a new constitution that created a bicameral legislature, a council of state to frame legislation, and a prince-president with a ten-year term. The barricades went up again in Paris, and the authorities crushed them and killed about two hundred people. At the end of 1852, Louis Napoleon took the final step and asked if the people wanted the Empire restored with Louis Napoleon Bonaparte as emperor. There were 7.5 million votes in favor, 640,000 opposed.

## France under the Second Empire

Napoleon III promoted economic development by setting up banking corporations and financing railroad and harbor construction. He pushed for free trade and reduced tariffs with Britain. In his time, the agricultural revolution completed its spread in France. He also sponsored the rebuilding of Paris so as to prevent future revolts. Narrow, winding streets gave way to broad boulevards such as the Champs-Elysées.

# THE WEAKENING OF THE CONCERT OF EUROPE

The Concert had never fulfilled Metternich's vision as a global policeman after Britain's refusal to work against revolutions, but it was a way of keeping general order, especially among the great powers. The Russian intervention in Hungary had proved the continued strength of the Concert. The three eastern powers (Prussia, Austria, Russia) were still strongly committed to the principles laid down by Metternich, even though Metternich was gone.

After 1848, weaknesses began to eat away at the security system:

1. The revolutions had exposed the weakness of the Austrian Empire. Its failure to reform and modernize would cause it to join the Ottomans as an underlying security problem. It made matters worse by adopting an aggressive and expansionist foreign policy.
2. Napoleon III believed in a Concert system of some sort but had imperial ambitions, wanted to support liberal and national causes,

and drew closer to Britain. Until 1866, the French Emperor was the most important international figure.

3. The "Vienna generation" that included Metternich, Nicholas I, and Castlereagh, had gradually passed from the scene. The new generation featured ambitious national unifiers such as Camillo di Cavour in Italy and Otto von Bismarck in Germany.

4. Britain slipped into "splendid isolation," especially after the Crimean War.

# The Crimean War

## The Causes of the War

The weakness of the Ottomans continued to threaten security. Napoleon III increased his popularity among French Catholic voters by declaring France to be the protector of the Christian holy places and people in the Eastern Mediterranean. In Bethlehem and areas of Jerusalem, Orthodox and Roman Catholic priests had battled with club and fist and broom over each foot of control. Under French pressure, the Turks restored the rights of the Catholics in Bethlehem. In June 1853, the Russians intervened in Romania to "protect" Greek Orthodox believers, who they had considered to be under their protection since the Greek War of Independence. The Russians also wanted some revenge on the Turks who had refused to turn over Kossuth and other Hungarian rebels fleeing the wreckage of the 1848–1849 revolution. Russia also felt that Austria owed it for help against Hungary and Prussia. The Turks after getting rid of the Janissaries had embarked on the *Tanzimat* (reorganization) in 1839. This included western-style universities, a postal and telegraph system, some opening to British trade, and legal reform based on the Napoleonic Code. These reforms may have instilled a false sense of confidence because they declared war on Russia. The Turks were beaten badly. Nicholas I tried to force a treaty on the Turks as he had in 1833, but Britain and France declared war. Napoleon III saw the war as the way to an alliance with Britain.

## The Conduct of the War

The war centered on the most important Russian naval base at Sevastopol on the Crimean peninsula, hence the name of the war. London and Paris directed the war by telegraphed instructions, a military breakthrough. Piedmont-Sardinia's chief minister **Camillo di Cavour** (Prime Minister 1852–1861) brought that nation into the war on the side of Britain and France so that it could vent its grievances at a peace conference and win possible allies for the future. For the first time, Austria took a stand against Russia in the Balkans. The clever Schwarzenberg had died, and it has never been clear what Austria thought it would gain with this maneuver. Considering its growing problems with national groups, the last things Austria needed were more non-German peoples. This move was of huge significance: it foreshadowed the Austro-Russian rivalry over the Ottomans' carcass. The Russians saw it as a deep betrayal: they had saved the Austrian empire in 1849 and 1850. Some said it hastened the death of Russian Emperor Nicholas I. About 500,000 soldiers died, evenly divided between the two sides. Most died of disease and not enemy fire.

## The Peace of Paris 1856

The Allies finally took Sevastopol, and the Russians agreed to peace talks. The terms 1) put Romania under international control; 2) affirmed the total independence of the Ottoman Empire and denied any Russian protectorate over the Greek Orthodox believers; 3) forced Russia to give up a little territory and cede the mouths of the Danube River to Turkey; 4) forced all to accept the authority of international commissions on navigation rights in the Straits; 5) neutralized the Black Sea and forbade warships from entering the Straits and naval bases on the Sea. These terms were against Russia, weakened the Russian fleet, and took away Russian territory.

# The Future of the Concert

The attempts to put the Prussian army on a war footing had shown the woeful inadequacies of its forces. Prussia would soon call for military reform and modernization. Russia was unhappy and particularly angry at Austria. It plotted to regain its military rights in the Black Sea. It was shocked at its poor performance and would start to transform its economy and society. Many doubted the fighting ability of the British forces. The British grumbled that France had tricked them and retreated into isolation. By contrast, Napoleon III came out as impressive.

# The Vision of Federative Polity

The historian Robert Binkley suggested that in these days, there was an alternative to the ever-increasing centralization of power in the nation-state. In the age of Napoleon III, there were mutualist socialists such as Proudhon, who opposed the state-centered vision of Marx, and church leaders such as

Döllinger who opposed the Pope's centralization of the Catholic Church. Only five countries (France, Spain, Portugal, Piedmont, and Greece) in Europe had undivided sovereignty with one monarch ruling over one territory by one title. All the others ruled over different lands with different laws (Norway/Sweden, Denmark/Schleswig-Holstein, England/Scotland/Ireland, Russia/Poland/Finland, Austria before 1849). External forces bound others: the Italian states bound by treaty with Austria, the structure of the German Confederation.

## The Last Congress of the Concert

Napoleon III tried to convene the great powers in Paris at the end of 1863 to find a solution for the problems in Poland, Germany, the Balkans, Denmark, and Italy. He unveiled an ambitious program of reorganization and compensation, but the British refused to go along. The Congress, and the Concert of Europe, fell through. The Crimean War opened a series of wars among the great powers that redrew the map of Europe and changed the balance of power. Metternich's Concert of Europe had kept the peace from 1815 to 1854, the longest period of peace in European history up to that point.

# NEW EXPLORATIONS IN CENTRAL AFRICA

In the mid-nineteenth century, central Africa remained unknown to the Europeans. The sources of the Nile and Congo rivers stirred special interest. The fierce climate and deadly diseases (especially malaria) served as effective barriers as did the frequent waterfalls and rapids. In the 1840s, European missionaries sent to Africa by the fervent societies reported huge mountains with snow and vast lakes.

In 1856, two British explorers **Richard Francis Burton** (1821–1890) and **John Hanning Speke** (1827–1864) set off from Zanzibar to find the sources of the Nile with 152 persons in their caravan. They reached Tanganyika in February 1858. Burton had fallen ill and paused, while Speke pressed on and found Nyanza, which he called Lake Victoria and the source of the Nile, in August 1858. Burton was jealous and denied that Nyanza was the source. By the time they returned to Zanzibar in March 1859, both were deathly ill. Speke recovered first and returned to Britain twelve days ahead of Burton. He gave a public address on the expedition and received most of the credit.

Speke led a well-financed voyage from 1860 to 1863 and established that Victoria was the Nile's source and sailed down the river in triumph. All of the explorers penned best-selling books. Burton, backed by the missionary David

Livingstone, denounced Speke. Just as Burton and Speke were going to have a debate in 1864, Speke died in a mysterious gunshot accident.

# FRENCH INVOLVEMENT AROUND THE WORLD

## Algeria

France had taken over Algeria in 1830, and Napoleon III expanded its influence. He allowed natives to choose French citizenship if they wanted. He hoped that this would make things more equal between the French settlers and the natives. He introduced railroads, advanced irrigation, and new crops.

## Lebanon

France also became involved in Lebanon. After the Second Egyptian Crisis, Ibrahim Pasha had withdrawn from Lebanon and the area was divided between the Druze and the Maronite Christians. The Europeans who had compelled the Egyptian withdrawal remained involved, with the British sponsoring the Druze and the French supporting the Christians. Violence grew. In 1859, the Maronite peasants rose up against the nobles in the area of Mount Lebanon and demanded the end to privileges in imitation of the French Revolution. Having achieved that, Christian peasants in other areas began to rise up against the Druze nobles. The Ottomans intervened to support the Muslims, and some 10,000 Christians died in Damascus, including the American consul.

Napoleon III invoked a three hundred-year-old treaty that allowed France to protect Christians in the Ottoman Empire. The great powers of Europe sent a mainly French force to Lebanon under the command of Beaufort d'Hautpoul, who had been Ibrahim Pasha's Chief of Staff in the 1830s campaigns. The French withdrew in 1861 after the Ottoman Empire had separated the Lebanon province from the Syrian state.

## West Africa

A Bordeaux-based trading firm had urged the government to expand French involvement in Senegal. The government established a "Plan of 1854" to expand control of the Senegal river and take control of the acacia gum trade from the Africans. In 1854, Napoleon III appointed **Louis Faidherbe** as governor of Senegal. Faidherbe trained groups of African riflemen, founded the port of Dakar, and oversaw the telegraph link between Dakar and the fort of St. Louis. He defeated the Trarza Moors who had levied tolls on goods coming down river from the African interior. He built more forts along the coast and expanded power and trade up the Senegal river. After arriving by steamship and breaking Umar's ninety-seven day siege of Fort Medina, Faidherbe signed a treaty with the Muslim leader gaining concessions down to the Niger river. He also extended French control to the Gambia river. Napoleon III's government funded a railroad to go from Dakar to the Niger.

## The Suez Project

Khedive **Ismail** of Egypt, the grandson of Muhammad Ali, succeeded to the viceroyalty in 1863. The U.S. Civil War had increased the value of his cotton crop fivefold. Ismail spent the bounty freely on personal and developmental projects. Egypt gained a new army, palaces, theaters, and opera houses. He commissioned the world premiere of Giuseppe Verdi's opera *Aida*.

**Ferdinand de Lesseps** had gained a ninety-nine-year concession to build a Suez Canal from the previous viceroy. It cost 287,000,000 gold francs and took ten years instead of the planned six. The Khedive supplied forced laborers. French and Turkish sources provided the money while Britain had nothing to do with it. Egypt received 40 percent of the canal company's shares. The Canal reduced the voyage to India and Far East by half. The New York *Herald* said prophetically that the Canal would bring equatorial African discoveries within reach of British colonization. Napoleon III had married the Spanish princess Eugénie in 1856 and she was on the first ship that traveled through the canal in 1869. The Khedive followed on his ship, then Emperor Francis Joseph of Austria, and then seventy other vessels.

## Indochina

During the T'ay Son rebellion in 1777, the fifteen-year-old Prince **Nguyen Anh** had taken refuge with the French Bishop Pigneau de Behaine. In 1787, Pigneau and Nguyen Anh's son Prince Canh arrived at Versailles and appealed to King Louis XVI of France for help. The King pledged several thousand soldiers, but with the French financial crisis, the soldiers were not funded. Pigneau was able to pay for six hundred French soldiers himself and returned in 1789, just after the Chinese intervention had failed. Nguyen Anh took back Saigon and constructed fortresses on the French model. Several Frenchmen became high mandarins. By 1802, Nguyen Anh had taken Hué and Hanoi and proclaimed himself emperor of Annam with a new capital at Hué in the middle of a thin strip of farmable land. The last T'ay Son ruler was tied to four elephants and torn apart. For the first time, Vietnam had been united. He kept the old Le dynasty officials running the government in Hanoi and the Red river delta. The Nguyen emperors began to develop the Mekong delta south of Saigon.

When Nguyen Anh died in 1820, there were four French bishops in Vietnam. His son tried to ban French influence and French missionaries. Upon learning of the revolution of 1848 in France, the Vietnamese Emperor launched a wave of persecutions that killed twenty-five European priests, three hundred Vietnamese priests, and about 30,000 Vietnamese Christians.

In 1858, Napoleon III ordered a major intervention. The French and Spanish navy bombarded the port of Tourane (Da Nang). The Europeans were not able to occupy Hué, but they did occupy Saigon in the south and three provinces around it in 1859. Under the **Treaty of Saigon** (1862) France gained three eastern provinces of Cochin China and an indemnity of 20,000,000 francs. It allowed the free exercise of Catholicism and opened three ports to French trade. The King of Cambodia, a Hindu state dependent on Annam and Siam, accepted a French protectorate in 1863. In 1867 the French occupied the three southernmost provinces to round out Cochin China.

# THE MEXICAN ADVENTURE

Two institutions had dominated Mexico after it gained independence in the 1820s: the church and the army. The creole elite ruled Mexico. Iturbide had declared himself emperor, but the republicans overthrew him in 1823. **Antonio López de Santa Anna** (1794–1876) led their military force. In 1832, Santa Anna took direct power. Mexico had invited a group of American settlers led by Stephen Austin to settle the sparsely-populated province of Texas. Other settlers soon followed, and by 1835 Texas had an English-speaking population of 35,000. In 1830, Mexico abolished slavery in Texas. The Texans "freed" their slaves, then signed them to lifetime contracts of indentured servitude. Cultures clashed, and Mexico soon tightened control by abolishing the self-governance of all the states in Mexico. The Texans rebelled in 1836, defeated Santa Anna's army, and won independence. In the following year, however, Mexico fought off a French attack on Vera Cruz in the "pastry war" when France sought to recover loans and damage claims against Mexico. The war cost Santa Anna a leg.

Texas wanted to join the United States. Jackson and Van Buren put it off because the United States had renounced any claim to Texas in its 1819 treaty with Spain when the United States gained Florida. By 1844, annexation fever was sweeping the United States, not only for Texas, but for the western areas claimed by Mexico and Britain. There were perhaps 700 Americans settled in California, where 7,000 Mexicans lived. Another 5,000 Americans in the Willamette Valley of Oregon dwelled in uneasy coexistence with 750 Britons. **James K. Polk** (President 1845–1849) swept aside Van Buren as the Democratic Party leader. Polk settled the Oregon boundary at the 49th parallel, and sent a force into an area of Texas still claimed by Mexico, provoking the **U.S.-Mexican War** (1846–1848).

Mexico's loss shook the creole ruling structure. Conservatives argued that Mexico had to return to its Hispanic roots, protect the church and army, promote the old aristocracy, and perhaps even import a European monarch. The Liberals installed reforms in the mid-1850s, but conservatives counterattacked.

England, France, and Spain signed the **London Agreement** in October 1861 to regain debts from the liberal government and send a joint military expedition if necessary. They were able to do this and defy the Monroe Doctrine because the United States was embroiled in Civil War from April of 1861. Quarrels among the signatories led to the English and Spanish dropping out. Napoleon III sent 7,000 French soldiers to Mexico. The forces of **Benito Juárez** (d.1872), a Zapotec Indian, defeated them on May 5, 1862. The French emperor then increased the force to 30,000. The French army captured Mexico City in June 1863 and installed Maximilian von Habsburg, the brother of the Austrian Emperor Francis Joseph.

Napoleon III had covered a number of bases: he had bolstered Catholic resistance to possible Protestant American expansion, he had ideas of a Nicaraguan canal to link the Pacific and Atlantic Oceans as well as a Central American empire. Empress Eugénie was happy to see the liberals crushed. It provided a valuable diplomatic link with Austria. What could go wrong?

The adventure turned disastrous. Maximilian had no popular support and quarreled with the church over control of its lands. The U.S. Civil War ended in 1865, and Washington demanded that the French withdraw. The Prussians whipped Austria in a war of 1866. The French pulled out in February 1867. Juárez's forces quickly captured Maximilian and executed him. Juárez then broke the power of the Church by ending its 10 percent tax and introducing state-run schools. He also sold off some of the Church's property.

# TIMELINE

| | |
|---|---|
| 1802 | Nguyen Anh proclaims Empire of Annam |
| 1808 | Louis Napoleon Bonaparte born |
| 1831 | Bonaparte brothers take over Civita-Castellana |
| 1832 | Santa Anna takes power in Mexico |
| 1836 | Louis Napoleon attempts takeover and is exiled to the United States |
| | Texas war of independence |
| 1840 | Napoleon I's bones returned to Paris |
| | Louis Napoleon attempts takeover and is jailed |
| 1845 | U.S. annexes Texas |
| 1846–1848 | U.S.-Mexican War |
| 1846 | Louis Napoleon escapes from prison |
| 1848 | Revolutions inspire Vietnamese emperor to massacre Christian missionaries |
| | Louis Napoleon elected President |
| 1851 | Louis Napoleon overthrows Assembly and rules as Prince-President |
| 1852 | Louis Napoleon becomes Emperor Napoleon III |
| 1854 | Napoleon III appoints Louis Faidherbe as governor of Senegal |
| 1854–1856 | Crimean War |
| 1858 | Speke finds Victoria Nyanza, source of the Nile |
| 1860 | Napoleon III intervenes in Lebanon |
| 1862 | French gain three Indochinese provinces in Treaty of Saigon |
| 1863 | French army takes Mexico City and installs Maximilian von Habsburg |
| | Congress of Paris tries to redraw map of Europe |
| 1867 | Juárez's forces take Mexico and execute Emperor Maximilian |
| 1869 | Suez Canal opens |

# KEY TERMS

Crimean War
Congress of Paris
John Hanning Speke
Louis Faidherbe
Suez Canal
Nguyen Anh
Treaty of Saigon
Antonio López de Santa Anna
Benito Juárez

# PRIMARY SOURCE DOCUMENTS

**Benito Juárez**, http://historicaltextarchive.com/sections.
php?action=red&artid=144

**Charles Dudley Warner**, http://www.fordham.edu/Halsall/mod/1875nile.
asp

**Alfred, Lord Tennyson**, http://poetry.eserver.org/light-brigade.html

# Chapter 15

## NATION-STATE BUILDING

In the late 1850s and 1860s, the alternative of federative polity collapsed, and the nation-state ruled supreme. Confederations or possible confederations were destroyed in Italy, Germany, Denmark, Scandinavia, and the United States.

# THE UNIFICATION OF ITALY 1849-1871

## Piedmont-Sardinia and Cavour

After his disastrous showing against Austria, Charles Albert was forced to abdicate in favor of his son **Victor Emmanuel II** (ruled 1849–1878). The new king shared his father's ambition of a united Italy dominated by Sardinia. His Chief Minister Cavour agreed. The revolutions of 1848 had proved that Sardinia could not take on Austria by itself. It needed a great power. Cavour began to woo possible allies. He carried out a number of liberal economic reforms to impress the liberal powers Britain and France, then he elbowed his way into the Crimean War on their side to win respect. Cavour was driven by the fear that Mazzini and Garibaldi were still out there in exile and determined to unite Italy as a republic. In 1856, a Venetian, a Sicilian, and a Lombard founded an Italian National Society to promote unification under the Sardinian king.

# The Plombières Agreement

On January 14, 1858, the Italian nationalist Felice Orsini threw three grenades at the carriage of Napoleon III as the French emperor traveled to the opera. The emperor was unhurt and Orsini was guillotined, but this incident renewed Napoleon III's interest in Italian nationalism, a cause he and his brother had backed in 1831. On July 20, Cavour met with Napoleon III at Plombières les Bains, a French spa. The European elite men of the nineteenth were always going to rest at spas, and no one would be suspicious when they "accidentally" ran into each other. They agreed that if Sardinia and Austria went to war, France would support Sardinia. If Sardinia won, it would get Lombardy, Venetia, Parma, Modena and part of the papal states. An Italian confederation under the Pope would be set up. This was in keeping with Napoleon III's vision of "federative polity." France would get Nice and Savoy. Plon-Plon would marry one of Victor Emmanuel's daughters. Napoleon III then secured Russian noninterference by promising to seek a revision of the 1856 peace treaty. Prussia would support Austria only if France attacked. The British were in the middle of an election campaign and then spent two months trying to put together a coalition government.

# The War of 1859 and the Armistice of Villafranca

Austria quickly blundered into war. Sardinia had called for volunteer soldiers, and many who answered were draft dodgers from Lombardy. Austria used this as an excuse to attack Sardinia, not realizing the danger. In June of 1859, the French defeated Austria at the bloody **Battles of Magenta and Solferino**. The Austrians (as in 1848) fell back to their formidable "Quadrilateral" bases. Napoleon III concluded a ceasefire at Villafranca because he feared the ambitions of Sardinia and did not want to attack Austria's powerful fortresses. Sardinia gained Lombardy, but Austria still held Venetia. Villafranca mandated an Italian Confederation under the Pope's leadership, as the French Emperor had envisioned. Cavour regarded the agreement as a double-cross. Uprisings in Tuscany, Modena, the Romagna, and Parma led to calls for direct union with Piedmont-Sardinia as they feared anything less would allow a counterrevolution as had happened in 1849. The Pope's Swiss Guards slaughtered the revolutionaries of Perugia. Napoleon III got Nice and Savoy in return for letting Sardinia take direct control of Tuscany.

# Garibaldi's Conquest of Naples

Even though he had wanted a republic and not a monarchy, Giuseppe Garibaldi returned from exile to help the Sardinians in the war against Austria. After the peace, Cavour secretly prepared Garibaldi for an expedition to Sicily. The King of the Two Sicilies had just crushed a nationalist uprising and the prospects for success seemed low. Garibaldi landed in Sicily with a thousand red-shirted guerrillas. Sicily rose in June and July 1860, and Garibaldi won control as his force grew to 57,000. Naples fell in September.

Napoleon III was in a delicate position: Catholics would not forgive him if he let Garibaldi take Rome, but the Pope had put his troops under the command of a French general who supported monarchism over the Bonapartes. Cavour feared renewed republicanism, reached a new deal with Napoleon III, ordered Sardinian troops into the Papal States, and destroyed the Pope's army. This left the Pope with a small state protected by Napoleon III's soldiers. Perhaps following the example of José de San Martín, Garibaldi turned over his conquests to Sardinia rather than fight for an Italian Republic. In February 1861 an Italian Parliament gathered in Florence, declared Victor Emmanuel II King of Italy, and defeated all proposals for a decentralized confederation. Only Venetia (still under Austrian control) and the small Papal State around Rome were left out of the new kingdom.

# The Completion of Italian Unity

Piedmont did not treat the rest of Italy, especially southern Italy and Sicily, well. It stamped out local customs and law codes and forced northern Italian dialects on them. There was great resentment in the south against the wealth and power of the north. Italy gained Venetia in 1866 after allying with Prussia against Austria in the wars of German unification. Austria crushed the Italian armies in the fighting but when Prussia won, so did Italy.

Napoleon III reluctantly continued to protect Rome so as to make French Catholics happy. Garibaldi tried twice to take Rome but failed. When the Franco-Prussian war broke out in 1870, Napoleon III pulled them out, and the Italians moved in. Pope Pius IX refused to recognize the new government and barricaded himself in his palace. His successors continued this policy until 1929. The Church moved in a very reactionary direction: the Pope issued the *Syllabus of Errors* in 1864 that condemned all modern movements. He also called the first church council in more than three hundred years, which became known as the First Vatican Council (or **Vatican I** for short). Controversially, and perhaps contrary to Church Law, the Council put through the **Doctrine of Papal Infallibility** stating that when the Pope speaks officially in matters of faith and dogma, God is speaking through him and he cannot be in error. Since this doctrine was proclaimed in 1870, the Pope has invoked this only three times.

## Austria's Attempt at Confederation

Austria's defeat caused the fall of the emperor's chief advisers. Francis Joseph announced that he would enlarge the advisory Imperial Council to include large property owners. He restored Hungary's administrative unity and Magyar as its administrative language. The Empire held communal elections in November 1860. Francis Joseph issued a quasi-constitution called the **February Patent** in 1861. This created a bicameral Imperial Council consisting of a House of Lords (appointed by the Crown) and a House of Representatives that would be elected by estates diets—that meant large landowners. This Parliament would have the right to initiate legislation and pass the budget. Magyars, Italians, and Croatians boycotted the first meeting of the Imperial Council in May 1861. The system soon broke down, and the constitution was suspended in 1865.

## Toward Political Liberalism in France

After 1860, Napoleon III opened up public debate and allowed the legislature to hold an annual debate on the state of the nation. His government eased the press laws. In 1861, the legislature gained broader rights on the budget. There were liberal educational reforms and the government legalized strikes. After the French foreign policy setbacks of 1867 and 1869, there was even more liberalization and more voted than ever before. Finally, the ministers of the government became fully independent of the Emperor and completely responsible to the Legislature in 1870. Opposition was growing, but the public endorsed Napoleon III's government with 83 percent of the vote in May 1870.

## Reform and Federative Attempts in Russia

The Crimean War deeply humiliated Russia. The new Czar **Alexander II** (ruled 1855–81) struck out in new directions to bring Russia back to the level of the other Great Powers. The 1861 emancipation reform did not create legal equality: peasants still had to pay head tax, were tied to the communes, were subject to corporal punishment, recruited for the army, and would be judged by customary law. The government lifted the restrictions slowly: recruitment in 1874, the poll tax in 1885, corporal punishment in 1904, and passport restrictions in 1906. The reform gave land to the farming serfs, but not to the household serfs. Peasants would obtain about half of the land that they had worked, but had to compensate the landowners for that land. Because serfs lacked cash, the government gave bonds to the landowners, and the serfs would repay the state over a forty-nine-year period. Reschedulings and reassessments led to a law of 1896 that in some cases extended payment into the 1950s! The government offered an alternative: the peasant could take one-quarter of the land he had worked and pay nothing. In practice, peasants received 18 percent less land than they had worked, and in southern Russia, it was 40 percent less on average. They would have no access to forests and rivers without an additional payment. The reforms affected 52 million peasants, including more than 20 million who worked on private estates. Almost one-third of the farmland in Russia was transferred to the peasants between 1861 and 1877. The government followed with judicial, military, and financial reforms that finally created a central Bank of Russia. Despite educational expansion, only 9 percent of Russian children between ages seven and fourteen were attending school.

There was growing unrest in Poland after 1860. Many Polish nobles continued to dream of Poland reunited with the Lithuanian and Ukrainian lands lost in 1772. Many of the nobles had left after the failure of the Polish revolution of 1831. That left a substantial radical group that wanted an independent Polish republic. Alexander was willing to make some concessions but did not grant the Poles as much autonomy as Finland. At the end of 1862, Russians tried to conscript Poles into the Russian army. Revolt broke out in January 1863 and lasted for over a year. Prussia and Russia signed the **Alvensleben Convention** to suppress the revolt. Prussia agreed to return any fugitive rebels to Russia for harsh punishment. The significance was that Russia, angry at Austria for the Crimean betrayal, was moving toward Prussia. Russia had backed up Austria in the 1849–1850 war of words over the Erfurt Union and could have blocked German unification.

Finland remained quiet. Russia gradually loosened Finland's economic ties with Sweden by creating trade relations, a common coinage, and a new capital in Helsinki. Out of gratitude, Alexander II summoned a committee of forty-eight (twelve elected by each of four estates). Demonstrations demanded a summoning of the full Finnish diet for the first time since 1809. Alexander granted Finland a favored position within Russia in 1863. He allowed a four-estate Diet to meet every five years. In 1865/66 Finland gained its own currency and bank.

# THE UNIFICATION OF GERMANY

The Industrial Revolution had spread to western Germany after 1850. Prussia had established a customs union in 1834 to make trade easier in parts of the German Confederation. Austria refused to join in the founding, but Schwarzenberg was about to force Austria's entry on its terms when he died in 1852. Vast iron and coal reserves existed in the valleys of the Rhine and Ruhr rivers. By 1860, the German customs union had become the world's second-largest coal producer, far behind Britain. Big private banks were founded and provided capital for new businesses. Many of these businesses were established by liberals, a few of whom had been leaders in the 1848 revolution and retained their nationalism. Germans inspired by the Italian example founded their own National Society that leaned toward Prussia playing the role in Germany that Sardinia had in Italy.

After Austria forced Prussia to back down at Olmütz in 1850, Schwarzenberg had reduced Prussia's power in the Confederation. Still, angry from Prussia's bullying in the Erfurt Union, most of the middle-sized states supported Austria. The Austrians insisted on a majority ruling absolutely, marginalizing Prussia and a minority of states. Prussia appointed Otto von Bismarck as its representative at the Confederation. Bismarck waged a one-man war against Austrian influence, from symbolic rights to smoking a cigar to undermining a Federal navy. Bismarck regularly threatened Prussia's secession from the Confederation. He undermined attempts to create a unified patent and commercial law. The Confederation seemed to be moving toward standard weights and measure and perhaps coinage and money. The Austrians had ways of striking back at Prussian interests. Switzerland had reorganized its confederation in 1848 and separated powers. Prussia ruled the Swiss canton of Neuchâtel, felt its rights were reduced, and threatened an invasion in 1856. Austria led the Confederation denying the Prussian army passage to Switzerland. Napoleon III called for a conference, and Prussia lost control over Neuchâtel. In 1862, Austria pushed for the state parliaments to send delegates to write a common German civil and criminal law code, but Bismarck, now Prime Minister of Prussia, torpedoed it. In August 1863, the Austrians tried one last time by summoning a meeting of all the German princes to strengthen the Confederation. Only the King of Prussia refused, but that was enough, as in 1849, to scuttle the project.

## The Prussian Constitutional Conflict

Frederick William IV suffered a series of strokes and went insane. His younger brother **William I** (ruled 1861–88) became regent in 1858 and then King in 1861. The peculiar Prussian electoral system from the Constitution of 1850 gave great power to the rich. Frederick William and his advisers had assumed that the richest men in Prussia would always be the great landowners, especially those who lived east of the Elbe River (the *Junkers*). This was little more than absolutism with a mask. But by 1858, the richest men were liberal industrialists. The liberals won about 210 of about 300 seats in the Prussian House of Representatives. They were cautious, and the Prussian House of Lords easily voted down the few reforms they passed.

Frederick William's mobilization of the Prussian Army during the Crimean War had been disastrous, and preparedness during the Italian War of 1859 was hardly better. Clearly, there was a need to reform the armed forces. In February 1860, William proposed a bill that would 1) double the size of the regular army; 2) lengthen the term of service to three years, followed by reserve service for another four to five years; 3) diminish the role of the independent civilian militia; and 4) increase the military budget by 25 percent.

The House of Representatives tried to reduce the level of military increase, but William misused the money and claimed total control over the army's organization. The left wing of the liberals now formed an American-style political party called the **Progressive Party**. In the elections of 1861, the Progressives won more than a hundred seats, the moderate liberals had about 150 seats, and the conservatives had almost none in the House of Representatives. The House refused to grant any money for the military unless William conceded. William called for early elections in 1862, but the Progressives gained even more seats. The conservatives clamored for William to repeal the constitution, but he knew that this could cause a great uproar. He even contemplated abdicating in favor of his more liberal son.

# Bismarck Comes to Power

**Otto von Bismarck** was born in 1815 in the East Elbian lands of Prussia. He became prominent in 1848 as a bitter opponent of revolution in Prussia and the Frankfurt Parliament. Unlike most *Junker* conservatives, he was a German nationalist. William called him in as a hard liner and his last hope. Bismarck considered how to outmaneuver the liberals. He had a series of secret conversations with German socialist leader Ferdinand Lassalle, a moderate who had disagreed with Marx. Bismarck thought that perhaps he could win over factory workers and miners to an alliance with conservatives against the factory-owning liberals. They reached no agreement, and Lassalle died in a duel in 1864. Bismarck formulated a theory of a "constitutional gap": government employees collect and spend money and can theoretically do it without legislative approval if so ordered. Bismarck appropriated the money to the military as the King wished. He could maintain this policy as long as economic times remained good, and he did not have to ask the parliament to raise new taxes. Bismarck looked to war and foreign affairs to break the deadlock.

What could the Progressives have done? They could have tried calling a tax strike, but that probably would have failed. They feared the rise of the radicals from 1848 whom in their view had destroyed the revolution. They made no attempt to organize the people or call for universal voting rights. Out of 17 million people in Prussia, only 340,000 (2 percent) voted. That was not sufficient to claim a mandate. The liberals were happy with the three-class franchise system.

# The Danish and Austrian Wars

## Schleswig and Holstein

Lord Palmerston, the British Prime Minister, once said there were only three men in all Europe who understood the complexities of the Schleswig-Holstein question: one was dead, one went mad, and Palmerston himself was the third but had forgotten all the details. The Danish province of Holstein was almost entirely German, so a representative of the king of Denmark sat in the German Confederation. Schleswig was two-thirds German but not in the Confederation. Schleswig and Holstein contained about one-third of all Danish land, 40 percent of the population, and about half of the economic resources. Four hundred years before, Danish leaders had elected the Duke of Schleswig-Holstein as King. The nobles of Schleswig-Holstein had agreed to join Denmark if the king promised that the two provinces would never be divided.

In 1846, Danish King Christian VIII declared that if his son Frederick VII had no legitimate sons (which was a virtual certainty because of his numerous sexual affairs with commoners) the Duchies of Schleswig-Holstein would be inherited along with the rest of Denmark. The German Duke of Augustenburg challenged this: he wanted the territories' inheritance considered under German Salic Law, which forbade inheritance from going through a woman and thus would make him heir to the Duchies. The Assemblies of the Duchies agreed and refused to accept Christian's letter.

At the beginning of 1848, Frederick VII became king, renounced absolutism, and agreed to a constituent assembly. The resulting constitution did not apply to the Duchies. The revolutions of 1848 had brought war as German nationalists in Schleswig-Holstein rebelled against King Frederick.

Prussia supported the rebellion, but when it pulled out, the Danish government crushed the uprising. The Concert of Europe met and agreed to the **Protocol of London** (May 1852). All the great powers recognized Prince Christian of Glücksburg as Frederick VII's heir to the entire kingdom including the Duchies. It forbade any closer Danish links with one Duchy alone and reaffirmed Holstein's position in the German Confederation. Augustenburg would receive some financial compensation.

King Oscar of Sweden pursued his own dreams. Sweden had intervened to help Denmark in 1848. In the 1850s, Oscar promoted the idea of a Scandinavian Confederation. Sweden would make a full military alliance with Denmark and when King Frederick died, Sweden would take control of Denmark, contrary to the London Protocol. The Danish Foreign Minister objected and demanded that any treaty obligate Sweden to defend Holstein. Oscar then tried to interest Napoleon III in the idea of having the great powers divide Schleswig, add the southern part to Holstein and make it a separate state for Christian of Glücksburg.

In 1863, Denmark put out a new arrangement that denied Holstein a veto right over laws for Schleswig and Denmark. This effectively took full control of Schleswig contrary to the London Protocol and the 1460 agreement. King Frederick died suddenly. Christian of Glücksburg took the throne, ending Swedish interest in the problem and the possible Scandinavian Confederation.

This arcane legal battle should never have led to war. But Bismarck was trying to win glory against the liberals of the Prussian Parliament, and Francis Joseph was trying to bounce back from the Italian defeat of 1859. Prussia and Austria declared war on Denmark and crushed the small country in a short war. Denmark lost the Duchies, and the Germans forced the Danish-speakers out of Schleswig. Austria wanted a separate independent state under Augustenburg because it was too far from Vienna to control. Bismarck instead got Austria to agree to the temporary **Convention of Gastein** (August 1865): Austria would administer Holstein, and Prussia Schleswig. Bismarck had lured Austria into a trap.

Bismarck met Napoleon III at Biarritz in October 1865 and hinted at concessions to France in the Rhineland and maybe Luxemburg. In April 1866, Prussia made a secret alliance with Italy against Austria, violating the German Confederation's constitution. Bismarck appeased liberals by calling for a democratic reform that would allow all men to vote for representatives to the Confederation. Bismarck always championed universal manhood suffrage because he saw that as things stood, the liberal middle class could outvote the conservative elite. If conservative peasants and artisans and the lower middle class gained equal voting rights, they would overwhelm the liberals. He saw how Napoleon III had used universal manhood suffrage to bolster his power. Bismarck's miscalculation was that he did not anticipate the rising numbers of socialist industrial workers in the future. Austria also gained Napoleon III's neutrality. The French emperor hoped that Austria and Prussia would wear each other out in a long war, and that he would be stronger as a mediator. The smaller states tended to support Austria because they feared Prussia more, but they could contribute little to the struggle. When the Confederation condemned Prussia's aggression, the Prussians seceded from the union.

## The Seven Weeks' War

The war went badly for Austria. Its military staff was behind the times. The Prussian breech-loaded "needle gun" could fire five to seven rounds a minute with the soldier lying down, while the Austrians could only shoot three to five rounds a minute and had to stand exposed. Because Austria had not built enough railroads, it could not move its troops fast enough to face the Prussians. At the **Battle of Königgrätz** (July 3, 1866), Austria lost badly on the same day that Prussian conservatives gained almost half the seats in the House of Representatives. Half a million fought in this battle and one-quarter were killed or wounded, a warning of the growing bloodiness of modern warfare.

Bismarck wanted a quick peace and lenient terms before Napoleon III could stick his nose into the situation. At the critical moment the French emperor had fallen ill. The **Peace of Prague** (August 1866) separated Austria from the rest of Germany and gave Venetia to Italy. The rest of the German Confederation suffered more. Prussia annexed some territories such as Hanover entirely. William felt bad about taking Hanover from a king who was blind and whose family's nobility was older than William's Hohenzollern family. The Confederation itself came to an end. Bismarck oversaw the creation of the **North German Confederation**: the twenty-two states north of the Main river joined together under Prussian pressure. The president of this confederation would always be the King of Prussia. It had a bicameral legislature: the Reichstag elected by universal manhood suffrage had budget powers and the right to approve or disapprove all laws but could not initiate laws. The Upper House (the Federal Council) was appointed by the princes and effectively controlled by Prussia. It could veto laws and had to approve amendments. The King would pick the ministers, and they were not responsible to Reichstag control.

## Effect on Austria

After the 1859 defeat in Italy, Austria had considered reforms. When Austria's domination of Germany ended once and for all on the field of Königgrätz, it needed to make peace with the Hungarians and set up a "Dual Monarchy" in the *Ausgleich* (Compromise) of 1867. There would be one imperial and royal army and joint responsibility for foreign policy, military affairs, and financial matters. Each half (Austria and Hungary) would have its own parliament and control over domestic affairs with its own cabinet of ministers. While this finally liberated the Hungarians, it made matters worse for the smaller nationalities, who were caught under two layers of government and began to agitate for independence.

### Effect on Prussia

If 1848 was one "turning point that failed to turn," 1862 to 1866 was another as Bismarck foiled the liberals. The Progressives split in October 1866 as the moderates joined others to form the National Liberal Party (NLP) which became Bismarck's main support until 1879. The NLP joined the conservatives in retroactively approving the illegal budgets that Bismarck had used from 1862 to 1866. The remaining Progressives still opposed Bismarck. The middle class, rather than asserting its own values as it did in other countries, instead sought to imitate the great aristocrats. Democracy was stunted. Bismarck's strategy was proved when elections were held under the new laws in 1867. The Progressives won only nineteen of 297 seats in the Reichstag.

# Problems of Unification

The three southern German states (Bavaria, Württemberg, and Baden) refused to join the North German Confederation. Bismarck had to create a situation where the other states would willingly ally with the Confederation against another threatening power. Napoleon III had been disappointed by the 1866 result and sought compensation if Germany united because he realized that the new power would be a colossus. He sought Luxemburg, Belgium, or parts of the Rhineland. This came to nothing. He made concessions to the liberals to get a French army reform bill through the Parliament, in contrast to the Prussians. He desperately tried to conclude an anti-Prussian alliance with Austria and Italy. The Austrians were still weak, and Hungary would not support a new war. Italy declined a French alliance. Bismarck kept Russia neutral by promising help in the growing disputes in southeastern Europe and in revising the 1856 Peace of Paris.

## The Franco-Prussian War

Bismarck decided it was time to move. Spain had been suffering unrest since the 1820s, and many felt that it should start over with a new king. Spanish leaders offered the throne to William I's Catholic cousin, much to France's alarm as it feared encirclement. At the spa of Ems, the French ambassador Benedetti spoke with the vacationing William I and got him to drop the plan. But in Berlin, Bismarck edited the text of the king's telegram (**the Ems Dispatch**) to make the words look much harsher and seem that William had insulted Benedetti. France declared war on Prussia on July 19, 1870.

The southern German states joined the Confederation troops, giving Germany a two-to-one advantage in troops with better supplies and better administration. The Germans captured Napoleon III and an army of 100,000 at Sedan. When the news reached Paris, revolutionaries overthrew the government and proclaimed a republic. The new leaders called on the people to resist the Germans. After a long siege, the Germans took Paris. France lost 580,000 killed, wounded, or taken prisoner. Bismarck demanded and got elections which resulted in the election of Adolphe Thiers as President.

The German princes gathered outside of Paris at the palace of Versailles and proclaimed William I as first emperor of Germany. The Empire's constitution was just the North German Confederation's constitution extended to more states. Bismarck became the Chancellor of the Empire. The **Treaty of Frankfurt** (May 1871) was a very harsh peace because unlike Austria, France would be irreconcilable, and Bismarck wanted to keep it down. Under the Treaty, Germany took the rich provinces of Alsace and Lorraine from France along with five billion francs of indemnity. There would be a German army of occupation until France paid. Bismarck figured it would take the French many years to pay this off. Russia got the straits clause of 1856 nullified so it could finally send its warships through the Bosporus and Dardanelles.

# NATION-STATE BUILDING IN NORTH AMERICA

## Civil War in the United States

Coming out of the Revolution, the United States had split along lines drawn during the mercantilist era by the British: the northern states depended on trade and manufacturing, while the southern states focused on growing slave-dependent cash crops such as cotton and tobacco. The invention of the cotton 'gin caused a great expansion of slavery across the South in cotton plantations. The abolition of slavery by Mexico caused a revolt by the Texas slaveholders, who first won independence from Mexico in 1836 and then joined the United States in 1845. The South kept a balance in the Senate through the 1840s: for each free state admitted, a slave state was admitted. The South was overrepresented in the House of Representatives, because the Constitution considered each slave to be three-fifths of a human being though the states did not permit slaves to vote. For the same reason, the South dominated presidential elections. Every president elected before 1860 was from a slave state or supported slavery.

By 1850, slavery was in trouble. The North grew harsher in condemning slavery as it began to build industry and immigrants swelled northern numbers. In 1853, the New York to Chicago railroad opened, shifting trade away from the Mississippi river. The newer states were not well suited to cotton farming: the South had taken what it could. A battle over free trade grew as the new northern factories wanted protection from British industry with high tariffs while the South feared a retaliatory tariff against cotton and other products.

The nation was held together, as it had been since independence, by concern over the western boundary. The United States and Britain jointly administered the sparsely-populated but fur-rich area of the Pacific territory between Mexico and Russian America to the north. There were growing calls for the United States to seize the entire Oregon territory. Then Mexican California suddenly sprang to the forefront. As the Irish potato famine began in 1845, some Irish resettled in California, and rumors began that Britain was about to buy California from Mexico and flood the land with Irish refugees. Unable to fight Britain and Mexico simultaneously, the United States split the Oregon territory, cutting off California from the British lands.

In the **Mexican War** (1846–48), the United States defeated Mexico and took the areas of California, Nevada, Arizona, New Mexico, and part of Colorado. Unexpectedly, gold was discovered in California and hundreds of thousands of "forty-niners" swarmed in hoping to get rich quick. It became apparent that the population was large enough for California to apply for statehood. Outnumbered at the polls, the slaveowners unleashed murder and terror to try to win their way, but the majority of Californians banned slavery in their state. The bitter fight shifted to Congress. California came in as the sixteenth free state, breaking the balance with the slave states, but the **Compromise of 1850** gave southern slaveowners greater rights in tracking down runaway slaves. Fighting broke out over whether Kansas would be a free or slave state. The Republican Party was founded as an anti-slavery party. Still, there could be hope of averting a war. Most places had freed slaves with some kind of compensation. Two-thirds of the southerners owned no slaves. But the elite believed things would never change, and most southerners feared losing their white privilege whether they owned slaves or not. The Supreme Court failed to resolve things with a pro-slavery ruling in the **Dred Scott Case** (1857) and lost credibility. In the 1860 presidential election, the Democrats split and nominated northern and southern candidates. The Republicans nominated **Abraham Lincoln** (President 1861–65) on a platform of no extension of slavery.

The South realized that if Lincoln were elected, more free states would be admitted, and the North would become stronger and stronger. The southern states had promoted the theory that individual states made up the union in 1787 and could leave when they wanted. When Lincoln won, South Carolina seceded from the Union, followed by six other slave states. They proclaimed the **Confederate States of America** (C.S.A.) that asserted in its constitution that slavery was a basic right and demanded two-thirds votes to take effective action.

In those days, there was a five-month lag between the election and the inauguration. This gap allowed the C.S.A. to seize most federal armories. When South Carolina bombarded one of few forts that had not surrendered in April 1861, Lincoln called for 75,000 volunteers and the **Civil War** was on. Virginia, Arkansas, North Carolina and Tennessee joined the C.S.A. rather than provide volunteers. The North had 23 million people against six million whites in the Confederacy. The North had better industry and finance. The North blockaded the Confederacy so cotton could not get out. The North made little progress in the first year as the Confederacy ordered conscription. For the first years, the C.S.A. armies went at the northerners in set battles. The North could replace soldiers easily, while the Confederacy's armies got smaller and more threadbare. The C.S.A. hoped that Britain and France would intervene. It was true that Napoleon III's dreams in Mexico and Central America depended on a Confederate victory. But the French Emperor deferred to Britain. Charles Francis Adams, son and grandson of presidents, ably represented the United States in London. Britain substituted Indian and Egyptian cotton for that of America. The Palmerston/Gladstone government was uneasy with a slave government and, finally, there was never a point where a southern victory appeared possible.

Lincoln decided that the soldiers needed a moral cause to fight for; the abstract of preserving the Union was not enough. Lincoln issued the **Emancipation Proclamation** (1863) setting slaves free without compensation to the owners. This only applied to the rebel states, so few slaves were freed at first. However, it increased U.S. support in Europe and encouraged slaves behind the lines to flee, revolt, and free themselves. After four bloody years of fighting, the North wore down the South and defeated it at a total cost of 600,000 killed and 400,000 wounded on both sides. Lincoln was assassinated by John Wilkes Booth, a Confederate sympathizer named after the great English reformer.

While the South was out, the Congress outlawed slavery in the **Thirteenth Amendment** to the Constitution. Congress passed tariffs to protect new industries up to 47 percent of the value of manufactured goods and encouraged settlement of the West in the **Homestead Act**. It granted land at 30,000 acres per member of Congress to support state agricultural colleges. It subsidized a transcontinental railroad, which was completed in 1869. In 1867 Russia sold Alaska to the United States for $7.2 million. The **Fourteenth Amendment** added American citizenship to state citizenship and defined it. The United States emerged as a solid nation-state that was industrializing rapidly.

# The Dominion of Canada

In the 1850s telegraphs and railroads began to link the Maritime Provinces to the Canadas. In the 1850s and 1860s British North Americans adopted a decimal currency in place of the British system. The Crimean War stimulated the Canadian grain industry as Britain was cut off from the Russian supply. The American Civil War meant even more demand for Canadian goods. Following the revolutions of 1848, Britain granted responsibility to Prince Edward Island, New Brunswick, and Newfoundland. The **Colonial Laws Validity Act** (1865) gave the colonial parliaments the right to amend their constitutions and even erect trade barriers against Britain. In the aftermath of the Oregon Treaty, the British had created a colony of Vancouver Island on the Pacific while the rest of the area remained unorganized and under the administration of the Hudson's Bay Company. This changed in 1858 when the colonial governor sent gold ore from the Fraser Canyon to the mint in San Francisco. Tens of thousands of Americans headed north, and the alarmed British colonial office, fearing American capture of the land, organized the interior into the colony of British Columbia. Subsequent gold rushes led to rapid development. British Columbia and Vancouver Island merged in 1866.

The 1860s saw sectional differences accelerating. Railroads had created enormous public debts with little tax revenue. This revived the earlier suggestion of a union. Ambitious politicians supported the idea. The British government, withdrawing into isolation, saw colonies as needless financial drags. The U.S. Civil War also raised issues of defense because Lincoln had created a massive army of 2.2 million men. What if the United States next invaded Canada, as some American officials were urging? Britain had neither the soldiers nor the money to defend Canada. It put heavy pressure on the colonies to accept union.

The 1867 **British North American Act** established the Dominion of Canada with elected provincial assemblies, a national parliament, and an appointed Senate that gave Ontario, Québec, and the Maritimes equal representation. Federative polity had triumphed in Canada. **John A. Macdonald** and George-Étienne Cartier, who preserved French-Canadian culture, were mainly responsible for drafting Canada's constitution. The Hudson's Bay Company turned over its western lands in 1869. Macdonald became Canada's first Prime Minister and persuaded Prince Edward Island and Manitoba to join the Dominion. In the west, British Columbia needed government aid to develop the area even as it feared U.S. annexation. It joined Canada in return for promises to build a transcontinental railroad and assume the debts of the colony. A Canadian Pacific Railway linked the Atlantic to the Pacific in 1885. These events marked the first peaceful granting of liberty to a colony.

# TIMELINE

| | |
|---|---|
| 1846–48 | U.S.-Mexican War |
| 1850 | California admitted to the United States |
| 1859 | France and Sardinia defeat Austria |
| 1859–67 | Constitutional crisis in Prussia |
| 1860 | Garibaldi takes southern Italy |
| | Lincoln elected President |
| 1861 | Kingdom of Italy proclaimed |
| 1861–65 | U.S. Civil War |
| 1862 | Bismarck becomes Prime Minister of Prussia |
| | Fraser Canyon gold rush begins British Columbia's development |
| 1864 | Austria and Prussia defeat Denmark and take Schleswig and Holstein |
| 1866 | Prussia and Italy defeat Austria and most of the German Confederation |
| | Prussia gains Schleswig, Italy takes Venetia |
| 1867 | British North American Act creates Dominion of Canada |
| | Compromise reforms Austro-Hungarian Empire |
| 1870–71 | Franco-Prussian War |

Italy takes over Rome

1871        German Empire proclaimed

# KEY TERMS

Camillo di Cavour
Giuseppe Garibaldi
Otto von Bismarck
Treaty of Frankfurt
Abraham Lincoln
Emancipation Proclamation

# PRIMARY SOURCE DOCUMENTS

**Giuseppe Garibaldi**, http://www.fordham.edu/halsall/mod/1860garibaldi.html

**Otto von Bismarck**, http://history.hanover.edu/texts/bis.html

**Emancipation Proclamation**, http://odur.let.rug.nl/~usa/P/al16/writings/emancip.htm

# Chapter 16

## REVOLUTION IN CHINA AND JAPAN

## The Taiping Rebellion

The Treaty of Nanjing was followed by similar treaties with the United States and France in 1844. The French insisted on toleration of Christianity, which had been prohibited in 1724. Trade boomed in Shanghai. Forty-four foreign ships entered Shanghai in 1844; ten times that number traded in 1855. Foreign residents practically took over the city by the 1860s.

The Chinese administration continued to deteriorate. More people organized secret societies against the Manchus, especially in the South. One of these rebels was **Hong Hiuxiu** (1814–64), a Hakka peasant who had failed the exam to join the civil service. This was not a surprise since 99 percent failed the test and Hong lacked the funds to bribe the test examiner. He had picked up some Protestant Christian tracts in Quangzhou and became convinced that God had chosen him to conquer and reform China. This was reinforced when he spent two months in 1847 in Quangzhou studying under an American missionary. He and his followers attacked Buddhist and Taoist temples and criticized Confucianism. In 1850, the police tried to arrest Hong in Guangxi province. Hong and his followers attacked the police.

This began the Taiping Rebellion, so called because Hong proclaimed himself as the founder of a new ruling dynasty, the T'ai P'ing ("Great Peace"). He ordered followers to show their opposition to the Manchus by abandoning the queue hairstyle. Hong denounced opium, tobacco, gambling, alcohol, adultery, prostitution, and footbinding of women. He called for equality of the sexes and literacy for the masses. The Qing rulers called them "long-haired bandits." In 1852, the untended Yellow River began a massive shift of hundreds of miles to the north. This was its first major shift since 1194 and caused tremendous destruction. The Grand Canal that linked the Yellow and Yangtze rivers became blocked in 1855. This suggested to many that the Qing had lost the "Mandate of Heaven" since natural events were supposed to indicate divine approval or disapproval of the regime. The rebellion moved north to the Yangtze river, then came down in boats and captured Nanjing in 1853. The Taipings destroyed Yongle's magnificent 260-foot Porcelain Pagoda. The peasants had hoped for land reform when Hong promised egalitarian communities such as his "brother" Jesus had created, but the Taiping plundering seemed to justify the Qing designation of bandit. The Taipings did not set up an adequate administration. They reformed the calendar and outlawed opium use. The Taiping army grew to half a million soldiers. Every province was in rebellion, but the bureaucracy remained loyal. The religious fanaticism alienated other secret societies. The Qing hired Mongol cavalry which protected Beijing from the Taiping attack. Seeing little help from the Qing, local scholar-landowners organized their own militias. In another context, they would have been called *caudillos*. Zeng Guofan organized the most significant one, then raised other armies and put them under his associates Li Hongzhang and Zuo Zongtang. For the first time under the Qing, armies were led by Chinese, not Manchus. The militias defeated the Taipings and reduced them to Nanjing and a few other areas.

The Taiping rebellion touched off other revolts. A secret society in Shanghai attacked the International Settlement in 1853 and held much of the city for over a year. The revolt destroyed the Chinese administration, and the foreigners chose their own inspector who would collect the trade duties on imported goods. There was more unrest as the Taiping rebellion inspired the Muslims in western China to rebel in 1855 and 1862. Bandits controlled much of the northeast in the 1850s and 1860s. The revolts killed millions and destroyed precious capital.

Chinese-European war broke out in Quangzhou after the Chinese authorities boarded a ship accused of piracy. The murky circumstances and the violence of the British response actually caused the Palmerston government to fall in Britain, but an election restored his strength and endorsed a military action. The British and French seized Quangzhou, sailed to the Hai river, and then up the river to Tianjin. The **Treaty of Tianjin** (1858) opened more ports to trade, including several up the Yangtze river, allowed foreigners to travel freely in China and set up embassies in Beijing. But then the government repudiated this treaty and killed British and French diplomats. In a separate agreement, Russia gained part of the Pacific coast and established their city of Vladivostok.

The British and French advanced in wrath on Beijing and burned the Summer Palace. The emperor fled and left behind his younger brother **Yixin** (or **Prince Gong**) (d.1898). Yixin signed a new treaty affirming the Treaty of Tianjin, paying damages to the foreigners, and opening Tianjin itself to trade.

# Cixi and Yixin

## European Assistance

The emperor died in 1861, leaving a five-year-old boy as emperor. He had provided for an eight-man regency. However, the former emperor's widow **Ci'an** and the young emperor's mother **Cixi, the Empress Dowager** (1835–1908) plotted with Yixin to overthrow the regents. When the court returned to Beijing, the three formed what amounted to a co-regency. Yixin moved into the estate that had once been Heshen's opulent mansion. The Taipings broke loose from Nanjing and raged down the Yangtze toward Shanghai. The westerners, who had originally sympathized with this "Christian" movement, now agreed that the Taipings were bandits. The merchant community paid for a Chinese force under the command of the American Frederick Ward. When Ward was killed in 1862, the British major **Charles Gordon** took command. Gordon and the independent militias penned up Hong in Nanjing. In 1864, Hong committed suicide and the war that had killed perhaps 30 million people was finally over. The northeastern bandits were suppressed by 1868. The Muslim rebels held out until 1878.

The Westerners now felt they were part of the Chinese order and should defend it. They helped reorganize accounts and administration. They assisted in building lighthouses, improving harbors and rivers, and setting up a postal service. Telegraph cables linked Vladivostok, Nagasaki, Shanghai, Hong Kong, and Singapore. While westerners benefited from all these things, they were also good for the Chinese economy and society. Yixin set up the first Ministry of Foreign Affairs in 1861, then a College of Foreign Languages in 1862 in Beijing and a school for western science and mathematics in Shanghai in 1863. Zheng Guofan died mysteriously in Nanjing while living in Hong's old palace. His proteges Li and Zuo played important military, political, and diplomatic roles for the next thirty years. In 1872, the government sent the first Chinese students to Europe and the United States. Customs revenues from Shanghai paid for this "Self-Strengthening Movement." These programs had mixed success. The shipyard and gunpowder plants established in the

1860s were so inefficient that it was cheaper to import ships and weapons. Like the Enlightened Despots, the scholar-landowners were not willing to transform society.

# Korea

Korea had become a vassal state to the Qing dynasty in 1637. In theory, it remained under Chinese domination, but Korea was virtually independent by 1800. Europeans tried to invade after the Korean government executed nine priests. The French in 1866 and the Germans in 1867 attempted expeditions but were driven off by the Koreans. Korea did not establish relations with any outside country until 1876, when it forged ties with Japan.

# The Genesis of Capitalism in Japan

Japan is the one country outside of Europe that generated capitalism on its own. A vital precondition was controlling population growth. The population was 30 million in the 1721 census and 32 million in the 1872 census. Crop production grew 65 percent from 1598 to 1834. The population in those years had grown by 45 percent, so labor productivity grew 14 percent. Land productivity also seemed to grow. Japan enjoyed 250 years without a serious war or revolution, though the disturbances grew more intense in the last hundred years of the shogunate. The shoguns had used guns to come to power in 1600 but then strictly forbade them. The shogun levied a rice tax of 30 to 50 percent that increased pressure on society. Japanese men and women delayed marriage, practiced contraception, and resorted to killing children in hard times. For some reason, Japanese women stopped bearing children in their middle thirties, much sooner than most women around the world. The average size of the household fell nearly 20 percent between 1800 and 1870.

There was a clear rise in the living standards, even for peasants. For example, cotton clothing became common. This helped to create a domestic market, unlike China. The shoguns prevented the great lords (*daimyo*) from piling up wealth by enforcing an "alternate attendance system" where the lords had to live every other year at Edo and leave their families as hostages. The high road from Kyoto to Edo was crowded with people and inns. This transferred wealth from the lords to the ordinary people and created many jobs. Large estates were broken down into smaller family-sized units. Rich peasants preferred to concentrate on the best land, rent out the rest, and invest profits in the new village industries of *sake*, cotton spinning, weaving, and dyeing. Some invested in tobacco or mulberry leaves to raise silk. This was in contrast to the pattern in the rest of the world where prosperity in land or trade usually led to the purchase of more land. Rich peasants challenged merchants and moved into trade by the late eighteenth century. Rice brokers, sake merchants, and pawnbrokers became richer than the samurai and the *daimyo*. Edo became an economic and cultural hub. The shogunate lifted the ban on foreign books in 1720.

While foreign merchants were confined to Nagasaki, a single large market was created in Japan. Like Britain, Japan is a series of islands and this aided transport and kept costs down. Sea transport had to grow because the shogunate deliberately destroyed bridges, imposed checkpoints, and banned wheeled transport from the roads to control the populace. Japan used coins and varieties of paper money. The rapid increase of the money supply outpaced the productivity growth and caused price inflation, especially in the first third of the nineteenth century. The volume of money in circulation grew by 80 percent from 1816 to 1841 and another 50 percent from 1841 to the 1880s. Rice markets in Edo and Osaka dealt in commodities futures just like Amsterdam. There was a high literacy rate: in 1850 perhaps 45 percent of men and 15 percent of women could read and write, more than Russia at that time and about the same as the American South. Most merchants lived under the control of the lenient shogun, not feudal lords. Japanese merchants enjoyed less confiscation or ruinous taxation and controls than most Asian merchants.

# The Opening of Japan

These social pressures and economic changes created an irresistible force that would break the immovable object of the shogunate. The old system was gradually decaying. Nobles fell into deep debt to the merchants. In 1814, the first **Shinto** ("the way of the gods") sect was established. Under Shinto, the Emperor, shut away in Kyoto by the shoguns, was the son of heaven. It stressed patriotism and faith-healing. Over time, about half the population of Japan would support Shinto, as it surpassed Buddhism.

There was growing pressure in Japanese society to expand foreign trade. The nobles hoped that foreign trade might restore their wealth; lesser lords were willing to enter careers in the army or the civil service. Merchants looking for money wanted to trade abroad. Patriots feared falling behind in military technology. The Japanese authorities were well aware of what had happened in China with the Opium War and its aftermath.

In 1853 and again in 1854, Commodore **Matthew Perry** sailed into Edo harbor with one-quarter of the United States Navy. He demanded that Japan open trade. Two earlier American negotiators had failed at this. Fishing ships in the North Pacific wanted to have a refueling and repair center. Japan had no navy and its coastal defenses could not withstand an American attack. The shogun's government (the *bafuku*) signed the **Treaty of Kanagawa** in 1854. This was not as severe as the Chinese Treaty of Nanjing, but did open two more ports to trade. The European countries now demanded that they receive at least equal treatment as the Americans. In 1858, the American diplomat Townsend Harris got the shogun's government to sign a new treaty opening more ports and allowing foreign travel in Japan. A crisis occurred when the Emperor refused to endorse the treaty. The powers of shogun and emperor were on a collision course. Complicating everything was the problem that the shogun Iesada was ill and physically weak, then died in 1858. He named Iemochi, a twelve-year-old boy, as his successor over the candidate of the xenophobes.

A number of warlords, especially the lords of Satsuma and Choshu in the southwest, saw the treaties as a way of overthrowing the shogunate if they could charge that the shoguns were weak and betraying Japan. Unlike the Emperor, the shoguns had a precise knowledge of the westerners' military capacities and knew what they had done to China when it resisted. An extremist samurai murdered the head of the *bafuku* council in 1860. In 1863, the Emperor summoned Iemochi to Kyoto (the first summons in 230 years) and issued an order to "drive out the barbarians." Lords launched private wars against westerners. Increased trade had disrupted the monetary system and the ratio of gold to silver. Intense foreign demand for Japanese goods caused their prices to rise and made them unaffordable to some Japanese. The antiforeign reaction that developed in Japan was nationalism instead of Chinese-style disdain. Two key differences between China and Japan were centralization and homogeneity. The westerners moved warships into Osaka Bay in 1865 and forced the Emperor to sign the treaties.

# The Meiji Restoration

Provincial lords built a new army from conscripted peasants rather than relying on the samurai. In 1866, the *daimyo* of Choshu illegally bought guns that were surplus from the U.S. Civil War and armed his troops. The new army was superior to the old army of the shogun. Iemochi died in 1866, and was replaced by Keiki, the candidate of the xenophobes. In January 1867, the Emperor died of smallpox at the age of thirty-six. There was suspicion that Choshu radicals had assassinated him, perhaps with an infected handkerchief, because he and Keiki seemed about to agree on a program to modernize the army on French lines and buy massive amounts of modern weapons from the United States. The new Emperor was **Mutsuhito** (ruled 1868–1912), only fourteen years old. Keiki resigned as shogun in November 1867 without designating a successor. Keiki may have expected to be named as a Prime Minister, but soldiers from Satsuma and Choshu flooded into Kyoto to block any such move. Reformers, chiefly young samurai from the outlying provinces, declared the emperor restored to full authority. There was a brief war between the Tokugawa supporters and the lords of Satsuma and Choshu, but the latter prevailed.

Mutsuhito presided over the *Meiji* ("Enlightened") era. The imperial capital moved from Kyoto to Edo (renamed Tokyo), and the Emperor took over the shogun's administration. The Emperor swore that the public would rule and that he would call an assembly. The warlords surrendered their territories and the Emperor gave them other areas to govern. This broke the traditional ties between the lords and their lands. The central government maintained its right to tax and control lands. In the **Five Articles Oath**, the Emperor swore to convene deliberative assemblies, have public discussion of issues, allow people to have the occupation of their choice and base laws on the just laws of Nature. He called for gaining knowledge to strengthen rule. Having used the xenophobes to gain power, the Emperor's supporters dropped all antiforeign policies.

Reforms rapidly transformed the government into a division among legislative, administrative, and judicial functions with a number of ministries. They divided Japan into three urban prefectures and seventy-two other prefectures. The warlords realized that centralization was necessary to resist the West.

The government continued payments to the samurai and warlords to keep them happy. Since they comprised up to 6 percent of the population, this was a considerable expense. Finances were very difficult at first: revenues covered only one-third of the 1868 budget. In 1871, the government introduced a decimal currency of yen throughout Japan. Agricultural taxes would be based on land value, not yields. Interest rates were high at 10 percent a year. The government jump-started the modern cotton industry and imported higher-quality fibers. The government ordered universal education in 1872. It developed Hokkaido island to the north. Japan adopted the western calendar in 1873 and accepted religious toleration. In the same year, the rice tax was converted to a money tax, costing 40 to 50 percent of peasant yields. The samurai class was abolished and all peasant dependency on the nobles was removed. The government compensated the samurai by giving them bonds. However, rampant inflation in the 1870s cut the real value of paper money in half. This reduced the tax bite on the peasants but ruined many of the samurai who were holding government bonds. The government initiated sharp deflation to bring this under control and established the Bank of Japan in 1882. There is an old saying that the revolution eats its children. This was never truer than in Japan. The samurai and *daimyo* had overthrown the shogun with the aim of taking control. Instead, they had lost their lands, peasants, and wealth. When the samurai plotted a war to loot Korea, the modernizers blocked that scheme because it would divert precious investment. Finally, a Satsuma samurai sparked a futile revolt that marked the final triumph of the merchants and rich peasants.

# Economic Takeoff

The government took the leading role in organizing and encouraging business, especially mining. It introduced the railroad in 1872 and built 1,349 miles of track by 1890. It paid for this by taking a foreign loan. The railroad was critical to development because of Japan's rugged terrain and expensive overland costs. The rickshaw was invented in 1869. It combined western technology with cheap labor and spread throughout Asia. There was a concentrated effort to reclaim land and make it more productive. Land productivity grew by 21 percent in the 1880s alone. Japanese used Western ships and learned Western navigational techniques. Price inflation caused the government to sell many industries at a discount in 1880. Those who were wealthy enough to buy these became captains of industry.

The House of **Mitsui** made the transition from shogun economic leadership to the new regime. It had started by making *sake*, then moved into moneylending and pawnbroking, opened dry goods stores, and finally became the official banker to the shogunate in 1691. A former supervisor of commerce in Nagasaki, **Iwasaki Yataro** (1834–85) set up the **Mitsubishi** House. He brought in foreign experts and French machinery to revamp the silk industry, which became an export along with tea. Before 1900, Japan had become an importer of rice, but had close to a trade surplus. Japan's coal production grew twelve-fold from 1860 to 1900. It also exported cotton cloth, spun and woven mostly by women and girls. By 1913, one-quarter of the world's cotton yarn exports came from Japan.

Japan first concentrated on its comparative advantage. It made *sake*, miso, and soy sauce that were immune to foreign imitation. Because it was a late industrializer, it skipped over much of the steam stage and went directly to electricity. In 1899, Japan revised the western treaties to make them more fair.

Like so many revolutions, the Japanese revolution was disguised as a restoration. The tide of revolution that had started on the shores of North America had come to rest on the coast of Japan.

# TIMELINE

| 1800 | Korea virtually independent |
|------|------|
| 1814 | First Shinto sect in Japan |
| 1850–64 | Taiping rebellion |
| 1852 | Yellow river shifts course |
| 1853–54 | Perry's trips to Edo end in Treaty of Kanagawa |
| 1855 | Grand Canal blocked |
| 1858 | Treaty of Tianjin |
| 1861 | Chinese emperor's death leads to co-regency of Ci'an, Cixi, and Yixin |
| 1867 | Shogun Keiki resigns, Meiji restoration |
| 1872 | Japan orders universal education |
| 1876 | Korea opens diplomatic relations with Japan |

# KEY TERMS

Taiping Rebellion
Matthew Perry
Treaty of Kanagawa
*daimyo*
Shinto
Five Articles Oath

# PRIMARY SOURCE DOCUMENTS

**The Taipings**, http://academic.brooklyn.cuny.edu/core9/phalsall/texts/taiping.html
**Matthew Perry**, http://www.fordham.edu/halsall/mod/1854Perry-japan
**Five Articles Oath**, http://afe.easia.columbia.edu/ps/japan/charter_oath-1868.pdf